The Garden
Succulents Primer

The
Garden
Succulents
Primer

Gideon F. Smith
Ben-Erik van Wyk

TIMBER PRESS
PORTLAND · LONDON

Published in 2008 by
Timber Press, Inc.

The Haseltine Building
133 S.W. Second Avenue, Suite 450
Portland, Oregon 97204-3527, U.S.A.
www.timberpress.com

2 The Quadrant
135 Salusbury Road
London NW6 6RJ
United Kingdom
www.timberpress.co.uk

ISBN-13: 978-0-88192-954-6

Project manager: Reneé Ferreira
Proofreading: Frances Perryer
Typesetting: Melinda Stark, Lebone Publishing Services
Reproduction: Unifoto and Resolution, Cape Town
Printed and bound by Tien Wah Press, Singapore

All cover photographs by Ben-Erik van Wyk except top of front cover by Norman Chan,
courtesy of iStock International Inc.

Catalog records for this book are available from the Library of Congress
and the British Library.

Contents

Acknowledgements

The authors would like to thank Reneé Ferreira, Eben van Wyk and the production team at Briza Publications for their excellent editorial and logistic support. The photographic contributions from the institutions and persons listed below are gratefully acknowledged. Thank you to our families, colleagues, post-graduate students and friends for support and companionship during field trips and garden visits. We greatly appreciate the efforts of gardeners and garden staff for the beautiful and diverse displays of succulents at the numerous botanical gardens that we have visited over a period of more than 25 years.

Photographic contributions

Photographs are arranged alphabetically from top to bottom and from left to right, according to photographer and page number. **Ben-Erik van Wyk**: 9abcdef, 11abcde, 13abc, 15abcdef, 17abc, 19abcde, 21abcdefghijkl, 25cd, 27abdef, 29acde, 31bc, 33abcd, 35abcde, 39abcd, 41bcd, 43abcde, 45ab, 47abcd, 49abc, 51abcde, 53abcd, 55bcdef, 57abcdef, 59abd, 61abc, 63c, 65abcdefg, 67abcdefgh, 69abcde, 71cdef, 73abcd, 75abde, 77abcd, 79abcdf, 81ac, 83abcdef, 85abcde, 87abcdef, 89abcde, 91abcde, 93abcdf, 95cd, 97abdef, 99acef, 101abcd, 103abcdef, 105abcd, 107abcdef, 109abcd, 111abcde, 113abcde, 115abcdef, 117abcdef, 119abcd, 121abcd, 123abcd, 125abcde, 127abcdef, 129abcdef, 131abcdef, 133abcd, 135abcdef, 137bcdef, 139abcdef, 141ab, 143acde, 145abcdef, 147abcd, 149abc, 151abcdef, 153abcdef, 155abcd, 157abcde, 159abcd, 161abcdef, 163abc, 165abce, 167abcdef, 169abcde, 171abc, 173abcdef, 175abcdef, 177abcdef, 179abcd, 181abcd, 183abcdef, 185abcd, 187abcd, 189ab, 191abcde, 193abc, 195abcdef, 197abcde, 199abcdef, 201acdefh, 203abcdef, 205abc, 207abc, 209abc, 211abcd, 213abc, 215abcd, 217ab, 219abc, 221abcd, 223abc, 225abc. **Gideon Smith**: 25ab, 27c, 29b, 31ade, 37abcd, 41a, 59c, 63ab, 71ab, 79e, 93e, 99bd, 111f, 137a, 143b, 159ef, 163de, 209d. **South African National Biodiversity Institute**: 55a, 97c, 171d, 201bf. **Frits van Oudtshoorn**: 95ab, 141cdef. **Alice Biemond**: 81b. **Silke Rügheimer**: 75c. **Anne Lise Schutte-Vlok**: 165d.

Introduction

About 3% of the flowering plants of the world are represented by a wealth of succulents of all shapes, sizes and descriptions. This plant life form is distributed over more than 60 different families, but with a significant concentration in about 15 of them. Furthermore, perhaps with the exception of forests, succulents make up a distinct and conspicuous component of many vegetation types, especially in seasonally dry and arid regions. It is therefore no surprise that they also play an important part in gardening and horticulture.

Writing an identification guide to all the succulents of the world (an estimated 10 000 species) would be a difficult task – there are simply too many to fit into one book! However, the task becomes much easier if we restrict ourselves to those succulents that are commonly grown in gardens. This unfortunately excludes many of the fascinating and rare gems that succulent plant enthusiasts enjoy adding to their greenhouse collections. Rare succulents are generally well covered in specialist books but the garden succulents are rarely featured as an entity on their own in gardening books.

The first step in identifying garden succulents is to become familiar with the main groups (families and genera). Fortunately, most succulent plant families are so distinctive that they are easily recognised. One need not be a trained botanist or horticulturalist to tell a cactus from a carrion flower or an aloe from an agave. An attempt is made in this book to show how very different the main families are and how easily they can be distinguished from one another. Once the family or genus is recognised, it becomes much easier to identify the plant to species level.

With this aim in mind, garden succulents are here divided into 10 main groups. The first eight groups correspond more or less to the current botanical classification of the plants. However, many plant families include one or two succulent members or are poorly known in horticulture. These are included in the two artificial groups ("unusual stem succulents" and "unusual leaf succulents") simply to give a wider coverage of genera and species.

The succulents can be classified according to the plant organ (leaves, stems, roots) that is fleshy. For the layperson perhaps the most useful subdivision of succulence is indeed based on these easy-to-observe structures. Therefore, reference is typically made to leaf succulents, stem succulents or caudiciform succulents (where the water-storing tissue is in the stem–root continuum). Many non-succulent plants, if grown with their fleshy roots exposed, would be referred to as caudiciform succulents. Leaves, stems and roots are not the only plant structures that can be succulent. Other, less conventional plant parts can also be succulent, such as the wiry but fleshy, twining inflorescence of the climbing onion (*Bowiea volubilis*). Different types of succulence are not mutually exclusive and plants that combine leaf and stem succulence, for example, are often encountered.

Uses of succulents

Domestic and amenity horticulture is by far the most common and widespread use to which succulents are put. In this regard the ease with which they can be grown and their ability to survive on very little aftercare and irrigation makes them favourite subjects in present-day horticulture where there is a strong tendency towards low-maintenance and water-wise gardening. However, succulents have many other uses in everyday life.

The most famous medicinal plant in the world is arguably *Aloe vera*, an ancient cultigen of North African and Arabian origin that has become popular as an ingredient of cosmetic products and more recently as a tonic drink. The bitter yellow juice is a traditional laxative medicine but the non-bitter inner pulp ("white juice" or gel) has become the most important product. This industry is estimated to be worth more than 110 billion US dollars per year. *Aloe ferox* is used in much the same way – the bitter purgative medicine, known as Cape aloes, has been wildcrafted since 1770 and gel products have also become popular. *Aloe arborescens* is used in Japan, where this southern African plant is known as "Japan aloe". Other succulents used in traditional medicine include the peyote cactus (*Lophophora williamsii*), a well-known hallucinogen that was used in traditional ceremonies. A product known as *kougoed* or *canna* is a traditional hypnotic that has been used for its mild sedative properties in the dry parts of southern Africa. It is made from *Sceletium tortuosum*, a member of the mesemb family (Mesembryanthemaceae). Several members of this family (such as the *asbos* or "ash bush", *Psilocaulon junceum*) have been used as a source of lye for making soap in the days before industrial caustic soda became widely available.

Food uses are many and varied. Edible fruits include prickly pear (*Opuntia ficus-indica*), pitaya (*Cereus peruvianus*) and the more recently commercialised dragon fruit (*Hylocereus undatus*). In the Cape, sour fig (*Carpobrotus edulis*, a member of the mesemb family) is much sought after for eating fresh or for making into jams and curries. The succulent leaves of the ice plant (*Mesembryanthemum crystallinum*) are used as salad, while the leaves and flowers of the *vetkousie* (*Carpanthea pomeridiana*) are an ingredient of traditional meat stews. The young stems of several prickly pear species (*Opuntia*) are eaten as crispy vegetables in Mexico. Alcoholic beverages such as tequila (from *Agave tequilana*) and pulque (from *Agave salmiana* among others) are produced from the fermentation or distillation of the de-leaved stems (*cabezas* or heads) of other species. A product made from naturalised *Agave americana* in the Karoo in South Africa is called "Agava".

Agave sisalana, along with *Agave lechuiguilla* among others, is a commercial source of natural fibres used in manufacturing ropes and mats, for example. Their dry flowering poles, and even the stems of columnar cacti, are used as fence poles and for the construction of dwellings and enclosures for domesticated animals.

Health products (*Aloe vera* gel)

Aloe medicinal products

Prickly pears (*Opuntia* fruits)

Sour figs and jam (*Carpobrotus* fruits)

Peyote cactus (*Lophophora williamsii*)

Sisal plantation (*Agave sisalana*)

Conservation

The threats to a number of succulent plant populations are manifold. These range from, among other things, unsound agricultural practices, urban expansion and industrial development to injudicious and non-sustainable collecting by enthusiasts, an increasing need for plant material by sources and suppliers of traditional medicines and sometimes simply ignorance about the plight of the environment in general.

It is an indictment against the unscrupulous hand of man that several species of succulents have become extinct. These include a few species of the mesemb family (Mesembryanthemaceae). One single-species genus, *Circandra*, is an example of a genus that has become extinct, possibly as a result of agricultural development. If care is not taken, some species of the curious stone plants with localised distributions (such as the species of *Argyroderma*) may go the same route. *Aloe* species such as *Aloe pillansii* (the giant quiver tree) and *A. polyphylla* (the spiral aloe) have become rare in nature and there are serious concerns about their long-term survival. Indeed, the conservation status of many succulents indicates that immediate steps should be taken to accurately determine the true situation. Areas of the world with a large diversity of succulents, many of them with highly localised distributions, require the most attention. These include the southern parts of Madagascar, the Canary Islands, parts of Arabia and North Africa, southern Africa (western parts of South Africa and Namibia), the arid southern parts of the USA and Mexico.

It is therefore imperative that all gardeners and landscapers take care not to obtain material from sources that are unable to show that it has not been harvested from the wild. With an increasing number of commercial nurseries nowadays offering succulent plants that have been grown from seed to the public, there is really no reason why plants should be collected illegally from wild populations. When you are rambling in the natural habitat of succulents, and other plants for that matter, please pay close attention to the well-known nature conservation maxims:

> **TAKE** photographs only
> **LEAVE** footprints only
> **OBSERVE** conservation regulations.

In situ conservation (conserving the species in their natural habitats) is always the best option, but *ex situ* conservation, where plants are propagated and cultivated outside their natural environment, can play an important role. Succulents such as the spectacular queen agave (*Agave victoria-reginae*) and the golden barrel cactus (*Echinocactus grusonii*) have become rare in nature but are now grown in large numbers in gardens all over the world. The same is true for the dollar plant (*Xerosicyos danguyi*), a member of the pumpkin family (Cucurbitaceae) from southwestern Madagascar. There are usually very good reasons why conservation legislation aims to protect specific plants and their habitats. So, please do not be tempted to transgress any rules or regulations. Do your part to ensure the long-term survival of rare species by insisting on plant material or seeds of garden origin. Remember that extinction is forever.

Giant quiver tree (*Aloe pillansii*) in nature

Giant quiver tree (*Aloe pillansii*)

Dollar plant (*Xerosicyos danguyi*)

Queen agave (*Agave victoria-reginae*)

Golden barrel cactus (*Echinocactus grusonii*)

Cultivation

Certainly one of the real charms of growing succulents is the ease with which they can be cultivated. Most species included in this broadly and often somewhat loosely conceived group of plants do not require green fingers to get and keep them going and growing beautifully. To be successful with succulents requires adherence to a very few golden rules only.

The first and most important pertains to their growing media. **Make sure that the plants are not subjected to wet feet in their dormant phase.** If there is one thing that fat-bodied plants generally cannot tolerate, it is being subjected to stagnant water in the "off season", which invariably coincides with their resting phase. Depending on the species and the conditions prevalent in their natural habitats, this could be either summer or winter. Therefore, if *Aloe plicatilis* from the winter-rainfall area of South Africa, for example, is to be grown successfully in summer-rainfall areas, it is imperative that the plants be kept reasonably dry in summer. This is usually best achieved by keeping such plants in pots in a cultivation house. The same is of course true for the hundreds of miniature mesembs from Namaqualand or the numerous exquisite small cacti from Mexico, most of which observe a similar less active growing phase in summer or winter. Predictably, the opposite applies to the magnificence of the succulents from summer rainfall areas. But there are always exceptions, even to this first golden rule. *Cyphostemma juttae*, the bottle-trunked wine-grape relative from winter-dry Namibia, does almost equally well in both summer and winter rainfall areas and it can withstand much more rainfall than predicted by its arid natural environment. Also bear in mind that, generally speaking, succulents can tolerate wet conditions much more effectively in the open ground than in restrictive containers where the soil surface is often covered with a layer of pebbles to prevent unattractive splashing of soil onto the plants. The same, really essential, inorganic or organic surface mulch does not have this sometimes devastating effect on plants grown in the open. One of the safest ways to ensure good soil drainage in pots and in open beds is to make sure that the soil mixture is friable. This can be easily achieved by simply adding sufficient sharp sand to the potting mixture.

The second golden rule applies to light. **Succulents usually excel in bright light conditions, with the exception of small, soft-bodied species, which prefer slightly filtered, but still bright sunlight.** Only by exposing succulents to bright light will they take on the magnificent leaf and stem colours that one finds in their natural habitats. Where they grow in nature, succulents often make use of nurse plants – that is, other often non-succulent plants that filter or shade out the most intense and damaging rays of sunlight. In few instances is this more obvious than in the case of the majestic *saguaro* or cowboy cactus, which most often starts its life as a tiny seedling growing under the shady protection of the desert-hardy palo verde trees in the Sonoran Desert of Arizona. Often only decades later will it push its trunk and arms beyond the canopy of the tree. Many carrion flowers and some miniature mesembs are difficult to grow unless they are offered some protection from direct sunlight. Furthermore, a plant that has been growing in a shade house will certainly be damaged by the intense direct rays of the sun, regardless of how low the percentage shade provided in the shade house. Plants used to full sunlight will develop unsightly thin stems or become deformed if suddenly moved to the shade.

Mass planting of *Aloe vanbaleni*

Aptenia cordifolia on a slope

Group of columnar cacti

The third and final golden rule pertains to plant food. **Succulents, especially those grown in containers, require a regime of supplemental feeding.** The soil in containers will eventually become leached of nutrients and it is imperative that it is regularly enriched by providing additional plant food. Care should be taken not to cause damage by excessive amounts of inorganic fertiliser. Small amounts at regular intervals are far better and more effective. Various organic fertilisers are available but ordinary good quality compost is an excellent way of ensuring that plants flourish and look their best.

Succulents are some of the most robust and strongest growers in the Plant Kingdom. But make no mistake: like most plant species, succulents also have their fair share of pests and diseases. Although the majority of succulents have evolved a remarkable range of defence mechanisms to protect them against predation, they are certainly not immune to attack by pests that range from microscopic organisms through to large mammals foraging on them. Interestingly, the defence mechanisms often contribute to the fascination of the species. Here one is invariably reminded of the beautiful and often ornately arranged spines and prickles adorning the leaves of aloes and the stems of euphorbias and cacti. Other defence mechanisms are not easy to observe as they may be contained in the chemical constituents of the sap and juices of the plants.

The best line of defence against pests and diseases is to make sure that the plants are flourishing. However, despite careful watering and feeding, some succulents may still be infected. Diseased or rotten parts may be carefully cut off and burnt, taking care to seal the wounds or to allow them to dry out. Commercial insecticides and fungicides are sometimes the only option. Follow the instructions and guidelines given by the manufacturer to ensure that the product is used in a safe and effective way.

Zürich Sukkulenten-Sammlung

Succulents in Padua Botanical Garden

Selected form of *Opuntia robusta* (right)

Garden mesemb (*Lampranthus roseus*)

Fairy crassula (*Crassula multicava*)

Dollar plant (*Crassula ovata*)

Propagation

Regardless of which group of plants a gardener is interested in, there are only a limited number of ways in which to multiply them. The two most popular mechanisms through which the number of plants in a collection can be increased are by means of seed or cuttings. Of these two, the taking of cuttings is by far the easiest and most succulents are eminently suited to this means of propagation. One of the great advantages of propagating plants with cuttings is that fairly large plants can be easily established directly in the spot intended in a garden. This makes some species, such as the shrubby *Aloe arborescens* or tree-like *Opuntia ficus-indica,* very popular for rapidly creating a bed or border that looks mature, virtually from the start.

Some representatives of certain succulent plant families are very particular as to the conditions required for the successful rooting of cuttings. In fact, with some species it could be virtually impossible to multiply them using vegetative means. On the other hand, obtaining new plants from cuttings could be as simple as removing a branch or truncheon with a hacksaw and unceremoniously sticking it into a hole in the ground where you want a new plant to become established. By observing a few simple rules that lie somewhere between these two extremes, it is quite possible to produce your own crop of succulents for your garden. The following description applies to the vast majority of succulents. Here is how to go about it:

- Remove a branch or rosette as cleanly as possible from the mother plant, for example by using a sharp knife or a pair of secateurs.

- Seal both wounds with a commercially available tree sealant. This is really only necessary if the cutting leaves a large wound on a tree-like specimen of, for example, *Aloe barberae.*

- Leave the cutting in the shade for a few days to allow the wound to dry out.

- Small cuttings can now be placed in a very well drained growing medium, such as sharp river sand, but the medium should be kept moist.

- Large cuttings can be established directly in the spot intended by simply digging a hole large enough to accommodate and support it.

- The bottom of the hole can be filled with a rooting medium, for example coarse sand, to ensure good drainage if the soil in your garden tends to be clayey, or poorly drained.

- Anchor and support a large branch in place by securing it with cables. Be sure that the cable is prevented from chafing the branch by covering it with rope, a rubber strip or any other fabric at the point of contact with the branch.

- Water a newly established cutting or branch only sparingly until new growth starts to emerge. Always bear in mind that succulents generally cannot tolerate wet, soggy growing media.

Succulent plant nursery

Aloe arborescens rooted cuttings

Hoodia gordonii seedlings

Gardening with succulents

A well-designed and established succulent garden creates a wonderfully relaxed energy in any open space, especially in a domestic garden. The warm, summer colours of a multitude of these species will imbue any landscape with rich, toasted shades that not only invite exploration, but also suggest peace and well-being.

A loosely landscaped succulent garden is relaxed and timeless. Succulent gardening also allows for surrounding oneself with plants with varied and wonderful provenances: real collectible talking pieces revelling in clear simplicity. But no two gardeners are alike. Everyone passionate about plants and gardens prefers to accessorise in their preferred style. But succulents have it all, from style to colour and, of course, form. These hardy plants therefore present the ultimate opportunity for visual variability, virtually in all facets of garden and landscape design. For example, with the hundreds of shapes and forms available, these fat-bodied plants allow for playfully emphasising different plant parts that, by effectively using changing light conditions, create incredible illusions of movement in the garden.

By growing heirloom succulent plants, such as the multi-annual *Agave americana* 'Variegata' with its long, twisted, snake-like leaves, or *Aloe barberae* with its towering trunk supporting a rounded, multi-crowned canopy, it is easy to exemplify quality and style. Such plants are also recognised for their toughness and durability, and certainly their colours and texture. Indeed, in the right place, that is, virtually anywhere, succulents add style, glamour and a touch of essential whimsy and eclecticism to any garden. The simplicity and honesty of the kind of garden that can be created with succulents is certain to strike a chord with every gardener.

Massive, large-growing succulents tend to anchor a garden. This is most evident when their chunky, symmetrical or irregular shapes are scattered haphazardly throughout the garden, suggesting timeless ageing that creates weight near the soil surface. However, not all succulents are large and chubby. Their versatility as garden subjects essentially knows no boundary. An amazing sense of near-subtropical opulence can also be created using these drought-resistant plant wonders. It would be difficult to transcend the sense of walking on a Mexican Mayan forest floor created by a dense stand of clumps of the soft-leaved *Agave attenuata* plants.

Lastly, if a mass display of colour is needed, then there are succulents to oblige. Few flowering plants can match the spring spectacle of a well-grown stand of mesembs – garden *vygies* (*Lampranthus* species) or dewflowers (*Drosanthemum* species) in full bloom. The annual Livingstone daisy (*Dorotheanthus bellidiformis*) or the perennial lobster flower (*Plectranthus neochilus*) are also useful for this purpose. The petals of mesemb flowers (family Mesembryanthemaceae) have the remarkable feature of reflecting sunlight to make an absolutely dazzling display of brilliant colour.

Mature cactus garden with *Echinocactus grusonii* in the middle

Lobster flowers (*Plectranthus neochilus*)

African milk trees (*Euphorbia trigona*)

Garden mesemb (*Lampranthus spectabilis*)

Exposed roots of
Cyphostemma cirrhosum

About this book

This book is arranged into a number of introductory chapters on succulents in general, followed by a series of comprehensive treatments of those plant families of which some or most of the species are succulent. **The main aim of the book is to introduce the various families of succulent plants, which are generally easily recognised by a combination of characters**.

Once the family to which a plant belongs has been identified, then the search for the names of the genus and species becomes much easier. Many of the large genera of succulents typically contain numerous species, and getting the identification down to the species level is often difficult without access to the latest specialist book on that particular genus. It is hoped that this broad overview of typical families, genera and selected species will serve as a first step towards identifying all the common garden succulents.

For each family, the typical characteristics (diagnostic features) are given, together with photographs illustrating the typical stems, leaves and flowers of representative genera and species. The main garden succulent genera are listed, followed by brief descriptions (and photographs) of the main genera and some representative species of each that are commonly encountered in gardens and rockeries. Note carefully the sometimes subtle differences between various types of thorns or different leaf types. Unrelated plants have sometimes adopted similar strategies for survival and may therefore look rather similar. However, closer inspection often reveals obvious differences. A good example is the superficially similar columnar cacti from America and the columnar spurges or euphorbias of Africa. The thorns and flowers are quite different.

On pages 22 and 23, a broad overview of the eight main succulent plant groups (= families) is given. These eight families account for more than 80 per cent of all succulent plants, so that the ability to recognise these families is a useful first step. The reader is encouraged to focus on the critical details characteristic of each of the main families. The last two groups (Groups 9 and 10) are included to accommodate families which contain only a few (but often well-known) succulent plants. Included here under "Unusual stem succulents" (Group 9) and "Unusual leaf succulents" (Group 10) are also a few unusual and interesting plants that are sometimes grown as novelties.

Where possible, we have avoided the use of complicated technical terms for plant and flower parts. However, some basic terms are explained on the opposite page. Identifying plants is not always easy. Careful observation is a good starting point, and when followed by perseverance, the enthusiast will gain experience and confidence, resulting in a deepening of the enjoyment that can be derived from growing these diverse and fascinating plants.

Opposite leaves

Alternate leaves

Rosulate (spiral) leaves

Distichous leaves

Inflorescence (flower cluster)

Raceme (stalked flowers)

Spike (sessile flowers)

Flower head (capitulum)

Areoles with spines (cactus)

Thorns (euphorbia)

Spines (carrion flower)

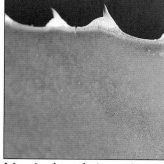

Marginal teeth (agave)

Guide to the main succulent

Group 1 Agavaceae: Sisal family, Century plant family (including Dracaenaceae)
Page 24
Leaf succulents
Aloe-like plants
Fibrous, persistent leaves
Flowers usually white or greenish

Group 2 Apocynaceae: Carrion flower family
Page 42
Stem succulents (often no leaves)
Often with milky sap
Waxy flowers (often with a strong smell)
Flowers often adorned with small hairs
Seeds with silky seed hairs

Group 3 Asphodelaceae: Aloe family
Page 64
Leaf succulents
Leaves relatively soft, die back
Often with a bitter yellow sap
Flowers often red and showy and borne in a
    candle-shaped inflorescence

Group 4 Asteraceae: Daisy family
Page 92
Stem or leaf succulents
Tiny flowers in dense groups (heads)
Flowers usually yellow, white or red and showy
Small fruits (achenes) with hairy plumes

Group 5 Cactaceae: Cactus family, Prickly pear family
Page 98
Stem succulents
Leaves absent (modified into spines)
Spines borne in star-shaped groups on felty cushions (areoles)
Stems without milky sap
Flowers large, showy, short-lived

plant groups (families)

Group 6 Crassulaceae: Stonecrop family, Plakkie family
Page 122
Leaf and stem succulents
Leaves in symmetrical arrangements
Flowers star-shaped or tubular
Nectar glands prominent, petals 4 or 5 (or multiples)

Group 7 Euphorbiaceae: Spurge family, Milkweed family
Page 166
Stem succulents
Stems with milky sap
Flowers usually small and inconspicuous
Fruit a small, three-valved capsule

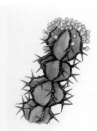

Group 8 Mesembryanthemaceae: Ice plant family, Mesemb family
Page 182
Leaf succulents
Leaves very thick, in opposite pairs
Flowers single, large and showy
Sepals green, few; petals colourful, numerous
Fruit a hygroscopic capsule (i.e. it opens when wet)

Group 9 Unusual stem succulents (various families)
Page 204
Bombacaceae: Baobab family
Dioscoreaceae: Wild yam family, Elephant's foot family
Hyacinthaceae: Hyacinth family
Passifloraceae: Granadilla family, Passion flower family
Pedaliaceae: Sesame family
Vitaceae: Grape family

Group 10 Unusual leaf succulents (various families)
Page 216
Geraniaceae: Geranium family
Lamiaceae: Mint family
Portulacaceae: Portulaca family
Welwitschiaceae: Welwitschia family
Zygophyllaceae: Devil-thorn family

23

Group 1

AGAVACEAE
Sisal family or Century plant family
(here including the Dracaenaceae –
the Dragon tree family)

DISTINGUISHING CHARACTERS The Agavaceae is a medium-sized family of mostly stiff-leaved, multi-annual rosette plants. It includes eight genera only (or ten, with the two genera of the Dracaenaceae included), of which *Agave* (century plants) has the most species by far. With very few exceptions, species of *Agave* bloom once only and then die. However, to make up for this horticultural "disaster" plants take many years to bloom, and when flowering takes place it is a striking and unforgettable sight. A rigid flowering pole of up to 5 or 6 m, often with numerous, prominent side-branches, is produced from the centre of a rosette of leaves and it is covered in hundreds, if not thousands, of flowers. In many species the flowers are in time replaced by small plantlets or bulbils that will drop to the ground, take root and ensure the survival of a single clone for many successive generations. The genus *Agave* and most of its relatives grow naturally in Central America, Mexico and the southern parts of the United States. These plants are restricted to the New World but are often confused with aloes (which in turn are found only in Africa and Arabia). Agaves have tough, persistent leaves, while aloes have soft, non-fibrous leaves that die back after a few years.

NOTES We are aware that *Dracaena* (dragon trees) and *Sansevieria* (bowstring hemp, devil's tongue) fit uncomfortably into the Agavaceae. For the time being, we group the two genera here, simply because they share with the Agavaceae the aloe-like growth form and fibrous leaves. The two genera are sometimes placed in their own family, the Dracaenaceae. More recently it has been proposed that the family should be included in the Convallariaceae which is restricted to the northern hemisphere, from Europe to Asia. It has also been suggested that species of *Dracaena* and *Sansevieria* should be lumped together into a single genus, *Dracaena*. The 120 species of the two genera are distributed primarily in the Old World tropics and subtropics, in forests and bushveld (savanna). Plants are small trees, shrubs or medium-sized, comparatively stemless succulents that multiply by means of aerial or subterranean runners. In both genera the leaves are crowded into rosettes at the tips of the stems and branches or at ground level. Most species bear numerous off-white flowers on branched or unbranched inflorescences. As in most lily-like plants, the flower parts typically consist of six members each. Species of both genera bear brightly coloured berries harbouring creamy-white seeds, in contrast to the black seeds of species of some related families. Succulent and non-succulent species of both *Sansevieria* and *Dracaena* are exceedingly popular among succulent enthusiasts for outdoor cultivation and as indoor pot plants.

Agave parryi

Flowers of *Agave hurteri*

Plantlets on sisal (*Agave sisalana*)

African dracaena (*Dracaena aletriformis*)

Brief notes on genera

Agave (century plants)

Species of *Agave* are typical succulents, consisting of a rosette of numerous erect or recurved, fat leaves that are armed with ferocious spines along their margins. Most species sucker freely, and herein lies a danger: some of them will spread easily and become weeds, smothering other plants in the process. A fairly small selection of species of *Agave* is available for sale in nurseries. These species are typically large, robust plants that spread readily from underground runners. They flower once and then die.

Beaucarnea (ponytail palm)

The well-known ponytail is a palm-like tree with a bottle-shaped stem and narrow, gracefully curved leaves. Some botanists include *Beaucarnea* with the genus *Nolina* in the family Nolinaceae, while others group it with Agavaceae or Dracaenaceae.

Beschorneria (beschornerias)

The species of *Beschorneria* are perhaps best known as multi-headed shrubs used as accent plants, rather than as succulents. Yet, their leaves are tough, fibrous, leathery and at least basally thickly succulent. These species do not die after having flowered.

Dracaena (dragon trees)

The stems are typically smooth, soft and fibrous inside. The tips of the branches bear crowns of broad or narrow, erect or recurved, shiny green, mostly non-succulent leaves. The horticultural appeal of most species lies in their leaves which could be variously variegated with yellowish or whitish longitudinal bands. In addition, the nocturnal flowers of many species are pleasantly fragrant, especially those of some of the popular indoor horticultural subjects, such as *D. fragrans*. *D. transvaalensis* has stiff, fleshy leaves.

Furcraea (false agaves)

Very few of these striking plants are regularly encountered in cultivation. *Furcraea selloa* (false agave) and *Furcraea foetida* (Mauritius hemp) have long, prominently or sparsely spiny, sword-shaped leaves. A single, multi-branched inflorescence is produced at the end of the plant's life.

Sansevieria (bowstring hemp, devil's tongue)

This is a genus of small to robust rosette plants with thick, leathery to distinctly succulent leaves. Plants are small to medium-sized succulent herbs. The leaves are very fibrous and, not surprisingly, have been and are still used locally for the production of rope and cordage. One species, *S. trifasciata*, from the Democratic Republic of Congo, is very popular as an indoor pot plant, primarily as a result of its beautiful, transversely and longitudinally variegated leaves. The rosettes of sansevierias cease to grow once they have flowered. However, the rosette does not die immediately, but take several years to wither away. In the meantime the rosettes offset prolifically.

Yucca (yuccas, Spanish daggers)

Cultivated species of *Yucca* either have numerous, long stems that are densely armed with sharp-tipped leaves, or are stemless plants that have flexible leaves mostly with margins adorned with white threads. These species do not die after flowering.

Agave attenuata

Dracaena draco

Furcraea selloa

Sansevieria trifasciata

Sansevieria pearsonii

Yucca gloriosa

Notes on species of Agavaceae

AGAVE

Agave americana (century plant, American aloe)

Perhaps the best known of all horticulturally important species of *Agave* worldwide is *Agave americana*. This is of course the big, blue-leaved species that will in time grow into the size of a small family car! The typical form is a rather untidy sprouting plant with long leaves that topple over as the plant grows to its massive dimensions. The plants flower only once after about 15 to 20 years and then produce a spectacular inflorescence of up to 6 or 7 m. The de-leaved stems of *Agave americana*, called pineapples or pinnas, can be distilled, yielding a high quality organic alcohol. In Mexico the pinnas of another species, *Agave tequilana*, is used for distilling tequila, which is very popular as the alcohol basis of cocktails such as margarita and tequila sunrise. *Agave americana* is exceptionally hardy and in cultivation will tolerate extreme climatic conditions. It thrives in severely hot and arid conditions, but also in high rainfall areas and even in very cold situations. At least two cultivars of *Agave americana* are commonly cultivated. The one has distinct yellow leaf margins and is known in the horticultural trade as var. *marginata*. The other cultivar, var. *mediopicta alba*, has a broad, white central section to its leaves.

Agave sisalana (sisal plant)

In contrast to *Agave americana*, the leaves of *Agave sisalana* are a dull to bright green, but never blue. Furthermore, they are borne erectly spreading and will hardly ever become drooping. *Agave sisalana* takes only about eight to 10 years, or even less, to reach flowering age. When this species flowers, a further distinction between it and *Agave americana* becomes evident: *Agave sisalana* generally does not form seed capsules, but produces a multitude of tiny, but rapidly developing plantlets in the places where the flowers were carried. These plantlets easily become detached from the inflorescence and will rapidly take root where they fall. This species is vigorous and robust in cultivation and also forms small colonies around a mother plant. Indeed, in a short space of time a colony is formed which constantly increases in size. But beware the unsuspecting visitor because, although the leaves have no marginal armature, they are tipped with tough, sharp spines. *Agave sisalana* is an important crop plant, producing valuable natural fibres. However, synthetic fibres have replaced much of the demand for sisal fibres and many plantations of the species were abandoned as a result of a low financial yield per hectare.

Agave americana

Agave americana var. *mediopicta*

Agave sisalana

American aloe (*Agave americana*)

Sisal (*Agave sisalana*)

AGAVE

Agave angustifolia (narrow-leaf century plant)

In some parts of the world, *Agave angustifolia* has been consistently known under the name *Agave vivipara*. As is the case with *Agave americana* and *Agave sisalana*, this species also rapidly forms small colonies of spiny plants. Single plants and colonies are generally smaller than in either of the aforementioned species, but their smaller size should not be misleading. Indeed, they are as ferocious as any other century plant. Their leaf margins are armed with small, needle-sharp spines that generally point towards the tips of the leaves. In contrast to *Agave sisalana*, *Agave angustifolia* produces viable seed in addition to a multitude of inflorescence bulbils. *Agave angustifolia* is used for a variety of domestic purposes in its native Mexico, but in other parts of the world it is used mostly in amenity horticulture and as a barrier plant around suburban dwellings. Apart from the typical form of *Agave angustifolia*, a horticultural variety with distinctly white or yellowish leaf edges, var. *marginata*, is also popular amongst gardeners. A well-grown specimen of this form in a container is a stunning complement to soften the harsh vertical and horizontal architectural lines ever present in the modern concrete jungle. *Agave tequilana*, the tequila agave, is a close relative of *Agave angustifolia*.

Agave victoria-reginae (queen agave)

Agave victoria-reginae is one of the most beautiful species of *Agave* found in horticulture. This species grows almost exclusively as solitary plants, and it does not form plantlets on its inflorescence. Traditionally propagation is therefore from seed, although some forms will sparingly form suckers. It has been observed though that some clones will spontaneously start sprouting side-shoots, especially when they are transplanted. This species is not quite as simple in cultivation as most other century plants. But again it seems to depend on the clone being cultivated: some are definitely easier than others. The charm and attraction of the species lie in its wonderfully white-striped, short, chubby leaves. These are terminally broadly-blunt, but end in one or more short, needle-sharp spines. The inflorescence of *Agave victoria-reginae* is single, unbranched and spike-like. It is somewhat thicker than a broomstick, but considerably longer.

Agave attenuata (elephant's trunk)

Although most species of *Agave* are stiff-leaved, there are a few exceptions to this generalisation. *Agave attenuata* is by far the most commonly cultivated soft-leaved species. It has pliable, thornless and gracefully recurved leaves and one can be forgiven for not immediately recognising it as a century plant. It forms a formidable inflorescence of some metres long that resembles the trunk of an elephant.

Agave parryi (mescal, Parry's century plant)

This small to medium-sized, compact species deserves to be cultivated more widely. The distinctly greyish blue leaves are arranged in neat rosettes that contrast sharply with globular and columnar cacti where they are grown together on a rockery. The leaf margins are armed with short, stout pungent thorns.

Agave victoria-reginae

Agave angustifolia 'Variegata'

Agave attenuata in flower

Agave parryi

Agave tequilana

BEAUCARNEA

Beaucarnea recurvata (ponytail, ponytail palm)

The ponytail or ponytail palm is a North American and Mexican plant that is known to some people as the bottle palm, bottle ponytail or elephant's foot tree. The species is sometimes included in the genus *Nolina* and is then known as *Nolina recurvata*.

When mature, the stem may reach a height of 10 m and the leaves may be up to 2 m long. A form of the species known as var. *intermedia*, however, has a mature height of only 2 m. This is the most commonly cultivated variety in many parts of the world. The plant has a distinctive bottle-shaped stem and clumps of leaves congested on the branch tips. Young plants grown in pots soon develop a thick stem and attractive head of leaves. The sparse clusters of creamy-white flowers can make a beautiful display when the plant is in full bloom. Each flower has six petals and six stamens. The fruit is a 3-winged capsule.

Cultivation may be either from seeds or stem cuttings, but the latter is preferred because sizeable plants can be obtained in a shorter period. The ponytail palm can be grown outdoors in warm dry regions but is more suitable for pot cultivation in cold areas.

BESCHORNERIA

Beschorneria bracteata (green-flowered beschorneria)

Not all the representatives of the family Agavaceae die after flowering. Species of the small genus *Beschorneria* fall in this category. Plants of *Beschorneria* typically form medium-sized or large clumping rosettes of characteristically soft, pliable and gracefully recurved leaves. The leaves are almost invariably a bluish grey colour and perfect for a white or silver garden, that is one where most plants grown in a specific area or bed have foliage that is various shades of white or grey. The disposition of the leaves varies among species: in some, like *B. yuccoides* (Mexican lily), they are held horizontally or erect whereas in others, such as *B. bracteata*, they are strongly recurved to drooping. The leaves of *Beschorneria* species are pleasant exceptions to those of most species of the family Agavaceae in that they are only minutely saw-toothed, unarmed and easy to prune. Indeed, although also rather fibrous, the leaves can easily be severed from the short trunk. If the old leaves are regularly removed from the trunk, the plants take on a palm-like growth form. Although many people find this a rather unnatural, disturbing practice, it testifies to the horticultural versatility of these plants. Species of *Beschorneria* flower regularly, producing long, reddish flower stalks with numerous, somewhat outsized dull yellowish green flowers. These stalks should be trimmed as close as possible to the main trunk after the flowers have been shed. *B. bracteata* is exceptionally hardy and will tolerate temperatures of well below 0 °C.

Beaucarnea stems

Beaucarnea recurvata

Beschorneria bracteata flowers

Beschorneria bracteata

Notes on species of Dracaenaceae

DRACAENA

Dracaena aletriformis (African dracaena)

This African species is a very popular accent plant that is the ideal choice for giving a lush tropical atmosphere to the garden or patio. The leaves are quite broad, flat, and tend to curve downwards. Older plants become much branched and several metres high. The inconspicuous flowers are borne in terminal clusters, followed by orange fleshy fruits.

Dracaena draco (dragon tree, dragon's blood tree)

The dragon tree or dragon's blood tree is certainly the best known of all the dracaenas. The common name is said to have been derived from the latex of some dracaenas which dries to a reddish resinous powder used as a colouring agent. This majestic tree is indigenous to the Canary Islands, but today it is cultivated in many tropical and subtropical regions of the world. It forms a thick, smooth, cylindrical bole up to 4 m tall, bearing numerous thick, erectly spreading branches. The branches give the crown of the tree a striking, symmetrically rounded appearance. In exceptional cases dragon trees can reach a height of 15 to 20 m, with a stem diameter of up to 4 m. Each branch is crowned by large rosettes of thin, pliable, pointed leaves which can reach a length of up to 1 m. The trunk of the tree remains unbranched until it produces an inflorescence. Although the flowers are rather dull-coloured, the yellowish orange berries are quite decorative. However, the fascination of the species certainly lies in its striking trunk which with age sometimes forms thick, solidified teardrops down its length, almost like molten wax sliding down the sides of a long-burning candle. In old specimens, the roots are quite formidable, often arising above ground on the lower part of the stem, stretching to the soil surface like thick pythons. The dragon tree prefers a subtropical climate and is susceptible to even light frost.

Dracaena fragrans (fragrant dracaena)

This is a popular foliage plant for a shady corner. Plants have slender stems and are sparsely branched, even when mature. The bright dark green leaves are long and relatively broad. As the name suggests, the creamy white flowers have a delightful fragrance, especially at night.

Dracaena transvaalensis (curly-leaved dracaena)

For a time, this species has been included in *D. aletriformis*, a commonly cultivated accent plant. However, in contrast to the latter species it is exceptionally drought-tolerant and a perfect plant to grow on a rockery in the harsh climate of savanna regions. Furthermore, its succulent leaves are rolled back lengthwise, probably as an adaptation to expose as small a portion as possible to the direct rays of the sun. *D. transvaalensis* is altogether a smaller plant than *D. aletriformis* and its stem does not reach the same circumference or height. This curly-leaved dracaena is naturally restricted to a small area in South Africa. In contrast to *D. aletriformis*, which has gracefully recurved leaves, those of *D. transvaalensis* are always borne erectly.

Dracaena draco

Dracaena draco

Dracaena aletriformis

Dracaena aletriformis

Dracaena transvaalensis

Notes on species of Agavaceae

FURCRAEA

Furcraea selloa (false agave)

One of the easiest ways of distinguishing cultivated species of *Furcraea* from the more widely grown *Agave* species is the shape of the bulbils or plantlets that form on the inflorescences after the flowers have been shed. In the case of *Furcraea* they are almost perfectly rounded, with only the slightest of indications from which end the leaves will develop, as opposed to the part that should be placed in the ground! In the case of *Agave*, the plantlets are almost perfectly formed miniature replicas of the mature plants. Furthermore, the inflorescences of *Furcraea* species often resemble overgrown versions of the open, multi-branched inflorescences of love grass species, included in the grass genus *Eragrostis*. The leaves of *Furcraea selloa* have a slightly rough texture, resembling that of emery board. The leaf margins are smooth for most of their length, with only a few scattered thorns towards the middle and base of the leaves. A beautiful form of the species, with yellow leaf margins, known as cultivar 'Marginata', is most often cultivated. These plants should be protected against sub-zero temperatures in wet winters, as they are not frost hardy under these conditions.

Furcraea foetida (Mauritius hemp, green aloe)

Furcraea foetida, with its long, uniformly green, sword-shaped leaves, is sometimes cultivated in large gardens. A form with whitish leaves, known as var. *mediopicta*, is popular in subtropical parts. This species is known as Mauritius hemp and is commonly cultivated in Mauritius and St Helena. So-called Cuba hemp (*F. hexapetala*), which is commonly grown in Central America for fibres and cordage, may not be distinct from *F. foetida*. Another species used for making ropes is the Central American cabuya (*F. cabuya*). Both these species are used to some extent as ornamental plants. However, *Furcraea selloa* seems to be favoured by gardeners as a result of its greater tolerance of low temperatures. Both species grow into massive, basally sprouting specimens.

Several other species are occasionally encountered in gardens and parks. These include *F. albispina, F. bedinghausii, F. elegans, F. flavoviridis, F. hexapetala, F. longaeva, F. macdougalii, F. pubescens, F. stricta* and *F. tuberosa.*

Furcraea selloa

Furcraea foetida

Furcraea foetida var. *mediopicta*

Furcraea foetida

SANSEVIERIA

Sansevieria aethiopica (common bowstring hemp)

Sansevieria aethiopica is one of the most widespread species of *Sansevieria*. Plants are proliferous through underground runners and carry their leaves in small rosettes. The leaves are folded lengthwise along the centre and are gracefully recurved. Like the other species in the genus, its horticultural charm lies in the attractively spotted leaves. It is a very hardy and useful, albeit rather sparse, groundcover. The flowers of *S. aethiopica* are very sweetly scented, especially at night.

Sansevieria hyacinthoides (African bowstring hemp)

The subtropical eastern seaboard and bushveld region of Africa is the natural habitat of *Sansevieria hyacinthoides*. The leaves are shaped like small shields, gradually tapering at both ends. Leaf colour varies widely, ranging from dull to dark green. Some forms have leaves that are beautifully mottled with light green patches. The large flowers of *S. hyacinthoides* are dull creamy white and quite pretty with their elaborately recurved, rather thread-like flower segments. The species is exceptionally adaptable to varying climatic regimes and grows very easily in dark, shady areas and also in bright sunlight.

Sansevieria pearsonii (spear plant, rhinoceros grass)

The savanna species *Sansevieria pearsonii* has very tough, sharply pointed leaves that are arranged more or less in a single row. The leaves are dull green, grooved lengthwise and resemble spears arising straight from the ground. Not surprisingly, one of the common names of *S. pearsonii* is rhinoceros grass – indeed only a rhinoceros would venture into a thick stand of the sharply pointed leaves. The inconspicuous flowers are borne on a short flower stalk that does not exceed the leaves.

Sansevieria trifasciata (snake plant, mother-in-law's tongue)

The exotic-looking *Sansevieria trifasciata* of Central Africa must rank as one of the most popular container plants in the world. It will tolerate much cultivation abuse and neglect without losing its fascination and charm. Indeed, it is often one of the few species of succulent, or any container plant for that matter, that will survive in a rather dark, dusty corner of a charming continental European restaurant. The main reason for its popularity is its ability to produce a wide range of forms with variegated leaves. This apparently occurs as a result of inherent genetic instability, allowing morphological expression in numerous mutated forms. The most commonly encountered form, known under the cultivar name 'Laurentii', has dark green leaves with lighter green transverse bands and yellow leaf edges. The structurally interesting leaves can reach a height of up to 1.5 m. The sharp but non-pungent leaf tips have given rise to the common name, mother-in-law's tongue. Its ability to maintain erect, bright green rosettes of sharp, tapering leaves regardless of treatment, has no doubt contributed to its horticultural popularity and value.

Sansevieria aethiopica

Sansevieria hyacinthoides

Sansevieria pearsonii

Sansevieria trifasciata

YUCCA

Yucca aloifolia (Spanish bayonet)

This species bears a close resemblance to the much more widely grown *Yucca gloriosa*, but it is a more dainty plant in all respects. The leaves are narrower, but no less formidable than those of *Yucca gloriosa*: they are very sharp-tipped and the margins are coarse, almost sawtooth-like. It is much more reluctant to flower in cultivation than *Yucca gloriosa*, but makes up for the lack of blooms by creating a specific "cowboy country" atmosphere in a garden. A cultivar, variously known in the horticultural trade as 'Tricolor' or 'Marginata', which has yellow leaf portions and a strong reddish tint as a young plant, is available. The species is widely known as Spanish bayonet.

Yucca elephantipes (palm-lily)

It has recently been shown that *Yucca elephantipes* is the correct name of the widely known *Yucca guatamalensis*. This species, the palm-lily, is a very popular pot plant in many parts of the world. It has long, pliable, erect to beautifully recurved leaves up to 1 m long. The leaves are rather thin, flat and hardly succulent. However, for a succulent lover the charm of the species lies in its stem, which in time will form a thick, fat, foot-like structure from which the branches arise. Old multi-stemmed specimens can reach an immense size, with long leafy branches reaching a height of 4 to 5 m. It does not flower as easily in cultivation as other *Yucca* species. A number of different leaf-colour forms are available in the trade. The most popular, 'Variegata', has yellow leaf margins, whereas the cultivar 'Jewel' has broad, light green central leaf portions and slightly darker green leaf margins.

Yucca filamentosa (Adam's needle, Adam's thread)

This species is stemless and has flexible leaves that bend downwards. The leaf margins are adorned with white threads that give it the look of a soft-leaved species of *Agave*. As with most *Yucca* species, the flowers appear to be much too large for the flowering stalk, giving the plant a lopsided appearance. Some strikingly beautiful cultivars with leaves with central or marginal yellow stripes are available under the names *Yucca filamentosa* 'Brighteye' or simply 'Variegata'. Although the leaves of *Yucca filamentosa* are pliable, their tips are deceivingly sharp and pungent. Its apt common name is Adam's needle or Adam's thread.

Yucca gloriosa (Spanish dagger)

The leaves of this species are extremely sharp-tipped and, not surprisingly, it is a popular hedge plant. Plants can reach a height of up to 3 m, but care should be taken that these large plants do not topple over. The young leaves are borne erectly, while the older, often dry, ones tend to bend down sharply, hugging the stems. The large flowers of this species are white, tinged with purple. The species is widely known as Spanish dagger. As with most other species of *Yucca*, this plant is very hardy and will tolerate very cold and dry cultivation conditions. A flowering plant of this species is shown on the family page.

Yucca elephantipes

Yucca elephantipes 'Variegata'

Yucca gloriosa 'Variegata'

Yucca filamentosa

APOCYNACEAE
Carrion flower family

DISTINGUISHING CHARACTERS Scented flowers are not uncommon in the Plant Kingdom. The sweet, subtle and often mystical scents arising from exquisitely beautiful carnations, roses and gardenias, to name but a few, are well known among gardeners and have certainly contributed to their popularity in horticulture. However, a few plants have opted for endowing their flowers with the smell of decaying flesh. This is but one of the striking features of carrion flowers: more often than not they smell like vermin! To further enhance their chances of attracting flies and bluebottles, the flowers of these plants look like putrid meat. They are almost never rosy pink or pure yellow. Instead they are often mottled with red and purple spots, contrasted against a dark cream or brown background. In addition, many carrion flowers have small, club-shaped appendages resembling fungal outgrowths that may break into a waving dance in the lightest of breezes.

NOTES It is not only the fragrance, colours and finer details of the flowers of these plants that interest botanists. Indeed, their overall shape and structure are equally intriguing. The beauty in their oddity has resulted in them today having a dedicated following of succulent plant enthusiasts across the world. But regardless of the fascination they hold for botanists and collectors, they remain notoriously difficult to identify and therefore to classify. This controversy starts at the family level. Although traditionally included in the Asclepiadaceae, recent advances in the knowledge of relationships amongst groups of plants seem to indicate that the carrion flowers are so closely related to the Apocynaceae (Oleander family) and the Periplocaceae (Khadi-root family) that all three should rather be placed together under the Apocynaceae. The largest concentrations of carrion flowers are found in southern Africa, eastern Africa and the Arabian Peninsula.

Brief notes on genera
Subfamily Apocynoideae

The genera *Adenium* and *Pachypodium* are two stalwarts of a narrowly circumscribed family Apocynaceae. They have indeed been included in this family for a long time.

Adenium (adeniums, impala lilies)

The species included in this genus would certainly have been some of the most popular succulent plants in world horticulture were it not for their distinct preference for mild to subtropical climates and concomitant difficulty to keep them out of doors in more severe climate regions of the world, where protection under glass is a necessity to ensure their survival. The trunks of the plants resemble those of miniature baobab trees, while the flowers are star-shaped and bright white or pink, or a combination of these colours.

Stapelia gigantea

Hoodia pilifera with fruit

Larryleachia marlothii

Quaqua incarnata var. *lutea*

Adenium multiflorum

Pachypodium (pachypodiums)

Although quite variable in size, all the species of *Pachypodium* have succulent stems that are variously armed with pungent spines. Trunk shape also varies considerably, with squat, compressed forms being found often, while other species carry small clusters of leaves near the tips of fat, very tall, branched or unbranched stems. Although the flowers of the species are quite beautiful, their attraction undoubtedly lies in the bizarre shape of their stems.

Subfamily Asclepiadoideae

The genera listed below have traditionally been included in the family Asclepiadaceae, which includes the well-known carrion flowers or stapeliads. They are nowadays treated as part of a broadly circumscribed family Apocynaceae, in the subfamily Asclepiadoideae. These plants are well known for the remarkable diversity of their interesting and intricate flowers. Only the more commonly cultivated genera are included here – giving only a glimpse of the remarkable diversity in the group as a whole.

Brachystelma (brachystelmas)

This group of over 100 species often has large, lantern-shaped flowers. In habitat the storage organs, a typical caudex or numerous fattened roots, are usually borne underground, but in cultivation they are exposed above ground because of their attractive shapes. The open flowers are characteristically flat or widely bell-shaped, rarely tubular as in *Ceropegia*.

Ceropegia (ceropegias)

These miniature plants are popular items for hanging-basket culture. The stems are generally very thin and wiry and the variously shaped leaves are thick and succulent. Caudiciform, tuberous storage organs are carried underground and, in some cases, intermittently along the length of the creeping or dangling stems. The peculiar flowers with their complicated structure are typically tubular, with an inflated base.

Fockea (kambro)

This is a small genus of only six species, locally referred to as "kambro". A plant of one species, *Fockea crispa,* is purportedly the oldest container plant in Europe. The above-ground parts of the plants are usually thin and twining, while the underground tuberous storage organs can be truly massive. The white and crispy tubers are a favourite snack and water source in parts of the dry Kalahari desert and are traditionally used to make jam. In cultivation, the tubers are exposed to show off their attractive shape and rough texture.

Hoodia (*ghaap*)

Species of *Hoodia* look uncannily like cacti, but once the species flower, there can be no doubt as to their affinity with other members of the carrion flower family. The stems are generally quite spiny, but the spines are not as sharp and pungent as those of cacti. They are also borne singly and not in clusters (on areoles) as is the case in cacti. There are 13 species. In many parts of southern Africa, the bitter stems (known as *ghaap*) are traditionally eaten to suppress hunger and thirst.

Pachypodium namaquanum

Hoodia pilifera subsp. *annulata*

Hoya (wax plants, wax flowers)

This genus includes the common and popular wax plant or wax flower species grown indoors in many parts of the world. The stems and roots are rather thin and non-succulent, but the large leaves are fairly thick. The common name of the plant derives from the texture of the flowers that look as if they have been freshly removed from a candle wax cast. The flowers are generally a whitish colour. *Hoya* is a large genus with over 200 species that occur mostly in Malaysia, New Caledonia, the Fiji Islands and Pakistan.

Huernia (huernias)

The 60 or more species of *Huernia* are all dwarf stem succulents that tend to creep along the ground. The stems are angled and smooth, but have prominent teeth-like protuberances along the angles. Flowers are borne at the base or the middle of the stems. They are usually spectacular, with ornate spots and characteristic smaller lobes alternating with the large, pointed main lobes. The flowers of some species have thick swollen rims; others have the flowers covered in numerous hairy structures.

Orbea (orbeas)

All the species of *Orbea* have smooth, angled stems. Most species grow as dense clumps consisting of numerous stems. The angles on the stems carry large, non-pungent teeth. Flowers are variously coloured, ranging from red, through brown to cream and yellow. The genus *Orbeopsis* and a number of its relatives were recently included in *Orbea*, making it a genus of about 50 species.

Sarcostemma (viney milkweeds)

The species of *Sarcostemma* generally have thin, wiry stems that scramble and twine into trees and surrounding vegetation. The stems are leafless and smooth. The flowers are small and fairly unobtrusive, with lime yellow lobes and a white corona in the middle.

Stapelia (stapelias)

Stapelia species are low-growing stem succulents that will in time form massive clumps. The stems of most species are covered in short hairs that give them a felt-like appearance. The flowers of stapelias are generally quite large and attractive.

Subfamily Plumerioideae

Plumeria (frangipanis)

It is really only the well-known *Plumeria rubra* and *Plumeria alba* and some of their cultivars, that need to be considered here. These and other species are the frangipanis of world horticulture. They grow as medium-sized to very large trees that are rather partial to subtropical and tropical climates. The frangipani, although indigenous to Mexico and neighbouring countries and islands of South and Central America, is inextricably linked to the paradise island of Hawaii, where ephemeral but strikingly beautiful necklaces or leis are woven from its flowers.

Sarcostemma viminale in a thorn tree

Flowers of *Sarcostemma viminale*

Stapelia pillansii

White frangipani (*Plumeria alba*)

Notes on species of Apocynaceae

Subfamily Apocynoideae

ADENIUM

Adeniums are attractive stem succulents with thick, strongly tapering trunks that are usually smooth and waxy on the surface. Leaves are borne in clusters towards the branch ends. What makes these plants particularly desirable is the spectacular, brightly coloured flowers. These are borne in dense groups, often when the stems are leafless. The species are found on the African continent and also in Arabia and Socotra. The genus is named after the city of Aden in the Republic of Yemen, which lies at the southwestern corner of the Arabian Peninsula. The Port of Aden has a 3 000-year history as an important trade centre, as it lies halfway between Europe and the Far East (on the major trade route through the Suez Canal). Two commonly cultivated species are the eastern and southern African *A. multiflorum* (impala lily) and *A. swazicum* (large-leaf impala lily). The northern Namibian *A. boehmianum* (pink impala lily) is of ethnobotanical interest. It is a traditional source of arrow poison – the vernacular name *ouzuwo* is the Herero word for poison. Indeed, the stems and roots of *Adenium* species contain heart glycosides and some are known to be very poisonous.

Adenium multiflorum (impala lily)

The impala lily is a thick-stemmed plant up to 3 m in height, with watery sap in the stems. The glossy green leaves are crowded on the branch ends. The flowers are bright red with white or pale pink in the central part. The oblong fruits split open at maturity to release the numerous hairy seeds. This species was previously known as *A. obesum* var. *multiflorum*. The impala lily in full flower (in September) is one of the most memorable sights that meet visitors to the famous Kruger National Park in South Africa.

Adenium swazicum (large-leaf impala lily)

This is a small shrub originating from the east coast of southern Africa. It was previously known as *A. boehmianum* var. *swazicum*. Plants can be grown from cuttings and they develop thick stems after a few years. The leaves are long and narrow, pale green and often have somewhat wavy margins. The attractive flowers are bright purple but those of some garden forms are reddish purple. Although fairly easy to grow, it is important to remember that adeniums are easily killed by over-watering. They should be kept dry during the dormant period in the winter months. In colder regions, these plants are grown in pots and are brought indoors in winter, as they do not tolerate frost.

Adenium multiflorum

Adenium boehmianum

Flowers of *Adenium multiflorum*

PACHYPODIUM

Pachypodium geayii (hairy-leaf pachypodium)

As is the case with most species of *Pachypodium*, *Pachypodium geayii* has a columnar growth form, with stems often being unbranched for several metres, before a small cluster of stems will eventually form at the tip of the trunk. Although in general appearance it essentially looks very similar to *Pachypodium lamerei*, which also occurs in Madagascar, it can be distinguished by its leaves which are up to 400 mm long and a much more greyish green colour, and the leaf margins which are consistently rolled down along the margins. The flowers of *Pachypodium geayii* are also white but smaller and less obtrusive than those of *Pachypodium lamerei*. Plants of *Pachypodium geayii* are increasingly popular in cultivation in areas that are not subject to severe winters. It has been offered for sale in nurseries for some years, but it has not yet achieved the same level of popularity as the much more widely grown *Pachypodium lamerei*. The likely reason is its slower growth rate and the fact that it appears to be slightly more demanding in cultivation.

Pachypodium lamerei (smooth-leaf pachypodium, Madagascar bottle tree)

This species has today achieved the status of easily the most widely cultivated of all the Madagascan, and even African, species of *Pachypodium*. It is sold virtually by the truckload, as large numbers are being raised from seed and shipped to plant nursery outlets where they fascinate gardeners in mild to tropical climates. Furthermore, with a little bit of care and protection, they can even survive reasonably well in areas with a more severe continental-type climate. The popularity of *Pachypodium lamerei*, which occurs naturally in western and southwestern Madagascar, is related to the ease with which it can be cultivated, and of course the spines of its architectural stems. Although it usually grows as single-stemmed specimens, it will branch from the base, or even higher up on the stems, if injured, for example in a cold spell through frost damage. The leathery but bright green leaves are accumulated near the tips of the stems, where they sprout almost horizontally. A useful feature of these leaves is that they are quite long, giving the plant a balanced appearance. *Pachypodium lamerei* is a perfect plant for container gardening, and the container need not be overly large. Even in rather small pots, plants do not show any signs of stress as they grow happily for years on end. The species is rather shy to flower in cultivation, but what it lacks in floral display, it makes up for in terms of its architectural form.

Pachypodium geayii leaves

Pachypodium lamerei leaves

Pachypodium lamerei

Pachypodium lamerei flowers

Pachypodium lamerei stem

Pachypodium namaquanum (Namaqualand pachypodium, elephant's trunk, *halfmens*)

The attraction of this species certainly lies in its rarity and therefore the desire to grow it well outside of its specialised natural habitat seems irresistible to some collectors! It is known as *halfmens* in Afrikaans (English: "half man" or "half human") as a result of the shape of the plant, which has a very tall, branched or unbranched, erect stem that bears clusters of leaves near the tip of the stem, which is always bent northwards. From a distance these plants look like human beings fleeing northwards on foot, with their heads thrust forward. The stems of the species are quite spiny and have a greater diameter towards the base, becoming thinner upwards. The flowers are tubular and carried in clusters near the tips of the stems, hidden among the simple leaves. The leaves have a beautiful frilly appearance. The species occurs in some of the most arid parts of northwestern South Africa and southern Namibia in the world-renowned Richtersveld. This gives a clue to the preferred growing conditions of the species: care should be taken not to over-water it at any time, and summer-rainfall growers should keep it under glass when the annual downpours start.

Pachypodium saundersiae (bottle tree)

This is one of the lower-growing species of *Pachypodium*. Its growth form is more squat than that of many other species of the genus and the white to grey trunk often looks like a massive blob of candle wax that has been left in the sun for too long. The leaves are a bright, shiny green colour and the leaf margins are usually distinctly wavy. The flowers are a waxy, white colour, with reddish purple flecks, and the free parts of the petals are dissected in the shape of a five-lobed star. It grows on rocky outcrops, or in the crevices among rocks and boulders. Its natural habitat is a north–south band in eastern southern Africa, from South Africa to Mozambique, northwards to Zimbabwe. It is a distinctly summer-rainfall species that favours mild temperatures, even in winter. The species is deciduous and sheds its leaves in winter. During this dry time of year the trunk can shrivel considerably and feel soft to the touch. Once the rains return, the trunk expands again as it once again becomes filled with water. As a result of the wonderfully architectural trunk, which can grow fully exposed or somewhat below ground level, *Pachypodium saundersiae* is an excellent feature plant for a container or in an open bed.

Pachypodium namaquanum in nature

Flowers of *Pachypodium namaquanum*

Pachypodium saundersiae

Flowers and leaves of *Pachypodium saundersiae*

Subfamily Asclepiadoideae

BRACHYSTELMA

Brachystelma barberae

This small herb of only about 100 mm height produces a large edible tuber of up to 200 mm in diameter, which becomes irregular in shape when old. The annual stems bear several hairy leaves. The smelly flowers are borne in dense clusters of about 25 – they are truly spectacular and bizarre, with the long slender petals of each flower remaining fused at the tips to form a cage-like structure. The lobes are reddish brown inside and white on the outside. Care should be taken not to over-water plants in winter, when they are in a resting phase.

CEROPEGIA

Ceropegia woodii (rosary vine, hearts-on-a-string)

This species is the ultimate in terms of adaptation to cultivation in hanging baskets. It develops small stone-shaped storage organs from which thin, wiry stems arise that will easily and quickly creep over the edge of a container. These stems are adorned with small, strikingly mottled heart-shaped leaves, making a small pot of this species the perfect Valentine's Day gift for a loved one! The pinkish purple flowers are small, shaped like miniature lanterns and decorated with long purple hairs. *Ceropegia woodii* is one of the easiest of all succulents to grow successfully. It can tolerate a lot of water as long as the soil mixture is friable and well drained. It generally prefers a mixture that is rich in organic material.

FOCKEA

Fockea angustifolia (Kalahari kambro)

This species is a traditional water source that sustained human life during the dry winter season in the desert. It has large, smooth tubers, narrowly oblong leaves with characteristic wavy margins and small greenish flowers.

Fockea crispa (*bergkambro*)

A cultivated specimen of *Fockea crispa*, a typical caudiciform plant, is claimed to be the oldest surviving container plant in Europe. A specimen of this species, which occurs naturally in the Little Karoo in South Africa, has been in cultivation at Schönbrunn near Vienna, Austria, since 1799. It is a traditional food plant and is known locally as *bergkambro* (English: mountain kambro).

Fockea edulis (common kambro)

This species has a massive tuber with a characteristic warty surface. The plant has numerous stems that bear relatively broad leaves and inconspicuous green and white flowers. Large specimens, with the attractive tubers exposed above the ground surface, are sometimes seen in succulent gardens and rockeries in warm regions.

Brachystelma barberae

Leaves of *Fockea angustifolia*

Ceropegia woodii

Flowers of *Fockea edulis*

Fockea crispa

Tuber of *Fockea edulis*

HOODIA

Hoodia gordonii (common *ghaap*, bitter *ghaap*)

This is the best known and most commonly cultivated species. It has also become famous because it is a source of raw material for numerous weight loss products, claimed to suppress appetite. The erect stems are covered in sharp, somewhat tapering spines. The flesh-coloured and disc-shaped flowers look like small radar antennae.

Hoodia flava (yellow *ghaap*)

The small-flowered *Hoodia flava* is just one of several *Hoodia* species that are suitable for use as rockery plants in dry regions or more often as container plants. Plants grow quite fast and produce numerous small yellow flowers, followed by the typical paired fruits so characteristic of the family.

Hoodia pilifera subsp. *annulata* (purple *ghaap*)

It is really very easy to confuse this species with a species of cactus when it is observed for the first time. The plants grow as large clumps not unlike those formed by the cactus *Echinopsis spachiana*, which is naturalised in parts of the habitat of *Hoodia pilifera* subsp. *annulata*. The stems are carried erectly and they branch and rebranch mainly from the base of the stems. The stems are cylindrical in shape and spiny, with each spine arising from a small swelling on the stem. The flowers are a dark purplish brown colour and are densely arranged along the upper parts of the stems. *Hoodia pilifera* subsp. *pilifera* differs in the shape and colour of the flowers – almost black and without a ring (annulus). The species is fairly easy in cultivation, provided it is protected from excessive rainfall.

HOYA

Hoya carnosa (common wax plant, wax flower)

Of all the several hundred species of *Hoya* that are known, only one or two are widely grown. By far the most popular one is *Hoya carnosa*, the common wax plant. In few other instances among cultivated succulents has a single species done so much to popularise a large genus. Indeed, this is the plant that is often found on windowsills in European shops and pubs, with the leaves virtually covered in layers of months-old dust. Numerous cultivars of *Hoya carnosa* have been described, many of them with beautifully silver- and gold-spotted leaves. Some cultivars even have curly leaves, which is not to the liking of all gardeners, as these plants tend to appear sickly. *Hoya carnosa* is one of the most tolerant of all species when it comes to cultivation conditions. It can suffer almost any abuse and will still thrive. It can be grown in virtually any size container, in any type of soil. However, it prefers a rich, friable soil, supplemented by copious amounts of decomposed organic material. It will grow happily in such a mixture for years on end, but the addition of a seaweed-derived organic plant fertiliser will increase the number of flowers produced. *Hoyas* should never be pruned, as new flowers are formed on the same spot year after year. Interestingly, pot-bound plants tend to grow and flower far more prolifically than specimens that are regularly repotted – they either die or take long to recover if the roots are disturbed.

Hoodia gordonii

Hoodia pilifera subsp. *pilifera*

Hoodia flava

Hoodia pilifera subsp. *annulata*

Hoya carnosa flowers

Hoya carnosa

HUERNIA

Huernia hystrix (toad plant)

An easy species to grow, *Huernia hystrix* has attractive frilly flowers about 20 mm in diameter that are freely formed towards the end of summer.

Huernia zebrina (zebra flower)

As the name indicates, the flowers of *Huernia zebrina* are decorated with beautiful stripes like those of a zebra. The characteristic bright red, thick, smooth rim of the flower adds to the attraction. Plants are fairly easy to grow in well-drained, friable soil provided they are kept pest free and well watered during the growing season and protected from cold in winter.

ORBEA

Orbea lutea subsp. *lutea* (yellow carrion flower)

Orbea lutea subsp. *lutea* has short, curved, semi-erect stems that are a light green colour mottled with purplish flecks. The flowers are uniformly bright yellow and exude a terrible smell of putrid meat. The species is remarkably easy in cultivation and it will grow in almost any type of soil. The short stems that all lean to one side usually indicate the direction in which new growth will form. This is one of the fascinating tendencies of the species, indeed of many asclepiad species: the plants seem to be able to "walk", as new stems that look exactly like the existing ones grow in the direction of suitable microhabitats. *Orbea lutea* subsp. *lutea* grows very easily from stem cuttings planted directly in the desired spot in the garden. For some years *Orbea lutea* was known under the name *Orbeopsis lutea*.

Orbea variegata (common carrion flower, Cape fritillary)

This is the well-known carrion flower of Table Mountain. From Cape Town it has been transported all over the world and is today perhaps the most widely cultivated of all the typical asclepiad species, commonly known as carrion flowers. It has fairly thin stems that can reach a length of almost 200 mm, but they are usually somewhat shorter. The stems are a dull, light green colour and are blotched with purple spots. Flower size and colour vary somewhat, but the flowers of the most commonly encountered forms usually have a light creamy yellow or green background colour adorned with brown, red or purple spots. Flower size varies from 40 to 90 mm in diameter. Although coming from a winter-rainfall area, it grows surprisingly easily in summer-rainfall areas too, without protection. The fruit are paired capsules, resembling the horns of an antelope. At maturity they split open to release numerous small brown fruits crowned with long white hairs.

Huernia hystrix

Huernia zebrina

Orbea lutea subsp. *lutea*

Orbea variegata

SARCOSTEMMA

Sarcostemma viminale (viney milkweed)

This viney milkweed is widely distributed in Africa. It is usually a robust climber that often festoons large trees in savanna regions, but more shrubby dwarf forms are sometimes encountered in very dry habitats. The fleshy leafless stems are repeatedly branched and rebranched and exude milky latex when broken. Small but attractive off-white flowers are borne in clusters near the stem tips. Plants are easily cultivated in warm regions but they tend to become untidy with age.

STAPELIA

Stapelia gigantea (giant carrion flower)

The giant carrion flower must rate as one of the most spectacular gems of the succulent world. The plant has leafless and thornless four-angled stems curling upwards like fingers on a hand. Enormous star-shaped flowers are borne near the base of the plant. They are yellowish to pale brown in colour and beautifully decorated with numerous wavy purple lines. The plant is easily propagated from cuttings, which should be left out for a week or two to form callus tissue before they are planted. For containers, a mixture of two parts good garden soil and one part sharp, coarse sand will ensure adequate drainage. A fair amount of water is tolerated during the active growth period in summer but the plant should be kept fairly dry during the resting period in winter.

Stapelia grandiflora (purple carrion flower)

This is another popular carrion flower that is cultivated in many parts of the world. It closely resembles the giant carrion flower but the flowers are usually much darker in colour (often a purplish brown) with conspicuous hairs along the rather broad lobes. The specimen shown here is one of many colour forms of the species, previously known as *Stapelia flavirostris*. The unpleasant smell emitted by the flowers is not really a problem when the plant is grown outdoors. Notice the blowfly and the numerous blowfly eggs that are visible on the surface of the flower. The flies and blowflies are attracted by the powerful smell and are fooled into thinking that they have discovered a rotting animal carcass. The surface hairs and colour of the flowers contribute to the deception.

Stapelia leendertziae (red carrion flower, *aaskelk*)

Another gem from Africa, *Stapelia leendertziae* is indigenous to South Africa and Zimbabwe. The pale green, creeping stems can spread for considerable distances along the ground. The remarkable flowers, almost the size of a hand, are often borne in pairs. They are bell-shaped and dark purple, with elegant, slender lobes. Succulent enthusiasts all over the world have succeeded in growing this unusual plant. The secret is simple: well-drained but rich soil, limited watering in winter but fairly regular watering during the growing season. Plants in their dormant state can tolerate fairly low temperatures but are easily killed by frost.

Stapelia gigantea

Stapelia grandiflora

Stapelia leendertziae

Subfamily Plumerioideae

PLUMERIA

Plumeria rubra (red frangipani)

Representatives of *Plumeria*, the frangipani, are some of the few species of the subfamily Plumerioideae that are popular in world horticulture. A number of characters of the frangipani, or pagoda tree as it is sometimes known, contribute to its popularity in horticulture: it has magnificently fragranced flowers, the colour of the flowers varies tremendously and the succulent stems are neat and smooth. Furthermore, it is often the preferred specimen tree for a garden where succulents are the subjects of choice. Frangipani trees only start to branch after they have flowered. Although this can take a few years, the wait is worthwhile as the flowers are truly beautiful. They are trumpet-shaped and the free floral parts are generally twisted or spiralled to one side. A piece of string can be strung through the mouths of the flowers and out at the thin ends to make a densely packed necklace or "lei". Although nearly 50 species have been described in *Plumeria*, fewer than 10 probably have grounds for being recognised as good species for cultivation. One of these, *Plumeria rubra*, has been used as the source of many of the hundreds of named cultivars available in the nursery trade. Their flowers are particularly variable but are consistently magnificently scented. Flower colour varies from intensely reddish pink with a yellow centre, through uniformly yellow to white. As with all frangipanis, the leaves of young trees are larger than those of large, mature specimens. Incidentally, this trait is also found in the unrelated *Aloe barberae*, a tree-like member of the *Aloe* family.

Plumeria alba (white frangipani)

The flowers of *Plumeria alba* are white with yellow centres. Flower size is variable and forms with flowers that can be as much as 60 mm across are known. *Plumeria alba* is a faster grower than *Plumeria rubra*, but the latter is often preferred as a garden tree as a result of the intense pinkish red colour of its flowers. Both *Plumeria rubra* and *Plumeria alba* can grow into very large, almost unmanageable trees that will produce copious amounts of leaf litter in the winter, as they are deciduous. As a result of the size of their shiny, non-succulent, boat-shaped leaves and the density of their canopies such large trees will discourage growth of a groundcover of any kind under them. Most species of *Plumeria* are very easy in cultivation – a severed stem can simply be placed in the soil where the tree is intended to grow. Before this is done, it should be left in the shade to allow the wound to dry. This will prevent stem rot setting in. As always, care should be taken that the soil mixture is well drained.

Plumeria rubra

Plumeria rubra

Plumeria alba

ASPHODELACEAE

Aloe family

Group 3

Distinguishing characters The Asphodelaceae, which consists of an exclusively Old World group of genera, comprises about 700 species, all of which are rosulate leaf succulents. Two easily recognisable and rather distinct groups are widely accepted in the family. The first is the subfamily Alooideae, which contains all the aloes and their close relatives, while the other, somewhat lesser known subfamily, the Asphodeloideae, includes the well-known red hot pokers (*Kniphofia* species), bulbines and their relatives. The Alooideae is characterised by a number of rather cryptic anatomical and chemical characters that need not concern us here. For the purpose of this discussion, the aloes and their relatives are an exclusively succulent-leaved group of which most species bear striking, dense to sparse clusters of brightly or dull-coloured inflorescences in the winter months.

Notes The Asphodelaceae includes some of the most popular succulents in cultivation today. Many species, such as the single-stemmed *Aloe ferox* (bitter aloe) and *Aloe marlothii* (mountain aloe) are perfect specimen plants, while the shrubby *Bulbine frutescens* is a very popular groundcover.

Brief notes on genera

Subfamily Alooideae

Aloe

The genus *Aloe* is restricted to Africa, Madagascar and southern Arabia. Aloes come in all shapes and sizes, from the lofty tree aloe, *Aloe barberae* (up to 20 m tall), to the tiny white grass aloe, *Aloe albida,* barely 100 mm high. There is great variation in the size and shape of leaves, ranging from broad and boat-shaped to narrow and grass-like. The leaves of some aloes are virtually without thorns, while others have sharp spines along the edges and sometimes also on the upper and lower surfaces. Likewise, the shape, arrangement and colour of the flowers vary considerably, from dainty, bell-shaped and pinkish white, as in some of the grass aloes (for example *Aloe myriacantha*), to robust, tubular and crimson-red as in the krantz aloe (*Aloe arborescens*). The combination of these characters serves to make aloes some of the most desirable and rewarding succulents to grow. Many of the large species of *Aloe* are popular in amenity horticulture, while the smaller species are popular as container plants in collections.

Fan aloe (*Aloe plicatilis*)

Aloe ferox × *Aloe arborescens*

Aloe speciosa

Aloe leaf showing gel and juice

Bulbine frutescens leaves showing gel

Kniphofia (garden hybrid)

Bulbine frutescens

Astroloba

Although the brownish green flowers of the few species included in this genus closely resemble those of some species of *Haworthia*, their mouths are never two-lipped. Plants typically form large clumps consisting of thin stems that are covered in small, mostly triangular leaves that inconsistently die back along the entire length of the stems. The leaves are typically hard in texture and spine-tipped. One species, *Astroloba rubriflora*, has red flowers.

Chortolirion

This genus includes one species only, *Chortolirion angolense*. It is a small bulbous plant with distinctly grass-like leaves. The flowers are two-lipped and closely resemble those of some species of *Haworthia*.

Gasteria (gasterias, stomach flowers)

This small genus of about 18 species is characterised by the leaves, which are usually heavily spotted or warted and tongue-shaped, and by the curved, greenish red flowers with their characteristic basal inflation (hence the name *Gasteria*, meaning "stomach"). The genus *Gasteria* includes many shade-loving species that are perfect for inclusion in greenhouse collections as potted specimens. Some species have the leaves in a spiral (as in most aloes), while others have them in two ranks or rows. Gasterias are popular houseplants because they are able to tolerate very low levels of light.

Haworthia (wart plants)

Haworthia species are definitely not grown for their flowers. Even though mostly strikingly two-lipped, their small, dull, dirty-white (rarely yellowish or pinkish) flowers can only be described as insignificant. However, what they lack in terms of flower size and colour, they make up for in more ways than one with their beautifully coloured and beautifully shaped leaves that range from apically flattened and soil-hugging to erect and strikingly white-banded or spotted. The plants resemble miniature aloes and they show remarkable diversity in size and shape. All species of *Haworthia* (and those of *Astroloba* and *Gasteria*) are indigenous to southern Africa.

Subfamily Asphodeloideae

Bulbine

Bulbines can be very easily distinguished from their cousins in the Alooideae in that their flowers consist of free segments, giving them an open, star-shaped appearance. Furthermore, the flowers display diurnal movement, that is, they close at night and open again the next morning. The filaments or stalks that carry the anthers (collectively known as the stamens – the male reproductive organs) in the flowers are very distinctive because they are densely bearded. *Bulbine* is sometimes confused with *Bulbinella*, but species of the latter genus are non-succulent and the stamens are not bearded.

Astroloba foliolosa

Chortolirion angolense

Gasteria excelsa

Flowers of *Gasteria acinacifolia*

Haworthia mutica

Flowers of *Haworthia truncata*

Bulbine latifolia in nature

Flowers of *Bulbine latifolia*

Notes on species of Asphodelaceae

Subfamily Alooideae

ALOE

Aloe arborescens (krantz aloe)

Plants grow as robust shrubs that are characteristically multi-branched. Each branch carries medium-sized to large rosettes of variously recurved leaves in terminal clusters. The stems are usually covered in the remains of dried leaves. Leaf margins are armed with small but tough teeth. The neat, cone-shaped inflorescences are densely packed with pencil-shaped flowers and are borne on unbranched stalks. Flower colour usually varies from orange to red, but yellow forms are also known. This extremely variable species, which occurs from the southern tip of Africa along the high mountains to Zimbabwe and Malawi, must rate as the most popular aloe in amenity horticulture and landscaping practices. It grows exceptionally easily from large or small cuttings.

Aloe aristata (torch plant, lace aloe)

Plants are solitary or clump-forming miniatures. In time clumps will multiply to consist of numerous tightly packed rosettes. The leaf surfaces vary from almost smooth to densely covered with small, slightly elevated white spots. These spots and the leaf margins carry soft, harmless teeth. The leaves commonly have short or long hair-like awns at their tips. The bow-shaped flowers vary from deep red to light pink and are surprisingly large for such small plants. Plants are easy in cultivation and can be used effectively as a groundcover, if planted *en masse*. Like species of *Haworthia*, it prefers dappled shade, but will also thrive in deep shade.

Aloe barberae (tree aloe)

This is a graceful tree with dark green, curved leaves borne at the tips of slender branches to form a wide crown. The flowers are borne in short racemes and vary from pink to orange. As the tallest of all aloes, this species has become very popular as a garden tree in large gardens and parks. It is also often grown as a container plant on patios or as specimen plants along walls. With age, the tree develops a tapering trunk and the leaves tend to become smaller than those of juvenile plants. New plants form easily from cuttings or truncheons, provided they are initially kept dry to prevent rot.

Aloe brevifolia (short-leaf aloe, blue aloe)

Plants typically form small to medium-sized mound-shaped clumps that consist of numerous tightly packed rosettes. The rosettes consist of small, angled, somewhat finger-shaped, bluish leaves. Numerous inflorescences carrying bright orange, pencil-shaped flowers are produced in summer. The species grows exceptionally well in Mediterranean-type climates (mild, wet winters and hot, dry summers). In summer rainfall regions plants need to be protected from too much rainfall at this time of year. Plants of this species should also be protected from subzero temperatures.

Aloe arborescens

Aloe aristata

Aloe barberae

Flowers of *Aloe barberae*

Aloe brevifolia

Aloe camperi (East African aloe, *groenaalwyn*)

Plants grow as robust, stemless rosettes that will in time produce numerous offsets near ground level. The leaves are a deep dark green colour, with characteristic small white spots on both surfaces. The leaf marginal spines are short, stubby and not very pungent. In many forms of this species, the spines are also green and not dark brown or black as is most commonly encountered in this genus. The flowers are borne in much-branched inflorescences, which consist of small head-shaped side branches. The flowers themselves are club-shaped – a character that is not commonly found in aloes. This East African species is remarkably tolerant of shady positions in the garden.

Aloe ciliaris (fringed climbing aloe, *rankaalwyn*)

Plants of *Aloe ciliaris* grow as massive dangling creepers or they will climb into and onto artificial support structures or surrounding vegetation. The stems are fairly thin and unable to support the rosettes that consist of widely spaced leaves that are hardly succulent. The leaves are stem-clasping and have distinct fringes of soft, white teeth near the point of attachment to the stems. The inflorescences are fairly short and stout and consist of large red flowers loosely arranged on a central axis. *Aloe ciliaris* occurs in the Eastern Cape Province of South Africa, an area that receives rainfall throughout the year. This is the ultimate creeping and climbing aloe and it can even be trained and trimmed into a neat, dense hedge.

Aloe dichotoma (quiver tree)

Plants are medium-sized to large, single-trunked trees that support large canopies consisting of numerous branches with terminal rosettes. The stems of the species are columnar or sometimes the shape of an inverted cone. The bark on older stems splits longitudinally to give rise to razor sharp, ragged edges. The leaves are fairly short and a distinctive greyish green. The leaf margins are armed with short, white, harmless teeth. The flowers, produced in winter, are fleshy and a bright, butter yellow. Of the southern African tree aloes, *Aloe dichotoma*, the quiver tree, is perhaps the most famous. The giant quiver tree (*Aloe pillansii*), a very rare species, differs in the larger and fewer branches and the much-branched inflorescences that are borne from the basal leaves in the rosette. The maiden quiver tree (*Aloe ramosissima*) is also similar but this species lacks a main trunk. In some parts of its natural habitat the quiver tree is locally common enough to form small forests. The San people of the parched desert areas used the hollowed-out stems as quivers for their arrows, hence the common name. In their way, these trees are just as unique and impressive as the Californian redwoods or the Amazonian giant water lily. Quiver trees are quite difficult to grow as garden succulents as they require hot temperatures and very well-drained soil. *Aloe dichotoma*, however, grows reasonably well as a garden tree in warm regions and makes an excellent pot plant on a warm patio. The plants should be kept dry during the resting phase and good drainage is essential.

Aloe camperi

Aloe camperi in flower

Aloe ciliaris

Flowers of *Aloe dichotoma*

Aloe dichotoma in nature

Aloe ramosissima

Aloe ferox (Cape aloe, bitter aloe)

The famous Cape aloe or bitter aloe occurs in the eastern parts of South Africa. This single-stemmed aloe is similar to the mountain aloe but the flowers are borne in a dense, erect, candelabra-like inflorescence. Bitter aloes are particularly common in the Mossel Bay area in the southern Cape of South Africa, where they have been harvested for centuries to produce an important medicinal product known as Cape aloes or Cape aloe lump. The traditional method of production involves removing the leaves and piling them in neat, erect stacks over a skin or plastic sheet placed in a hollow in the ground. The yellow juice that exudes from the cut end is dried over an open fire to form a dark brown crystalline solid, still used in the pharmaceutical industry as a purgative. Experienced harvesters will not remove more than about eight leaves from each plant, so that the resource is used on a sustainable-yield basis. *Aloe ferox* is a popular garden succulent and can be grown in almost all warm and temperate regions, provided that it is protected from heavy frost. Propagation is only possible from seeds, as the plants are almost invariably single-stemmed. Multi-stemmed specimens (propagated from stem cuttings) are commonly encountered in gardens but these are usually hybrids with *A. arborescens* and not the pure species. *Aloe ferox* are available is a wide range of growth forms and natural colour variants. A form of the species previously known as *A. candelabrum* is particularly popular because of its gracefully down-curved leaves and coral red flowers. Various shades of orange or yellow and even pure white are sometimes seen in gardens.

Aloe humilis (spider aloe, hedgehog, crocodile-jaws)

Plants grow as large clumps consisting of a multitude of small rosettes. The leaves are densely covered with numerous soft, white, harmless teeth. The inflorescences are very large for these miniature plants. A limited number of flowers that appear distinctly oversized for such small plants are carried on robust inflorescences in the summer months. This species occurs naturally in the arid Eastern Cape Province and is also a component of subtropical thicket, in areas with a somewhat higher rainfall. It has also been recorded from the Little Karoo, a large arid valley between two mountain ranges in South Africa's southern Cape. *Aloe humilis* grows very well as a windowsill plant in small containers.

Aloe krapohliana (dwarf aloe)

This species, commonly known as dwarf aloe or *dwergaalwyn*, grows as small, single rosettes or occasionally a specimen will divide into two or more heads. The leaves are short, narrow and beautifully banded transversely with alternating bluish and greyish brown zones. The leaves are incurved, giving rise to the spherical or soccer ball-shape of the rosettes. The leaf margins are armed with very small, white teeth. The racemes are commonly unbranched and up to six can be produced simultaneously from a single rosette. Flower colour ranges from uniformly crimson-red to deep orange with yellow mouths. The species occurs in a broad strip along South Africa's arid winter-rainfall west coast, stretching inland for about 100 km. This is a strikingly beautiful species, especially when in flower in late winter because its inflorescences and flowers are very large for such a small plant. *Aloe krapohliana* is reasonably easy in cultivation, especially if grown from seed. It has a distinct preference for winter rainfall, and then only very little.

Aloe ferox (typical form)

Aloe ferox ("candelabra" form)

Aloe ferox (white-flowered form)

Aloe humilis

Aloe lineata var. *lineata* (lined aloe)

The species, known as lined aloe or *streepaalwyn*, grows as single stemmed specimens that occasionally form offsets along the length of the trunks. The stems are usually covered in the remains of old, dried leaves. The leaves are bright to brownish green and carry distinct reddish longitudinal lines. The leaf margins are armed with strong, pungent brownish teeth. Several fairly tall inflorescences are produced from a single plant. The buds on the inflorescences are almost completely enclosed by large floral bracts. Flower colour ranges from dull orange to bright red. The variety *lineata* is widely distributed in the Eastern Cape, where it flowers in spring to early summer. In contrast to most other species with which it occurs in the Eastern Cape thickets, *Aloe lineata* var. *lineata* tends to flower in summer and not winter. This is a good plant to have in your garden if you desire aloe flower colour in summer. But of course, the red-lined leaves make the species attractive throughout the year. It adapts well to coastal gardens.

Aloe littoralis (mountain aloe, spotted mountain aloe, Windhoek aloe)

Common names are often not very specific so it comes as no surprise that *Aloe littoralis* is also known as mountain aloe, or *bergaalwyn*. It is a conspicuous feature of the rocky hills in the capital city of Namibia, hence the alternative (and less ambiguous) name "Windhoek aloe". Plants grow as large, single-stemmed specimens that can reach a height of up to 3 m. The trunk is covered in a skirt of dried leaves. The rosettes consist of boat-shaped leaves that are often densely incurved, while the oldest living leaves tend to fan out horizontally from the stem. The leaves of young plants are copiously white-spotted, but these spots disappear almost entirely once plants reach maturity. The leaf margins carry sharp, triangular teeth that arise from a whitish base. The inflorescences are multi-branched and carry sparsely arranged flowers along their lengths. Flowers are pinkish red and often lined with yellow. This species occurs in South Africa, Botswana and Namibia and flowers in summer. It is one of the most stately single-stemmed summer-rainfall aloes. It shares a summer-flowering period with only a small group of other species.

Aloe longistyla (karoo aloe)

Aloe longistyla, the karoo aloe or *ramenas*, usually grows as solitary specimens, but occasionally a plant divides into two to three rosettes. These rosettes are small and compact and easily fit in under low karoo bushes in its natural habitat. The leaves are fairly small and short and carry soft, scattered teeth often on whitish spots. The flowers are extremely large for such a small plant and are densely clustered on a short flower stalk. The stamens, that is, the male parts of the flower, extend well beyond the flower mouth. The flowers are dull to bright red. The species grows in the dry central karroid regions of South Africa where it flowers from midwinter to late winter. To many people, particularly collectors, the small miniature aloes are some of the most desirable species to grow. This certainly applies to *Aloe longistyla*, which is magnificent in cultivation if grown to perfection. However, it is rather particular when it comes to growing conditions, and especially dislikes too much water. It is also exceedingly prone to mite (an arachnid) infestations.

Aloe lineata

Flowers of *Aloe lineata*

Aloe longistyla flowers

Aloe littoralis in flower

Aloe longistyla with fruits

Aloe marlothii (mountain aloe)

In the northern parts of South Africa and adjoining parts of Botswana, the robust, single-stemmed *Aloe marlothii*, the mountain aloe, often dominates the landscape as far as the eye can see. In time, plants will grow into very large, majestic specimens with large boat-shaped leaves arranged in massive rosettes. The margins and both surfaces of the leaves of *Aloe marlothii* are usually covered in sharp, dark brown spines. A unique feature of this aloe is the horizontally slanted peduncles on which the yellow, orange or red flowers are arranged. These peduncles form perfect perches for sunbirds attracted to the copious amounts of nectar. This archetypal aloe is a distinctive winter-flowering species in its habitat, brightening the landscape when little else is in flower.

When not in flower, this single-stemmed aloe can easily be mistaken for the bitter aloe (*Aloe ferox*). As is the case with *A. ferox*, the species also has numerous regional (natural) variants and colour forms. A form of *A. marlothii* occurring in the KwaZulu-Natal province of South Africa (previously known as *A. spectabilis*) has the flower clusters less slanted than the normal form but the bright yellow colour of the open flowers is a useful feature to identify this form and to distinguish it from *A. ferox* (in which the buds and open flowers are the same colour). A natural form with bright red flowers is also known.

Aloe marlothii is an important plant in African traditional medicine and is one of the most important of all sources of traditional veterinary medicine. The leaf gel has numerous uses and is commonly applied to treat wounds and skin conditions in cattle and other domestic animals. When taken internally, the bitter yellow juice is strongly purgative. Dried juice of this species was indeed once a commercial commodity (known as Natal aloes) but the quality is inferior to that of the more chemically uniform Cape aloes. *Aloe marlothii* is almost exclusively propagated from seeds (that germinate and grow very easily) because the plants are rarely multi-stemmed. For the best results, a hot, subtropical climate is required but plants can be successfully grown in a warm spot in the garden (against a wall, for example). Good drainage is essential, and plants should be kept quite dry during the resting phase.

Aloe microstigma (speckled aloe)

Plants of the speckled aloe or *gevlekte aalwyn*, as *Aloe microstigma* is popularly known, grow as medium-sized rosettes that are borne on stems that may reach a height of about 500 mm. The stems are covered with the remains of old, spent leaves. The leaves are narrowly boat-shaped and generally carried in an upright position. Both leaf surfaces are characteristically spotted with numerous small, white speckles. The leaf margins are armed with short, brownish teeth. The flowers are carried on a fairly tall, elongated, cone-shaped inflorescence. Flower colour varies widely, from uniformly red to uniformly yellow. However, inflorescences with reddish orange buds and yellow open flowers are most commonly found. The species is widely distributed in a west–east band that runs through the Little Karoo of South Africa and is one of the most common aloes. The plants are often locally dominant, and when in flower the hills are alive with colour provided by their tall, often multi-coloured, inflorescences.

Aloe marlothii (red-flowered form)

Aloe marlothii ("spectabilis" form)

Aloe marlothii (normal form)

Aloe microstigma

Aloe rupestris (bottlebrush aloe)

This is a tall, single-stemmed aloe that can reach a height of 8 m in exceptional cases. It has relatively narrow leaves and orange to red flowers with bright red stamens. Plants are easy to grow from seed and cuttings and have become very popular as a garden aloe in warm and temperate regions, where it will survive light frost. *Aloe rupestris* is unfortunately susceptible to white scale – any infestation should immediately be treated with contact insecticide to prevent serious damage.

Aloe striata (coral aloe)

The coral aloe is an old favourite amongst gardeners because of the ease with which it can be cultivated. It is has smooth, sea-green to turquoise leaves lined with a pink, spineless margin and bears clusters of coral orange flowers in spring.

Aloe striata × *Aloe maculata* (garden aloe)

One of the interesting features about aloes is that most of the species are interfertile and readily hybridise. This may be confusing to botanists and gardeners who want to identify garden aloes. There are aloe breeders who specialise in creating beautiful new aloe cultivars with desirable traits – plant size, flower number, flower size, colour intensity, time of flowering and especially ease of cultivation are all important considerations. One example of a popular garden hybrid is the cross between *Aloe maculata* (a spotted aloe) and the closely related *Aloe striata* (the coral aloe). It appears that there are actually several different clones in horticulture – evidence that the two species have been crossed more than once. The plants are easily propagated by sucker shoots, they are robust and easy to grow and they make an attractive display in winter or early summer.

Aloe tenuior (climbing aloe)

This distinctive aloe has thin elongated stems that gradually form dense masses. It has become a popular garden plant because of the ease with which it can be cultivated. Propagation is equally simple – cuttings root very easily. The flowers are small and vary from yellow to red. In time it will grow into a large tangled mass of stems.

Aloe thraskii (dune aloe)

The dune aloe is a striking plant that is well known to holidaymakers along the east coast of South Africa, because it is always found on sand dunes near the sea. It has large, deeply channelled, downturned leaves that almost touch the stem. The yellow flowers are borne in short, dense, erect racemes, grouped together in much-branched panicles. Few aloes can rival the graceful beauty of this species, which deserves to be planted more often, especially in coastal gardens. Since it is well adapted to sea breezes, *Aloe thraskii* is an excellent choice for coastal gardens.

Aloe rupestris plant

Aloe rupestris flowers

Aloe striata

Aloe maculata

Aloe thraskii

Aloe tenuior

Aloe variegata (partridge-breasted aloe, falcon feather, tiger aloe, *kanniedood* aloe)

The English common names of the species – partridge-breasted aloe, falcon feather and tiger aloe – make sense once one has seen the plant in its natural habitat: the dark blackish to greyish green leaves are indeed beautifully mottled with white flecks. Plants are fairly small and even mature specimens fit comfortably under the low canopies of karroid shrublets. The triangular leaves are arranged in three distinct rows and have a conspicuous central keel on the outer side. The leaf margins are unarmed, but do have whitish, finely toothed, horny ridges. The slightly curved flowers are laxly arranged on a short inflorescence. Flowers are pinkish red, or rarely yellow. The species is widely distributed in the central Karoo and adjacent arid parts of South Africa where it flowers in mid- to late winter. This was one of the first aloes to be cultivated in Europe, following its discovery and introduction to that continent. Even today it is a popular windowsill plant. It is a truly delightful species to grow, but be sure not to over-water it. An interesting feature of *Aloe variegata* is its large seeds – the largest in the genus – which have conspicuous, white papery wings.

Aloe vera (Barbados aloe)

Aloe vera is a relatively small aloe with short stems and soft, practically thornless leaves that characteristically curve graceful near the tips. The leaves may have a few spots near the base or may be quite heavily white-spotted in the small form of the species known as Chinese aloe (this form is widely cultivated in China, Thailand and other eastern countries). Plants soon form dense clusters if left unattended, but gardeners usually remove any suckers that are formed in order to increase the size of the specimen. The yellow (rarely red) flowers are borne in sparsely branched inflorescences. The long, tubular flowers typically hang down after they have opened.

This famous aloe is widely cultivated on a commercial scale for the production of aloe gel used in tonic drinks and cosmetic products. Indeed, *Aloe vera* has become one of the most important of all medicinal plants and the annual turnover of the industry has been estimated to exceed 120 billion US dollars. Some people refer to it as *Aloe barbadensis* but the oldest and correct name is definitely *Aloe vera*. It is believed to have originated in North Africa, from where it was first distributed to Spain and other Mediterranean countries and then to Central America. It has gradually become an important crop plant – first in Texas, where the industry originated, and later in Mexico and various countries of Central America. Today, thousands of hectares are cultivated under irrigation in the southern parts of North America, Central America and more recently also in China.

The plant has attractive (mostly yellow) flowers but it is a sterile cultigen (an ancient clone selected by humans) that rarely if ever forms seeds. It is, however, very easily propagated by the countless suckers that form around mature plants. These suckers (called "pups" in the USA) are simply removed and replanted. *Aloe vera* has become popular as a garden plant in recent years. A well-tended plant can be useful as a regular source of aloe leaf for making homemade tonic drinks or cosmetics for hair and skin care. Simply "fillet" the leaf by cutting away the bitter outer rind and then liquidise the clear inner parenchyma (the aloe gel) in a blender. The plant will tolerate the occasional and careful removal of a few leaves at a time.

Aloe variegata

Aloe vera in flower

Aloe vera plantation

ASTROLOBA

Astroloba foliolosa

This is a multi-stemmed succulent forming small clumps. The main charm of the plant lies in the ornate leaves that overlap each other in neat spirals – the flowers are fairly inconspicuous. The leaves are broad and stem-clasping at the base, have a yellowish green colour and are spiny at the tips. As is the case with many *Haworthia* and *Astroloba* species, these plants prefer light shade. They are not frost tolerant and need to be watered sparingly. The species is found naturally in the Eastern Cape Province of South Africa.

Astroloba herrei

The plant resembles a miniature branched aloe, with erect, greyish green leaves borne on elongated stems. The tubular flowers are borne in long slender racemes. The tips are yellow and the bulbous flower bases are covered with a white spongy tissue.

Astroloba rubriflora

Because of the unusual colour and shape of the bird-pollinated flowers, *Astroloba rubriflora* was previously considered to be a genus on its own and the only species was known as *Poellnitzia rubriflora*. The leaves are similar to other species of *Astroloba* in being spirally arranged, very hard in texture and spine-tipped. The slender racemes bear numerous red flowers that are all turned upwards. They are tubular in shape, with a narrow mouth surrounded by flaps or valves that regulate access to the copious amounts of nectar. In nature, this succulent has a localised distribution in the Worcester-Robertson Karoo of South Africa.

CHORTOLIRION

Chortolirion angolense (onion aloe)

This is a small, grass aloe-like bulbous plant that has only its thin leaves exposed above ground level. The leaves are often curled to form interesting, curled rosettes. The leaf margins are adorned with very fine teeth and the leaf bases are white-spotted. Like most grass aloes, the roots of the species are spindle-shaped, that is, they taper to both ends. The flowers are borne on an invariably unbranched flowering stalk. In appearance, the flowers closely resemble those of some species of *Haworthia*. The seed capsules of *Chortolirion* are tapered in their apical half. This inconspicuous aloe relative is mainly grown as a curiosity and can easily be overlooked in the rockery (or perhaps mistaken for a small onion). In its natural distribution area (the grasslands of tropical and arid southern Africa), the plants are very difficult to locate even if you know they are there! The narrow leaves closely mimic the grasses amongst which they grow. In the flowering season, the chances of finding the plants are better, as the tiny spikes of white flowers are easier to spot.

Astroloba foliolosa plant

Astroloba rubriflora

Astroloba herrei flowers

Astroloba rubriflora flowers

Chortolirion angolense plants

Chortolirion angolense flowers

GASTERIA

Gasteria carinata

This is a relatively small plant that proliferates to form clumps 500 mm or more in diameter. *Gasteria carinata* is one of the most variable of all the species. The leaves are usually arranged in rosettes but sometimes they remain distichous (two-ranked) as in the juvenile stage. The surface may be variously spotted and warty, but smooth-leaved forms are also known. The flowers are medium-sized and relatively narrow. They are characteristically borne on a single (unbranched), slender raceme. *Gasteria carinata* and G. *disticha* were the first two species to reach Europe in the late seventeenth century.

Gasteria batesiana

This species is a small succulent rosette up to 100 mm tall that may proliferate to form large clumps. It typically has firm, brittle and markedly warty leaves, which are often very dark green to almost black. It is similar to *G. carinata* (especially in bearing simple racemes) but the flowers are much larger, up to 40 mm long. *Gasteria batesiana* was in cultivation in Europe for a long time before the natural populations were relocated in South Africa.

Gasteria bicolor

Gasteria bicolor typically has a short leafy stem up to 200 mm long, with rounded leaves that end in a tiny spine (mucro). The leaves are densely spotted and have sharp, bony, saw-edge margins. Flowers are usually borne in branched panicles with up to eight side branches. The flowers are small (up to 20 mm long) and have a prominently swollen "stomach" which may be up to 9 mm in diameter. Plants are easily grown in cultivation and have become popular as houseplants.

Gasteria excelsa

This is the largest of the species and the solitary rosettes can reach a diameter of nearly 1 m. It is a very robust plant. The leaves are smooth with only faint spots and typical knife-edge margins formed by white cartilaginous teeth. The massively branched inflorescence adds to the curiosity value of this species – it may reach about 2 m in height and diameter. A single, well-grown plant typically bears more than 2 000 flowers! Compared to the large size of the plant, the flowers are surprisingly small (only about 25 mm long). The flower is swollen for two thirds of its length and ends in a narrow green tubular mouth. The brittle leaves of this species provide an easy method of propagation. Even small fragments of leaves can proliferate to form new plants. The plants adapt well to low light conditions and have become very popular as a garden plant in warm regions (and a houseplant in colder parts of the world). In the book *Gasterias of South Africa* by Ernst van Jaarsveld, three cultivars are described: 'Cala', a form with short wrinkled leaves, 'Gaika', a large form with striated leaves and 'Nqancule', a large form with very sharp leaf margins that can easily cause severe injury.

Flowering plant of *Gasteria batesiana*

Gasteria batesiana flowers

Gasteria bicolor flowers

Flowering plant of *Gasteria bicolor*

Leaves of *Gasteria excelsa*

HAWORTHIA

Haworthia attenuata var. *attenuata*

These plants grow as small rosettes that consist of numerous fairly thin, tapering leaves that are mostly borne erectly with the terminal portions slightly incurved. Both leaf surfaces are densely covered with small, white warts or tubercles, giving them a rough appearance. The flowers are carried on a rather tall, thin, wiry inflorescence. The flowers are a dirty white colour with a greenish brown tinge. This species is very proliferous and will quickly multiply into large, multi-headed specimens. It is perfect for cultivation in small pots or in the open ground where, surprisingly, it will withstand rather low temperatures.

Haworthia cooperi var. *dielsiana*

Plants form small rosettes that consist of fat, somewhat globular leaves, generally with large windows at their tips. The leaf surfaces are smooth and the plants grow well sunken into the ground, unlike some of their relatives that grow above the ground. The small, bright white flowers are fairly large for a species of haworthia and are carried on a short inflorescence. The flowers are distinctly two-lipped. This species is easy in cultivation, and can even tolerate the occasional very cold spell associated with subzero temperatures.

Haworthia cymbiformis

This *Haworthia* species is quite variable in the shape and size of both the rosettes and the leaves. Plants grow above the ground level and are generally easy to recognise by their pale green, translucent leaves that are usually distinctly boat-shaped, with short, hair-like bristles at the tips.

Haworthia glabrata

Plants grow as small open, rosettes that consist of numerous tapering leaves. Both leaf surfaces are densely covered with small, green warts or tubercles, giving the leaves a rough appearance. The flowers are carried on tall, thin, wiry inflorescences. The flowers are a dirty white colour with a greenish brown tinge. This species is quite proliferous and will quickly multiply into large, multi-headed mound-shaped specimens. It is perfect for cultivation in small pots or in the open ground where it will withstand very low temperatures. It prefers dappled shade and can be used effectively as a groundcover.

Haworthia maxima (= *H. pumila*)

As the largest member of the genus, these plants are easily recognised by their robust rosettes (the size of a large man's fist) and conspicuous warty leaf ornamentation. The flowers are rather atypical, as they are dull yellow to grey in colour and almost symmetrical (not markedly two-lipped). Plants should be watered sparingly during the summer months.

Plant of *Haworthia attenuata*

Flowers of *Haworthia attenuata*

Plant of *Haworthia cooperi*

Plant of *Haworthia cymbiformis*

Plant of *Haworthia maxima*

Flower of *Haworthia maxima*

Haworthia reinwardtii

This species is easily recognised by the elongated stems bearing relatively narrow incurved leaves ending in sharp tips. The leaves are densely covered in transversely oblong white tubercles (similar to those of *H. attenuata*).

Haworthia retusa

Plants have small, bright green leaves that have distinctive, flattened tips. The leaf tips are adorned with numerous longitudinal windows, allowing filtered sunlight into the leaves. The flowers are a fairly bright white colour and are carried on a thin inflorescence. The most desirable of the horticulturally popular species of *Haworthia* are indeed those that have window-leaves. This species, which can be proliferous from the base, is quite easy in cultivation, but requires protection from over-watering and low temperatures.

Haworthia ×*rigida*

This is the name given to a group of garden hybrids thought to be derived from crosses between *H. glabrata* and *H. tortuosa*. As it is one of the most popular of all garden haworthias, numerous named cultivars have been developed. Plants usually have dark green to reddish leaves that are characteristically hard and rigid in texture. The leaf surfaces vary from smooth to variously grooved or warty. New plants are easily propagated from stem cuttings or simply by division.

Haworthia tessellata subsp. *tessellata*

Plants are extremely variable but mostly consist of small, triangular leaves. The leaf surfaces could be smooth or rough, but invariably sport a grid-like network of light green markings, particularly on the upper surface. The two-lipped flowers are a dirty white colour and are borne in a thin inflorescence. The species has the widest geographical distribution range of all haworthias, particularly above the climatically severe inland escarpment. Its major claim to fame is its ability to tolerate very low temperatures without showing any signs of damage.

Haworthia truncata (horse teeth)

This is an unusual species because the leaves remain two-ranked and do not form rosettes as in other *Haworthia* species. The leaf tips are typically blunt as if cut off with a knife. The flowers are the same as those of most other species. It is often grown as a curiosity.

Haworthia viscosa

Plants have thin, erect or creeping stems that are entirely covered with small, overlapping, triangular leaves. The leaf surfaces could be quite rough or almost completely smooth. The tips of the leaves are often bent downwards in a typically roof-tile arrangement. As is the case with most species of *Haworthia*, the flowers are a dirty white colour and insignificant. The leaves of *Haworthia viscosa* vary in colour, but are generally a deep matt green or sometimes somewhat yellowish green, especially if grown in exposed positions. In its natural habitat in some of the arid parts of the Eastern Cape this species often grows in the protective shade of small karroid bushes. It is perfect for pot culture, for example on a windowsill.

Haworthia reinwardtii

Haworthia retusa

Haworthia ×rigida

Plant of *Haworthia truncata*

Plant of *Haworthia viscosa*

Subfamily Asphodeloideae

BULBINE

Bulbine frutescens (burn jelly plant, stalked bulbine)

Plants are small, multi-branched, low-growing shrubs that carry numerous pencil-shaped, almost wiry leaves. These soft leaves are borne erectly and are filled with a thin, watery, soothing juice. The shrubs are branched and rebranched to eventually create large clumps that are perfect as a groundcover. The flowers are most commonly yellow, but an orange flowering variant, known as cultivar 'Hallmark' is also widely grown. An interesting recent introduction to the horticultural market has yellow flowers with a brown central stripe down the centre of the yellow floral segments. Plants are very easy in cultivation and can be easily grown from cuttings that require little encouragement to set root and flourish. This species, which is widely distributed in southern Africa, is very cold tolerant. It is one of the most useful of all garden succulents, because it grows rapidly and flowers over a long period. The gel in the leaves is useful as a first aid treatment for minor cuts and bruises.

Bulbine latifolia (rooiwortel)

Plants are mostly solitary and consist of rather large rosettes carried at the ends of short stems. The leaves are bluish green and deeply channelled and consequently boat-shaped in cross-section. The stems are covered in the remains of dried leaves, a character most often associated with the cousins of bulbines, the true aloes. The leaves are soft, but firm and strongly recurved. The bright yellow flowers are fairly densely packed on a single, unbranched inflorescence. The species differs from a close relative, *Bulbine natalensis*, in being a more robust plant with bluish green leaves. It is also somewhat more difficult in cultivation than *Bulbine natalensis*. Furthermore, the epicentre of its geographical distribution range lies further south. This is the largest of all the species of *Bulbine*.

Bulbine natalensis

Plants grow as solitary or once- or twice-branched rosettes. The leaves are a bright, light green and fairly broad. The soft leaves are filled with a soothing juice that can be applied to burns and grazes. The tips of the leaves often die back in times of drought, resulting in the upper parts of the leaves becoming brown, papery and grass-like. The flowers are borne on short stalks along a single axis. Flower colour is invariably bright yellow and typical of those of bulbines in general. This species is exceptionally easy in cultivation, and although it originates from the subtropical eastern coastal areas of South Africa, will even withstand subzero temperatures. It also does very well in light to fairly deep shade. When grown *en masse*, it makes for an interesting and useful groundcover.

Bulbine frutescens 'Hallmark'

Bulbine frutescens flowers

Bulbine latifolia plant and inflorescence

Bulbine natalensis (with *Aloe ciliaris*)

Bulbine latifolia (left) and *B. natalensis* (right)

ASTERACEAE
Daisy family

Distinguishing characters When the daisy family is mentioned it is not immediately associated with succulence. In contrast, at first mention it is usually associated with sunflowers (*Helianthus annuus*) or some of the popular garden plants such as gazanias (*Gazania krebsiana*) or gerberas (Barberton daisies, *Gerbera jamesonii*).

All the species of the daisy family are characterised by having their flowers arranged in a distinct, head-shaped inflorescence referred to as a capitulum. Therefore, the "flower" of any daisy is not a single flower, but in fact often a collection of hundreds of closely packed flowers. Those on the periphery of the head are termed ray florets, whereas those on the flattened, central part are termed disc florets. The ray florets typically endow the daisy flowers with its bright colours, but in some species even the ray florets are dull-coloured or reduced, as in the case of some succulent species such as *Senecio rowleyanus*.

Notes With over 20 000 species included in the Asteraceae worldwide, it is not surprising that almost every conceivable growth form known for flowering plants is found in the family. Most of the few hundred daisies with succulent leaves (or stems) occur in Africa (including Madagascar), and in Mexico. Growth forms of these succulents range from small trees and shrubs through miniature tuberous plants and leafless curiosities with pencil-thin stems to soil hugging creepers and window-leaved twiners. However, all of these are united through the common presence of head-shaped flower clusters.

Brief notes on genera

Kleinia

Species included in this genus should arguably be returned or transferred to *Senecio*. The differences between the two genera are rather obscure and can only be seen in anatomical details of the ovary wall. Most of the 40 species currently recognised in *Kleinia* are stem succulents, and most are restricted to Africa and western Asia (including the Canary Isles, Madagascar, Arabia and India).

Othonna

The classification of and relationships amongst the species included in this genus are in many instances still poorly understood. More than 60 of the 150 species of *Othonna* are succulent. The genus is more or less restricted to southern Africa.

Senecio

Of all the daisy genera, *Senecio* is one of the most diverse as far as growth form is concerned and also the one most commonly referred to when succulents of this family are discussed. It has about 1 250 species worldwide, of which more than 100 are succulent.

Cape daisies *(Osteospermum jucundum)*

Senecio elegans

Othonna lyrata with flower heads

Othonna retrofracta with typical fruits

Kleinia fulgens

Cocoon plant (*Senecio haworthii*)

Notes on species of Asteraceae

KLEINIA

Kleinia galpinii

As there are many species of *Kleinia* in cultivation, space limitations will only allow two examples. The first one is the spectacular but relatively poorly known *Kleinia galpinii*. This species is an excellent choice for warm gardens as it has attractive rosettes of waxy grey-white foliage and colourful (and relatively large) flower heads. Leaves on the flowering stalk are smaller than the basal leaves. The florets are light to dark orange and smell of apricots.

Kleinia stapeliiformis

When not in flower, plants of this species can be very easily confused with representatives of the succulent Asclepiadaceae. The stems in particular of *Kleinia stapeliiformis* look uncannily like those of a species of *Stapelia*, among others, but when these small, clump-forming daisies produce their crimson red inflorescences at the tips of the stems there can be no doubt that they are daisies. But like many carrion flower species, their seeds also have soft, fluffy white appendages that assist with dispersal. The flowers of *K. stapeliiformis* are devoid of the usually much larger ray florets, but in the case of this species it does not matter: the small, bright red, star-like disc florets are strikingly beautiful and produced in abundance.

OTHONNA

Othonna capensis (little-pickles)

At least one of the species of this rather poorly known genus has become very popular in general horticulture. *Othonna capensis* is a low-growing species that answers to all the requirements for being the perfect groundcover. It forms a thick mat of succulent leaves and grows very quickly. As a carpet-forming creeper it is very useful as a soil binder, especially in denuded areas prone to soil erosion. The leaves of the species are rather short and thick and very succulent. In situations where plants receive bright, direct sunlight, the normally light green leaves turn a beautiful shade of purple. Plants flower profusely, carrying bright yellow inflorescences on short stalks. The long ray florets tend to curl back when flowers age.

Several shrubby species of *Othonna* are occasionally encountered in succulent gardens and collections. These plants vary from small (less than 0.2 m) to over 2 m high. The leaves are usually hairless and simple but may be variously toothed. Flower heads are typically pale yellow and lack ray florets. Well-known examples (mostly from South Africa) include *O. amplexicaulis*, *O. amplexifolia*, *O. arborescens*, *O. carnosa*, *O. cherifolia* (from North Africa), *O. cylindrica*, *O. furcata* (from Namibia), *O. retrofracta* and *O. triplinervia*.

Plant of *Kleinia galpinii*

Flower head of *Kleinia galpinii*

Kleinia stapeliiformis

Othonna capensis

SENECIO

Senecio articulatus (candle plant)

The narrow leaves of this stem succulent soon shrivel and die, leaving the thick green fleshy stems as the only permanent structures above the ground. The leaf scars have decorative purple lines but the flower heads are small and inconspicuous.

Senecio barbertonicus

This species must qualify as one of the most beautiful of all succulent shrubs or small trees. It has a dense crown of branches that are mostly covered with small, pencil-shaped leaves that glisten light green in the sun. The "flowers", or more correctly the inflorescences, are bright yellow and are borne in slender clusters.

Senecio ficoides

The plant is a small shrublet with strongly tapered, succulent leaves that have a grey waxy bloom on their surfaces. Small clusters of cream-coloured flower heads are borne on the branch ends.

Senecio macroglossus (wax vine)

As an attractive succulent vine (climber), this species has few rivals. It has beautifully ornate leaves resembling those of the common ivy creeper (*Hedera*). The flower heads are relatively large, with pale yellow or cream-coloured ray florets.

Senecio rowleyanus (string-of-beads)

This curious plant has thick fleshy leaves that resemble glass beads. They are borne on elongated creeping stems. The flower heads are relatively large and attractive, with white or cream-coloured disc florets but no ray florets.

Senecio tamoides (canary creeper)

The well-known canary creeper is a prolific grower that can be trained to cover a fence or any other garden structure, trail over a drab-looking cliff or simply left to form a bush enlivening an unsightly spot in the garden. The margins of its large, more or less heart-shaped, shiny green leaves are nicely sculptured and long lasting: it does not produce an inordinate messy leaf-drop. The flower heads of *S. tamoides* are bright yellow and are borne in small clusters. This species also has large ray florets contributing to its popularity in horticulture. Once it becomes overgrown it is very easy to trim plants into the desired size or shape since the greenish stems are soft and thornless and respond well to pruning. *S. tamoides* is likely to be indigenous to South Africa, but has become naturalised in several parts of the world, for example along the French Riviera where it grows as a component of the coastal bush vegetation.

Senecio articulatus

Senecio ficoides

Senecio barbertonicus

Senecio macroglossus

Senecio rowleyanus

Senecio tamoides

CACTACEAE
Cactus family

Group 5

DISTINGUISHING CHARACTERS The Cactaceae is the second largest of all the succulent plant families. It has close to 1 500 species and some 100 genera and, not surprisingly, has provided taxonomists with numerous classification difficulties. Although it can be a daunting task to distinguish among the different cactus genera and species, it is a fairly simple task to recognise a cactus. These plants are characterised by areoles, small spot-like cushions or budding organs that variously cover the plant body. Three, five, ten or even tens of cactus spines arise from each areole. In the Plant Kingdom no other plants have areoles, and any growth of a cactus (stems, flowers, roots etc.) arises from these small, sometimes deceivingly innocent-looking cottony balls. Cacti are typical stem succulents and generally leafless. The fruits are so-called one-celled berries, the seeds being embedded in the pulp with no walls or separations. Cactus plants may not appeal to all horticulturists, but they often bear strikingly beautiful flowers, compensating for their rather surly appearance. It is therefore not surprising that cacti have a dedicated following among collectors and growers worldwide.

NOTES There are numerous specialist books dealing with the identification of cacti. An overwhelmingly large number of genera and species are commonly cultivated as container plants but relatively few can be considered as common garden succulents. Only a small selection of genera and species that are commonly found in gardens is highlighted here.

Brief notes on genera

Astrophytum

There are only four species in this distinctive genus. These rather small cacti have rounded (globose) or shortly cylindrical stems, characteristically decorated with minute, chalky scales that give them a dotted appearance. Another feature is that spines are sparse or even absent in mature plants.

Cephalocereus

This is a small genus of columnar cacti with only three species. The erect stems are un-branched or sparsely branched at the base. The areoles bear hair-like, often silvery grey bristles. An interesting feature is the presence of a group of specialised floral areoles towards the ends of the branches in mature plants (technically known as a *cephaleum*). The shiny, nocturnal flowers are borne only on these floral areoles and not on other parts of the plant.

Opuntia robusta

Cowboy cactus (*Carnegia gigantea*)

Stem of *Pereskia* showing areoles

Flower of *Hylocereus triangularis*

Parodia magnifica

Leuchtenbergia principis

Cleistocactus (silver torch cacti)

Several tree-like members of the genus *Cleistocactus* are popular garden succulents. They are easily recognised by the slender erect stems and especially the narrowly tubular, usually red or purple flowers. The common name "silver torch cactus" refers mainly to the most popular garden species, *C. strausii*. Also common in cultivation is the so-called "golden rat's tail cactus", *C. winteri*. It has spreading and creeping stems clothed with short golden spines. The 30 to 50 species of *Cleistocactus* occur naturally in South America.

Cereus (queen of the night, night blooming cereus)

In many parts of the world these easily propagated columnar cacti are appreciated as specimen plants, especially in formal gardens. The common name "queen of the night" refers to the large, nocturnal flowers that open at night, attracting bats as the pollinating agents. There are about 40 tree-like or shrubby species, all indigenous to South America and the West Indies.

Disocactus (including *Aporocactus, Nopalxochia* and many species of *Epiphyllum*)

The species of *Disocactus* are often showy plants with a spectacular display of large flowers borne on long slender (flat or rounded) stems. Unfortunately, the correct names of these plants are confusing. Three species are particularly well known and popular as garden succulents. The so-called rat's-tail cactus is now known as *Discocactus flagelliformis* (previously called *Aporocactus flagelliformis*). The well-known Christmas cactus (*Disocactus ackermannii*) with its large red flowers is now included in the genus *Disocactus* but was previously known as *Nopalxochia ackermannii*. It is almost indistinguishable from the popular and widely cultivated orchid cacti (*Disocactus* ×*hybridus*). These plants have flattened, almost spineless stems bearing spectacular flowers in a multitude of colours. Many thousands of cultivars are available. They were previously included in the genus *Epiphyllum* and are still widely known as epiphyllums or epi's. However, the genus *Epiphyllum* is now restricted to only a few species with white or sometimes yellowish flowers, of which *E. oxypetalum* is the most familiar to succulent plant enthusiasts.

Echinocactus (golden barrel cacti)

The few species included in this genus today have rounded plant bodies that are mostly distinctly ribbed. The stems of the large-growing species are usually barrel-shaped. The ribs are densely adorned with pungent spines.

Echinopsis (torch cacti)

As a result of recent taxonomic changes, this is now an amazingly diverse genus, the species of which cover a wide variety of different growth forms. Plants are generally rather robust growers, thrive on neglect, and range from small and globular to large and columnar. Many species are grown in amenity horticulture, especially those with large flowers borne on relatively small, rounded stems. The flowers are sometimes larger than the plants!

Cleistocactus winteri

Cleistocactus smaragdiflorus forma *rojoi*

Disocactus martianus

Disocactus ackermannii

Epiphyllum (night blooming cactus)

The 15 species are epiphytes and can be grown in the fork of tree trunks in suitable climates. They have rounded stems that become flat and two-ribbed in mature plants. The flowers are nocturnal, large and usually white or cream-coloured. Note that the more commonly encountered epiphyllums, also known as epi's or orchid cacti, are nowadays included in the genus *Disocactus*. The majority of the modern cultivars with their red, pink or bi-coloured flowers belong to one species, *Disocactus ×hybridus*.

Ferocactus (barrel cacti)

It is not surprising that this is one of the most popular genera of garden cacti. The plants are exceptionally hardy and typically have robust stems and large, often brightly coloured thorns. The stems are rounded (globose) in young plants but may become thick and elongated in older plants. Flowers are yellow to pink in colour but tend to be small and rather inconspicuous.

Gymnocalycium (chin cacti)

The more or less 50 species in the genus are all small globular plants from South America. Many of them have short-lived but attractive flowers borne in groups. One species, *Gymnocalycium mihanovichii*, is well known because various stem colour forms are sold as grafted pot plants.

Hatiora (Easter cacti)

The popular and well-known Easter cactus (*Hatiora ×gaertneri*) belongs to this small genus of only four species. The plants are mostly epiphytes with cylindrical or flat stems that are characteristically segmented. Spines are soft and bristly and often absent. The bell-shaped flowers are regular (actinomorphic), with a short basal tube and spreading petals. The Easter cactus may be confused with the superficially similar *Schlumbergera ×buckleyi* (variously known as lobster's claw, Christmas cactus or orchid cactus – but see *Disocactus* and *Epiphyllum*). *Hatiora* is called Easter cactus because it flowers in the northern hemisphere spring (which corresponds with Easter in that half of the world). *Schlumbergera* species flowers in the northern hemisphere winter (hence the common name "Christmas cactus"). Furthermore, the flowers of *Hatiora* species are regular (not skewed) and the stamens do not protrude beyond the petals as in *Schlumbergera*.

Mammillaria (nipple cacti)

Of all the commonly cultivated cacti, those that belong to *Mammillaria* are perhaps the easiest to distinguish as a genus. The plant bodies are mostly globular or slightly elongated and consist almost exclusively of nipple-shaped protuberances carrying soft, harmless or pungent spines. Unlike most other cacti, the flowers are produced not from the areoles but from tufts of soft spines situated between the areoles. The small flowers often form a brightly coloured halo around the stems.

Ferocactus glaucescens

Ferocactus latispinus

Gymnocalycium monvillei

Hatiora ×gaertneri

Mammillaria bocasana

Mammillaria camptotrica

Myrtillocactus (myrtle cacti)

This is a genus of three or four species of tree-like cacti from Mexico and Guatemala. The plants have robust, ascending stems bearing numerous small flowers – up to nine per areole.

Opuntia (prickly pears)

Species are generally easy to recognise as the plant bodies are often divided into jointed, cylindrical or flattened pads. The flowers are fairly large and basally quite fleshy and the fruits of some species are edible and considered as a delicacy by some.

Pachycereus (organ pipes)

This is a small genus of columnar species that will produce really statuesque plants in time. As with many columnar species, the mature stems and branches tend to be less spiny, while the ribs of young plants are profusely adorned with short, but prominent, prickly thorns.

Parodia

Parodia is a genus of up to 50 species, all of which are indigenous to Argentina and Brazil. The plants are usually small, with rounded or, less often, elongated stems. The hairy and bristly spines are often bright yellow.

Rhipsalis (rope cacti)

Members of this genus of mostly shade-loving, thin-stemmed plants are perfect subjects for a succulent lover's hanging basket. It is the only cactus genus with indigenous African, Madagascan and Sri Lankan representatives.

Schlumbergera (Christmas cacti, orchid cacti, lobster claws, crab cacti)

The well-known orchid cactus, lobster claw, crab cactus or Christmas cactus, *S. truncata*, belongs to this genus of six epiphytic plants. In nature (southeastern Brazil) these plants grow on tree trunks and cliff faces. The attractive pink or red flowers vary from almost regular in some species to markedly asymmetrical (zygomorphic). Differences between *Schlumbergera* and the similar-looking Easter cactus (*Hatiora*) are discussed elsewhere (see *Hatiora*).

Stenocactus (brain cacti, ribbed cacti)

Members of this small genus of about 10 species are easily recognised by the stems that are decorated with very numerous, narrow ribs. The spines are often strongly flattened and the flowers are relatively small.

Myrtillocactus cochal

Opuntia microdasys (yellow form)

Pachycereus marginatus

Parodia herteri

Notes on species of Cactăceae

ASTROPHYTUM

Astrophytum myriostigma (bishop's cap)

The stems of this species are globose or shortly columnar, with four to five prominent ribs (up to 10-ribbed in the var. *tulense*). Most plants are covered in a dense layer of white chalky scales. The flowers are yellow, sometimes with a red or orange throat. The bishop's cap or bishop's hat is a very distinctive species that originated in northeastern Mexico.

Astrophytum ornatum (monk's hood)

Young plants have a single, rounded stem that gradually lengthens and may reach 1 m in height in old plants. The stem typically has six to eight ribs, with several spines borne along the ribs. Pale to deep yellow flowers appear in summer.

CEPHALOCEREUS

Cephalocereus senilis (old man cactus, old man of Mexico)

This is the best-known species, with simple or sparsely branched stems reaching heights of up to 12 m when conditions are favourable. Typical are the silver-hairy stems and woolly flower-bearing area (cephalium) situated at the side of the stems in mature plants. The nocturnal flowers are off-white with pinkish lines.

CEREUS

Cereus jamacaru (queen of the night)

Cereus jamacaru is perhaps the most popular and best-known columnar cactus. This is a large plant with bluish, strongly ribbed stems and attractive white flowers. A monstrose form of the species (it has abnormal growth resulting from a mutation) is sometimes encountered in cultivation. It has somewhat flattened and multi-ribbed stems. The fruits are edible and in some parts of the world this species or a close relative (known as *C. peruvianus*) is being developed as a crop plant. In some countries it is illegal to grow the species, as it tends to become invasive.

Bishop's cap (*Astrophytum myriostigma*)

Monk's hood (*Astrophytum ornatum*)

Old man cactus (*Cephalocereus senilis*)

Cereus jamacaru (monstrose form)

Cereus jamacaru (normal form)

Fruits of *Cereus jamacaru*

DISOCACTUS

Disocactus ackermannii (=*Nopalxochia ackermannii*) (red Christmas cactus)

The correct name of the well-known red Christmas cactus is *D. ackermannii*. The plant consists of flattened (two-angled or partially three-angled) stems bearing very small spines only when young. The beautiful tubular flowers are typically solitary and bright red. The Christmas cactus is sometimes confused with red colour forms of the similar-looking orchid cactus (*Disocactus ×hybridus*, usually referred to as *Epiphyllum*).

Disocactus flagelliformis (=*Aporocactus flagelliformis*) (rat's tail cactus)

This is one of the most popular cacti – perfectly suited to hanging-basket cultivation. It thrives in semi-shady positions that still receive bright light. The stems are finely ribbed and covered in harmless, bristle-like spines. Fairly large reddish or pinkish flowers are borne on the thin, rat's tail-like stems. Like so many other cacti, species of this genus are being hybridised and selected in an effort to make improved cultivars available to the horticultural trade.

Disocactus ×hybridus (=*Epiphyllum* cultivars) (orchid cacti, epiphyllums, epi's)

The well-known and popular orchid cactus, with its bewildering range of cultivars and colour forms, has been removed from the genus *Epiphyllum* and placed in the genus *Discocactus*. The plants are still widely known as epiphyllums or epi's (see *Epiphyllum*). Seedlings have rounded, spiny stems but in adult plants, the stems are spineless, flat and leaf-like, with toothed or scalloped margins. The large, colourful flowers (white, pink, purple, orange, red or variously bi-coloured) open in the daytime. Some cultivars have colourful stems.

ECHINOCACTUS

Echinocactus grusonii (golden barrel cactus, mother-in-law's cushion)

The best-known species of the genus *Echinocactus* is *E. grusonii*. As a result of its large, spiny, globular growth form it is commonly known as the mother-in-law's cushion, or golden barrel cactus. It sports a large, massively globular plant body that is distinctly ribbed and covered in sharp, pungent spines. The crown of the plant body is decked out with a yellow furry substance, and in the flowering season it carries small, bright yellow flowers. A form with white spines is also known.

Red Christmas cactus (*Disocactus ackermannii*)

Rat's tail cactus (*Disocactus flagelliformis*)

Orchid cactus (*Disocactus ×hybridus*)

Golden barrel cactus (*Echinocactus grusonii*)

ECHINOPSIS

Echinopsis oxygona (Easter lily cactus, sea urchin cactus)

Plants of this species have rounded, distinctly ribbed stems that gradually form clusters. The typically large and showy flowers are various shades of pink, depending on the cultivar. In some books, the plant is still listed by the old name, *Echinops multiplex*.

Echinopsis spachiana (torch cactus)

Two of the species of cactus discussed here are popularly known as "queen of the night", *Echinopsis spachiana* being one of them. Its growth form, a clump of numerous erect, ribbed, spiny stems, makes it near perfect as a hedge plant. Furthermore, it requires virtually no care after planting and its water needs are minimal. The large, white, short-lived flowers appear in summer. The torch cactus is a noxious weed in South Africa.

Echinopsis chamaecereus (peanut cactus)

Another very commonly cultivated cactus is *Echinopsis chamaecereus*. It is popularly known as the peanut cactus, in reference to its short, stubby stems that resemble unopened peanut pods. The species is exceptionally easy in cultivation and more than likely the first cactus to be grown by most cactophiles. The large, showy flowers of modern cultivars are every possible hue of red, orange and even purple. Grafted plants with brightly coloured stems are sold as curiosities.

EPIPHYLLUM

Epiphyllum anguliger (fishbone cactus)

The fishbone cactus is an interesting epiphyte from southern Mexico with flattened and deeply toothed stems. Very large, yellow and white, strongly scented flowers appear in late autumn.

Epiphyllum oxypetalum (night blooming cactus)

There are about 15 species of *Epiphyllum*, of which *E. oxypetalum* is perhaps the best known and most widely cultivated. It is an epiphyte with flattened stems and spectacular white flowers that open at night. To thrive, the plant requires rich but well-drained soil, warm temperatures and regular watering. The many cultivars known as orchid cacti or epiphyllums now belong to the genus *Disocactus*.

Easter lily cactus (*Echinopsis oxygona*)

Flowers of *Echinopsis spachiana* (torch cactus)

Echinopsis chamaecereus

Yellow-stemmed form of *E. chamaecereus*

Torch cactus (*Echinopsis spachiana*)

Fishbone cactus (*Epiphyllum anguliger*)

FEROCACTUS

Ferocactus glaucescens (blue barrel cactus)

This species has a single rounded stem that is characteristically bluish grey in colour. The spines (and flowers) are yellow.

Ferocactus histrix (porcupine barrel cactus, electrode cactus)

Although it has rather drab flowers, this barrel-shaped cactus has attractive thorns – very long but relatively narrow, resulting in areoles with a spider-like appearance.

Ferocactus latispinus (broad-spined barrel cactus)

The broad and recurved spines of this species are quite distinct. The single stems are usually rounded but may become elongated with age. Another feature is the prominent, sharp-edged ribs that may be spiralled in some cultivars. The flowers are usually yellow or purple.

Ferocactus pilosus (red-spined barrel cactus)

This clump-forming species originates from northern Mexico. It has characteristic elongated stems bearing large and colourful thorns. The flowers are various shades of orange.

GYMNOCALYCIUM

Gymnocalycium mihanovichii (red cap, plaid cactus)

A large number of species are cultivated, but this one is the best known because of the brilliantly coloured forms that are sold as grafted plants. Since the stems lack chlorophyll, they are unable to survive if they are not grafted onto a suitable green rootstock. Various cultivar names include 'Red Cap' or 'Hibotan', 'Pink Cap' and 'Yellow Cap'.

HATIORA

Hatiora gaertneri (=*Ripsalidopsis* ×*gaertneri*) (Easter cactus)

The plant is an epiphyte with flat stems that are characteristically segmented. Spines are soft and bristly and often absent. The bell-shaped flowers are regular (actinomorphic), with a short basal tube, spreading petals and short stamens that do not protrude beyond the petals. The Easter cactus flowers in the northern hemisphere spring and can therefore easily be distinguished from the similar-looking *Schlumbergera* species, which flower in winter (hence "Christmas cactus"). Easter cactus has regular flowers, while Christmas cactus typically has irregular (zygomorphic) flowers with long stamens.

Ferocactus histrix

Ferocactus pilosus

Gymnocalycium mihanovichii (red)

Gymnocalycium mihanovichii (pink)

Easter cactus (*Hatiora ×gaertneri*)

MAMMILLARIA

Mammillaria bocasana (powder puff cactus)

A popular and attractive species clothed with a mixture of white hairy bristles and reddish curved spines resembling fish-hooks. The plants form large clumps at maturity and bears small, pale pink flowers.

Mammillaria elongata (golden stars, lady finger cactus)

Mammillaria species are generally grown form their perfectly rounded plant bodies. Stems of this clump-forming species, however, are typically elongated and sparsely clothed with soft, yellowish spines. A cristate form known as "brain cactus" is also commonly cultivated. The small flowers are dull yellow.

Mammillaria geminispina (whitey)

This clump-forming species is easily recognised by the silvery white, spreading bristly spines and perfectly rounded stems.

Mammillaria gracilis (thimble cactus)

Mammillaria gracilis is one of the small mound-like cacti. It consists of small globular to somewhat elongated plant bodies that are strikingly adorned with soft, white bristles on the nipple-like stem globules. The flowers are a rather disappointing dull yellowish colour.

Mammillaria magnimamma (nipple cactus)

The distinctive features of the genus *Mammillaria* are clearly shown by this attractive species. It has a rounded plant body with a circle of pink flowers arising from between the areoles and not on them as in all other cacti.

MYRTILLOCACTUS

Myrtillocactus geometrizans (myrtle cactus)

This Central Mexican species is commonly cultivated. It is a much-branched plant that may reach 4 m in height and 3 m in width. The stems are blue-green and the thorns are typically reddish-brown, turning grey with age. Up to nine tiny flowers, creamy white in colour, are borne in groups of up to nine on each areole. The small fruits are raisin-like and edible when ripe. *M. cochal* is closely similar but has green stems, black thorns and pale yellow flowers tinged with green.

Mammillaria gracilis

Mammillaria magnimamma

Mammillaria elongata (normal form)

Mammillaria elongata (cristate form)

Myrtle cactus (*Myrtillocactus geometrizans*)

Flowers of *Myrtillocactus geometrizans*

OPUNTIA

Opuntia ficus-indica (prickly pear, Indian fig)

The prickly pear is a popular specimen plant – tough, drought-hardy and even frost-tolerant. It is often used as a live hedge and is widely cultivated as a commercial crop for the edible fruits. Numerous cultivars are available and the flower colour varies from orange to purplish red. The fruits are equally variable, ranging from green to yellow, orange or red. They are technically berries, with numerous hard seeds embedded in the tasty fruit flesh. In parts of Africa, the prickly pear has become an aggressive invader but it has also become a favourite food for elephants, which devour the fleshy stems, thorns and all. The dethorned pads are chopped up and fed to domestic stock in times of drought. The fruits, in the form of prickly pear syrup, were once an important source of sugar in rural areas. In some parts of the world the economically important cochineal insect is harvested from the pads as a source of natural red colouring.

Opuntia imbricata (chain-link cactus, chain cholla)

The pads of this ferociously spined species with its beautiful pinkish red flowers are cylindrical rather than flattened, but do not make it less dangerous as a rapid spreader. The plant is a tall and slender, with stems that may bend downwards. Stem segments become detached from the plant quite easily and rapidly root and flourish into new shrub-like plants.

Opuntia microdasys (rabbit-ears, bunny-ears)

Not all species of *Opuntia* have pads armed with long, sharp spines. *Opuntia microdasys* is a case in point. However, the lack of long, sharp spines may be misleading: the small areoles that cover the plant bodies are thickly set with minute spines that can cause severe irritation to the unsuspecting person who may bump into it. This Mexican native is a popular pot plant and rockery subject and, with its palm-shaped pads that are successively joined to the tips of the pads, has acquired the rather innocent and apt common name "bunny-ears". There are several variants – some with brown spines, others with yellow or white spines.

Opuntia stricta (Australian pest pear)

It is amazing how rapidly some exotic succulents can become established weeds in a foreign country. *Opuntia*, the predominantly Mexican cactus genus, has certainly played its part in providing countries such as South Africa and Australia with their share of problem plants. Most *Opuntia* species are noxious weeds in these countries and it is illegal to cultivate them. This species is a low-growing, most commonly almost creeping cactus, consisting of numerous smooth, shiny green, jointed pads dotted with sharp and ferocious spines. The pads become detached quite easily and rapidly root in a new location. Its initial popularity in amenity horticulture is easy to understand: the plants bear beautiful yellow flowers in profusion. Although most succulent collectors nowadays realise the dangers in cultivating and carelessly discarding this species, it is rapidly colonising suitable habitats.

Opuntia ficus-indica with cochineal

Opuntia macrocentra

Opuntia imbricata

Opuntia microdasys (white form)

Opuntia stricta

Opuntia stricta flowers

PACHYCEREUS

Pachycereus marginatus (organ-pipe cactus, Mexican fence cactus)

Pachycereus marginatus is one of the easiest of the columnar species to grow and with time it will form tall stems that appear thornless from a distance. In contrast to the large thorns of *P. pringlei*, those of *P. marginatus* are small and somewhat hidden along the ribs of the stems. The growth form makes it perfect for planting as a hedge, a purpose for which it is used in its native Mexico.

Pachycereus pringlei (giant Mexican cereus, Mexican giant)

In contrast to the flattened pads of species of *Opuntia*, many cacti have prominent, jointless stems that tower towards the sky, eventually branching and re-branching into a symphony of organ pipes. *Pachycereus pringlei* is a species with such a growth form. However, it is rather slow growing and will take many years to reach a massive size. Particularly when young, this columnar cactus has beautiful white spines that contrast sharply with the dull-green, ribbed stems.

PARODIA

Parodia leninghausii (golden ball cactus, yellow tower)

The golden ball cactus is an old favourite garden succulent indigenous to southern Brazil. It was previously known as *Notocactus leninghausii*. It has a single rounded stem that gradually become elongated and clustered. The spines are characteristically finely bristly and golden yellow to pale brown. Lemon yellow flowers are produced in summer.

RHIPSALIS

Rhipsalis baccifera subsp. *mauritiana* (rope cactus, mistletoe cactus)

Not all the species of the Cactaceae are drought-resistant monstrosities that can tolerate and happily survive in protracted dry periods. Indeed, some species are confined to high rainfall areas where they often hide as epiphytes in trees or against cliff faces. But one thing that they all have in common is that the growing medium in their habitats is invariably well drained. The only indigenous African cactus, *Rhipsalis baccifera* subsp. *mauritiana* is an example of such a species. Unlike the columnar or globular cacti of the New World, it is a rather small plant. The species typically grows in subtropical or even tropical thicket vegetation where it occurs as an epiphyte in the branch forks of trees or as lithophytes growing against the sometimes sheer cliff faces. This species has an exceptionally wide distribution, occurring in South America, most countries of sub-Saharan Africa, most islands off the African east coast, including Madagascar, Mauritius and Seychelles, and even Sri Lanka. The species of *Rhipsalis* are generally not very attractive and they hold little fascination for the collector. The flowers are small and white and these are eventually replaced by small mistletoe-like fruits which seem to remain on the plants forever. The stems of the plants are thin and almost wiry, and are sparsely covered in soft, white prickles.

Pachycereus pringlei

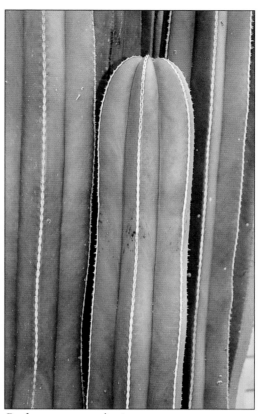

Pachycereus marginatus

Golden ball cactus (*Parodia leninghausii*)

Rhipsalis baccifera subsp. *mauritiana*

SCHLUMBERGERA

Schlumbergera ×buckleyi (=*S. truncata* × *S. russelliana*) (Christmas cactus)

This well-known hybrid is extremely popular as a pot plant and several millions of plants are sold each year. Flowering occurs in winter. It is very often confused with *Schlumbergera truncata* (which has almost identical flowers) but can easily be recognised by the rounded (crenate) teeth along the stem margins. These are markedly toothed (serrate) in *S. truncata*.

Schlumbergera russelliana (Christmas cactus)

The flowers of this species are almost regular (actinomorphic) and are deep pink in colour. The stamens and style are shortly exserted and protrude for a short distance from the petals. It is sometimes confused with the pink-flowered Easter cactus (*Hatiora rosea*) but the latter has regular flowers with short stamens. Furthermore, *Hatiora* species flower in spring, not winter.

Schlumbergera truncata (Christmas cactus, orchid cactus, lobster claws, crab cactus)

This epiphytic orchid was previously known as *Zygocactus truncatus*. It is the well-known and popular orchid cactus (but see *Disocactus* and *Epiphyllum*), also commonly called lobster claws. The flat and jointed stems are indeed reminiscent of the jointed legs of a lobster. The brightly coloured flowers are characteristically skewed to one side and are borne in profusion in autumn to winter. As a result, the plant is also known as Christmas cactus to distinguish it from the closely similar but spring-flowering Easter cactus (*Hatiora* species). (This distinction works well in the northern hemisphere but has led to considerable confusion in the southern hemisphere!) The whorls of petals are widely spaced, giving the impression of several flowers that have been inserted into one another. The orchid cactus is easily cultivated. It requires rich, well-drained soil and should be watered regularly. Several modern cultivars are available.

STENOCACTUS

Stenocactus multicostatus (brain cactus, wave cactus)

The small plants remain single or are sparsely clustering with age. The rounded stems are pale green, with up to 120 thin and decorative ribs. The flowers are white to purplish pink. Common names for this species include "brain cactus" and "wave cactus". It was previously known as *Echinofossulocactus multicostatus*.

Schlumbergera ×*buckleyi*

Hatiora rosea

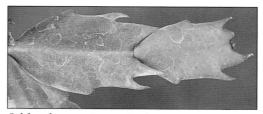

Schlumbergera truncata stem

Stenocactus multicostatus

Group 6

CRASSULACEAE
Stonecrop family or *Plakkie* family

DISTINGUISHING CHARACTERS Most members of this family are characterised by having thick, fleshy leaves typically arranged in symmetrical, opposite pairs or neat *Aloe*-like rosettes. It is this characteristic of neatly and symmetrically arranged leaves that make it easy to recognise members of this family. The flowers usually have four or five petals (or multiples thereof) and the fruits are made up of four or five separate parts (carpels). An interesting feature is the prominent nectar glands within the flowers.

NOTES The foliage of the stonecrops (*plakkies*) and their relatives together with their exceptional drought tolerance are probably the main reasons for their popularity in horticulture. The wide range of leaf shapes, sizes and textures contributes to their appeal amongst specialist succulent growers and gardeners in general. There are between 33 and 37 genera in the family and more than 1 100 species.

Brief notes on genera

Adromischus

This is a small genus with very fat, greenish grey leaves, characteristically with pale green or reddish spots and narrowly tubular, purplish pink flowers.

Aeonium

This Macaronesian genus has slightly fleshy leaves arranged in neat rosettes situated on long, slender stems. The yellow flowers are borne in dense, terminal clusters.

Aichryson

A group of 15 species found in Macaronesia and Morocco. *A.* ×*domesticum* is a common cultivated ornamental that was once popular as a decoration for windowsills.

Chiastophyllum

The single species of this genus is *C. oppositifolium*, a plant originally from the Caucasus region. It is a very popular garden ornamental known as lamb's tail. A profusion of yellow flowers are borne in drooping clusters.

Cotyledon

This well-known genus has fleshy leaves that are not deciduous (in contrast to those of *Tylecodon)* and the shape varies considerably. The large, tubular flowers are relatively uniform and vary from yellow to red.

Crassula

In terms of number of species this is the largest and most variable *plakkie* genus in Africa. The flowers are small and star-shaped, usually creamy white but sometimes pink or red. Growth forms in the genus are extraordinarily variable.

Flowers of *Aeonium arboreum*

Cotyledon orbiculata

Crassula pellucida

Crassula rupestris

Dudleya

There are about 40 species in this North American genus, some of which have become popular garden plants. All have glabrous (hairless) leaves and closely resemble species of *Echeveria*. Most, if not all, dudleyas respond to a winter rainfall regime.

Echeveria

These plants have small, grey rosettes of fleshy leaves, and creamy yellow or red flowers. There are more than 150 species, all from the warm parts of the New World (especially Mexico and South America). *Echeveria* is easily distinguished from *Cotyledon* by the axillary inflorescences (in *Cotyledon* species, the flowering stalks arise on the tips of the branches). Various segregate genera have been described, such as *Thompsonella*, a group of three Mexican species.

Graptopetalum

A genus of 12 species found in North America. The plants have neat rosettes of leaves that closely resemble those of *Echeveria* species, but the upward-facing, star-shaped flowers are easily recognised. The best-known species amongst succulent enthusiasts is *G. paraguayense*, which is not from Paraguay but from western Mexico! *Graptopetalum* species hybridise freely with other genera of the family to form intergeneric hybrids.

Greenovia

This small genus of four species from the Canary Islands has spread to other parts of the world as popular cultivated ornamentals. *Greenovia aurea* is commonly cultivated.

Jovibarba

A close relative of *Sempervivum*, but the six European species can be distinguished by having six or seven fringed sepals on each flower (nine to 20 sepals and not fringed in *Sempervivum*). There are two well-known cultivated ornamentals: *J. heuffelii*, which multiplies by the older rosettes that split into two, and *J. globifera*, which produces suckers (offsets, "hen and chickens").

Kalanchoe

Representatives of this genus are widely distributed in the Old World, especially Africa and its associated islands. The plants are variable in growth form and include shrubs, perennial herbs, annuals or climbers (vines). Despite the variable leaves, it can easily be distinguished from other genera by having four or eight rather than five or ten flower parts. Some of the species are viviparous – they produce tiny plantlets on the leaves that break off and become established as new plants.

Lenophyllum

The five or six species occur naturally in the warm parts of North America. They are popular as cultivated ornamental succulents. An example is *Lenophyllum reflexum*.

Monanthes

Species of this genus are indigenous to an area that stretches from Morocco to the Canary Islands (including Salvage Island). The plants are dwarf succulents that are commonly cultivated in gardens. The solitary flowers are relatively large, have small petals and are borne on slender stalks. Examples are *M. polyphylla* and *M. laxiflora*.

Echeveria species

Kalanchoe thyrsiflora

Kalanchoe sexangularis

Flowers of *Kalanchoe sexangularis*

Monanthes polyphylla

Pachyphytum

Plants of this genus of 12 Mexican species closely resemble *Echeveria* and differ from it only in details of the flowers – the presence of two scale-like appendages on the inside of each petal. Cultivated species include *P. oviferum* and *P. glutinicaule*.

Rosularia

The 27 species of this genus are found in North Africa, southern Europe and western Asia. The cultivated species (such as *R. chrysantha, R. pilosa, R. sempervivoides* and *R. sedoides*) usually have taproots and the leaves are borne in rosettes. The flowers are often yellowish or red and they have five to eight petals.

Sedum (stonecrops)

This is a large genus from the northern temperate regions with a few species in Madagascar and Mexico. The plants are generally small, and may be confused with crassulas. However, the flowers of most of the cultivated species are yellow or cream in colour. *Sedum* species have two rows (circles) of stamens; *Crassula* species have only one. In general the leaves and flowers of these plants are showier than those of many crassulas. The generic limits of *Sedum* are disputed and several splinter genera have been recognised, including *Hylotelephium, Orostachys* and *Rhodiola*. Species such as *S. roseum* (roseroot) and *S. acre* (wall pepper or common stonecrop) have edible leaves that are used in traditional medicine.

Sempervivum (houseleeks, live-forever)

This is one of the best-known genera of the cold northern regions. The plants (known as houseleeks) typically form small rosettes like miniature aloes, but the flowers are borne on elongated stalks and can be rather showy. Sempervivums are commonly grown in shallow soil on pillars, rock faces and flat roofs because of their uncanny ability to withstand extreme drought and frost, and it is widely believed that they will ward off lightning.

Sinocrassula (Chinese stonecrop)

A small genus of five species found from the Himalayas to southwestern China. It is closely related to *Sedum*. The plants are popular ornamentals, especially *S. yunnanensis*.

Tylecodon

A close relative of *Cotyledon,* but its species all differ in being deciduous, that is they shed their leaves. Its representatives are all indigenous to southern Africa. The tubular flowers, ranging from yellow to red, closely resemble those of *Cotyledon* species.

Umbilicus (navelworts)

A genus of 18 species found in North Africa, the Middle East and Europe. *U. rupestris,* commonly known as navelwort, penny pies or wall pennywort, is a well-known and popular garden succulent.

Villadia

About 30 species have been described in this genus, which is found from Texas southwards to Peru. One of the best-known and popular species is *V. batesii*.

Pachyphytum hookeri (=P. aduncum)

Hylotelephium (Sedum) sieboldii var. *ettyense*

Sedum obtusatum

Sedum 'Little Gem'

Sedum treleasii

Rhodiola rosea (=Sedum roseum)

Notes on species of Crassulaceae

ADROMISCHUS

Adromischus caryophylaceus

The species has fleshy leaves with horny margins right around them and usually with dark purple spots. The flowers are white, tinged with pink.

Adromischus cooperi (plover eggs)

"Plover eggs" is a very popular species amongst succulent enthusiasts and is often seen in cultivation. The thick fleshy leaves with their clavate shape and spotted surfaces are very distinct. Pale pink flowers are produced in summer. Unlike *A. cristatus* (which may have similar leaves) there are no root-hairs on the stems.

Adromischus cristatus (crinkle-leaf plant)

The wavy leaf-ends of the species make it easy to distinguish from other *Adromischus* species. The leaves are more or less cylindrical and, as is the case with most species of the genus, vary from uniformly light green to light green variously mottled with deeper green spots. Short, brown aerial roots often develop where the leaves are attached to the stems, giving the plants a rather unkempt appearance. It is very easy in cultivation and will readily grow from detached leaves.

Adromischus maculatus

The name of this species is somewhat misleading, as the leaves are not consistently red-spotted. In fact, the flat, rounded leaves of some plants are a uniform light green colour, usually with a distinct red margin. The leaves are in small, but dense clusters on stems that can reach a length of about knee-high. It grows easily and flourishes in winter-rainfall conditions.

Adromischus maximus

One can be excused for confusing this large-leaved species with a *Cotyledon*, because the large, rounded leaves usually do not show the purple spots so characteristic of *Adromischus* species. Older plants are branched and may form relatively large cushions (and therefore require quite a large pot). The inflorescences are long, with numerous small pink flowers. Propagation can be done from leaf cuttings but stem cuttings are much faster. Water plants sparingly in the dormant season.

Adromischus umbraticola

This miniature species has short, fleshy, often sunken, underground stems. The long erect flowering stalks bear several pinkish flowers pointing sideways.

Adromischus cooperi

Adromischus cristatus

Adromischus maculatus

Adromischus maculatus flowers

Adromischus maximus

Adromischus maximus

AEONIUM

Aeonium arboreum (tree aeonium, velvet rose)

Aeonium arboreum grows as large, shrub-like plants that have smooth stems with clusters of leaves restricted to the tips of the stems. The club-shaped leaves are soft, flattened and only somewhat fleshy. The flowers are very small, bright yellow and densely clustered into inverted cone-shaped clusters. The plants originate from the Atlantic coast of Morocco.

Aeonium arboreum 'Atropurpureum' (black rose)

This cultivar of *Aeonium arboreum* is in all features identical to the pure species with the exception that its leaves are almost pitch black. The same or similar cultivars are known in Europe by the names 'Zwartkop' or 'Schwarzkopf'. It is often listed as a cultivar of *Aeonium manriqueorum* and not *A. arboreum*.

Aeonium canariense (giant velvet rose)

The giant velvet rose is a robust plant that grows to a height of more than a metre. It is suitable for landscaping (both indoors and outdoors) and is suitable for pot cultivation. The slightly hairy leaves are borne in large rosettes. Large clusters of pale yellow flowers are produced in summer.

Aeonium haworthii (pinwheel)

Aeonium haworthii is one of the most popular and widely grown aeoniums. It is a clump-forming species that may reach a size of more than half a metre high and wide. The small flowers are pale yellow. Plants thrive in full sun and require well-drained soil. Water sparingly, even in the growing season.

AICHRYSON

Aichryson ×domesticum (youth-and-old-age)

This is a popular plant for windowsills and has been grown as a houseplant in Europe for a very long time. It has rounded silvery leaves and clusters of attractive, bright yellow flowers, each with about eight to ten narrow petals. The plant is a hybrid between *A. tortuosum* and *A. punctatum*.

Aichryson tortuosum (gouty houseleek)

Aichryson tortuosum is a perennial sub-shrub indigenous to the Canary Islands. It has crowded, fleshy and downy leaves. The small yellow flowers typically have eight petals.

Aeonium arboreum 'Atropurpureum'

Aeonium arboreum

Aeonium 'Zwartkop'

Aeonium haworthii

Aeonium canariense

Aichryson tortuosum

CHIASTOPHYLLUM

Chiastophyllum oppositifolium (lamb's tail)

Various leaf colour forms of this single species, commonly known as lamb's tail, are cultivated. The plant can easily be recognised by the toothed leaves and the drooping clusters of small yellow flowers.

COTYLEDON

Cotyledon barbeyi (hoary navelwort)

At maturity this species has smooth stems with the leaves arranged on the top third of the stems. The leaves of *Cotyledon barbeyi* are variable in size, shape and texture. The most beautiful form, which also grows strongly in cultivation, has leaves that appear somewhat sticky. The flowers of this *Cotyledon* are consistently red and have distinct basal swellings. It is widely distributed in subtropical climates, from the eastern seaboard of southern Africa northwards to East Africa and Arabia.

Cotyledon orbiculata (plakkie, pig's ears*)*

This is the most widespread and variable of all the species. Numerous regional forms and clones are in cultivation. The leaves are mostly large and rounded, thick and fleshy and vary from bright green to silver-white as a result of surface wax. The attractive orange to red flowers are bell-shaped and are borne in clusters. The individual flowers are pendulous, hanging down when open. The five petals are fused into a tube, with the tips gracefully curled back. Copious amounts of nectar are produced by the cup-shaped nectar glands, which are situated at the base of each of the free carpels (fruiting leaves). It is therefore no surprise that these plants are mainly pollinated by sunbirds.

A form of the species with undulate leaf margins is cultivated in Europe under the common names "silver crown" or "silver ruffles". This plant is sometimes known as *Cotyledon undulata* but it is nowadays regarded merely as a variety of *C. orbiculata*. Wild forms with lobed leaves resembling the antlers of a deer are also becoming popular.

Cotyledon tomentosa (bear's paw)

The species and its two subspecies (subsp. *tomentosa* and subsp. *ladismithiensis*) are easily distinguished from all other *Cotyledon* species by the densely hairy leaves. The plants are often very small, but occasionally may reach a height of up to 0.5 m. The subspecies *tomentosa* differs from the other subspecies in the presence of several large brown teeth near the leaf tips. The flowers are dark red but similar to those of other species.

Cotyledon barbeyi

Cotyledon orbiculata

Cotyledon orbiculata (cultivar with lobed leaves)

Cotyledon tomentosa var. *ladismithiensis*

CRASSULA

Crassula arborescens (silver dollar, silver jade plant, Chinese jade)

The leaves of these medium-sized shrubs are almost invariably coin-shaped in outline and a light silvery blue colour due to a layer of waxy surface scales. This distinguishes it from the superficially similar *C. ovata*. Common names include silver jade plant, silver dollar and Chinese jade (but both this species and the closely related *C. ovata* originally came from South Africa). The small, whitish, star-shaped flowers are carried in ball-shaped clusters and appear in winter. These turn light brown when they fade and tend to be persistent on the plants for quite some time after flowering. Propagation is very easy from stem cuttings. A group of well-grown specimens of *C. arborescens* makes a beautiful display in any garden and can be used as an effective silver-white backdrop for smaller succulents. Plants also grow well in large containers and may be used as a specimen plant because of the thick trunk that develops with time.

Crassula arborescens subsp. *undulatifolia* (wavy silver dollar)

It is easy to recognise this naturally occurring subspecies by the distinctive wavy margins of the leaves. The plant is indigenous to southern Africa and has become popular as a garden succulent. It tends to be less robust than the typical subspecies.

Crassula capitella subsp. *thyrsiflora*

These plants grow naturally in southern Africa and are small perennials with several branches of up to 0.4 m high when in flower (but often much smaller). The leaves are borne in rosettes and are sometimes neatly arranged in four ranks (as shown opposite) or sometimes in a spiral. They are bright green but may take on various brownish or reddish hues, especially when the plants become stressed through lack of water. The inconspicuous flowers, mostly cream but occasionally tinged with pink, are borne in a long, spike-like cluster.

Crassula coccinea (rock flower)

This is a small perennial shrub with erect branches that grows up to 0.6 m high. The leaves are broad and flat, with small hairs along the margins. They are arranged in four neat rows along the stem and remain on the stems when they dry up. Bright red or very rarely white flowers are formed in flat-topped clusters on the stem tips. The flowers are relatively large and tubular and superficially resemble those of *Kalanchoe blossfeldiana* (but *Kalanchoe* species have four petals, not five as in *Crassula*). This striking plant occurs naturally on the edges of rocky sandstone plateaux in the fynbos region near Cape Town and environs, where it flowers during December and January. It is one of the most spectacular *Crassula* species and is relatively easy to grow, provided it is given acid sandy soil and copious amounts of water in the winter months. In some books the plant will be found under its older name, *Rochea coccinea*. Plants are not very long-lived and would have to be replaced with new ones every two to three years.

Crassula arborescens

Leaves of *Crassula arborescens*

Crassula arborescens subsp. *undulatifolia*

Crassula capitella subsp. *thyrsiflora*

Crassula coccinea

Flowers of *Crassula coccinea*

Crassula columnaris

A small gem of the succulent world with a rounded to elongated plant body made up of broad and tightly overlapping leaves. The stems are only up to 10 mm long. Plants are variously coloured to blend in with the harsh, dry and rocky habitat in which they grow. Flowers are borne in dense rounded heads directly on top of the plant (often partly hidden among the upper leaves). The flowers are white, pale yellow or tinged with red. When not in flower, *C. columnaris* is difficult to distinguish from the closely related *C. barklyi* (rattlesnake crassula). Mature specimens of the latter are invariably branched, while *C. columnaris* plants remain unbranched or have short axillary branches at the base. There are numerous other dwarf crassulas that are occasionally grown as curiosities, such as *C. alpestris*, *C. namaquensis*, *C. nudicaulis*, *C. orbicularis*, *C. pyramidalis* and *C. sericea*.

Crassula deceptor

Another dwarf *Crassula* species that rarely grows taller than 80 mm. It differs markedly from *C. columnaris* in the numerous side branches that are formed and also in the flower cluster (technically a round-topped thyrse) that is borne on a slender stalk, high above the plant body. The individual flowers are small, cream-coloured and inconspicuous. The leaves are also quite distinctive – they have blunt tips covered in warty structures and form four neat rows, resulting in a four-angled column. The leaves vary in colour from green to grey to brown and are dotted with small spots (hydathodes), which become more prominent in stressed plants. The plant is widely distributed in Namibia and the dry parts of South Africa.

Crassula multicava (fairy crassula)

The plant is easily recognised by the very broad and rather flat, round leaves that are invariably decorated with small spots. They are borne horizontally and are often yellowish-green. Small white or pale pink, star-shaped flowers are borne in profusion in sparse clusters. The commonly grown form of the species usually has four petals rather than five (as in *Kalanchoe*). *Crassula multicava* is remarkably tolerant of shade and will thrive in the shade of an evergreen tree where it can be planted effectively as a groundcover. This species will grow easily from cuttings produced from either the leaves, stems or spent inflorescences. It is similar to *C. streyi* but the lower surfaces of the leaves are not purple.

Crassula muscosa (shoe-lace plant, moss cypress)

This peculiar crassula has thin trailing stems covered with minute overlapping scale-like leaves. It resembles a club moss or miniature cypress. The plants are usually pale yellowish green to pale brown in colour. The tiny flowers are inconspicuous but the colour and texture of the stems contrast beautifully with other plants on the rockery.

Crassula columnaris

Crassula alpestris

Crassula nudicaulis

Crassula deceptor

Crassula multicava

Crassula muscosa

Crassula ovata (dollar plant, jade plant, jade tree)

Plants grow as densely leaved robust shrubs, which in appearance resemble miniature baobab trees. The leaves are coin-shaped or slightly elongated and usually a bright light green colour. The flowers are carried in ball-shaped clusters and although quite small, create a feast of pinkish colour. Flowering occurs in early to midsummer (the similar *C. arborescens* flowers in midwinter). Plants grow very easily from stem or leaf cuttings – in fact, where either of these are dropped they will take root and produce new plants. This is one of the most popular and useful of all garden succulents. *Crassula ovata* is sometimes still referred to by the old name *C. portulacea*. Examples of garden cultivars include 'Basutoland' (white flowers), 'Crosby's Compact' (dwarf plant with purple leaves), 'Dwarf Green' (reddish leaf margins) and 'Sunset' (leaves with yellow stripes and red edges).

Crassula pellucida (pink buttons, trailing crassula)

The trailing crassula is an attractive ground cover that has become popular as a garden plant (not only in succulent gardens). It has small, broad leaves and sparse clusters of small white or pinkish flowers (see photograph on the family page).

Crassula perfoliata (propeller plant)

There are four varieties of this attractive and commonly cultivated species. The var. *minor* has sickle-shaped, laterally flattened leaves. The bracts on the flowering stalk are blunt and flower colour varies from white to pink to bright red. Var. *perfoliata* and var. *coccinea* are similar in the narrowly boat-shaped leaves and the sharply pointed bracts on the flowering stalk but the former has smaller white flowers, the latter larger and red. The var. *heterotricha* differs in the branched, more shrub-like habit. The leaves are usually oblong but may also be laterally flattened as in var. *minor*. The flower colour is usually white but is sometimes tinted pink inside. These plants are very useful garden succulents because they combine highly decorative foliage with attractive flower clusters.

Crassula perforata (skewer plant)

The plant is a slender, sparsely branched, scrambling and spreading perennial herb or shrublet that may reach a length of 0.6 m. Old leaves are persistent on the stems. The peculiar feature of this species is that the leaves are completely fused in pairs and surround the thin stem, like pieces of meat on a skewer – hence the common name. The leaves are flat, green to silvery in colour, with a conspicuous reddish horny edge. The cultivar 'Pagoda' has bright green leaves with white edges on rigid erect stems. Cream-coloured to pale yellow flowers occur in a dense elongated cluster partly hidden by leaf-like bracts and with no obvious stalk (peduncle).

Crassula rupestris (bead vine)

This species may be confused with *C. perforata* because the leaves may sometimes be fused at their bases, giving the effect of a vegetable rosary (hence the common names buttons on a string, bead vine, necklace vine or rosary vine). However, it is a much-branched, rounded shrublet up to 0.5 m in height and the old leaves tend to drop off. The leaves are flat or concave above but distinctly convex below. Another difference is the rounded (rather than elongated) and conspicuously stalked flower clusters, which may be cream-coloured, pink or tinged with red.

Crassula ovata

Crassula perfoliata var. *coccinea*

Crassula perfoliata var. *coccinea* flowers

Crassula perfoliata var. *perfoliata*

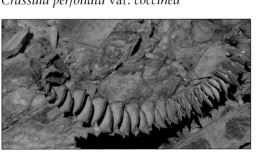

Crassula perforata

Crassula rupestris

Crassula sarcocaulis (bonsai crassula)

This species is easily confused with *C. tetragona* (especially with the subsp. *robusta*, which may have a similar, bonsai-like appearance) but the flowers are larger, with the petals up to 6 mm long. Furthermore, it has glandular hairs on the stems, at least below the flower clusters. The flowers are white to cream as in *C tetragona*, but can sometimes be tinted with red. Two subspecies have been recognised in *C. sarcocaulis,* which are easily distinguished by the leaf shape: narrow and pencil-shaped in subsp. *rupicola* and much broader and distinctly flattened in subsp. *sarcocaulis*. The main branches of subsp. *sarcocaulis* are markedly thicker (up to 50 mm in diameter) than those of subsp. *rupicola* (up to 10 mm in diameter). These plants occur naturally in southern Africa, from Malawi southwards to South Africa. They are grown as shrubby garden succulents or container plants that may reach a height of 0.6 m.

Crassula streyi (purple-leaved fairy crassula)

This is an attractive spreading perennial that makes an excellent groundcover. It is similar to *C. multicava* and is often confused with this species. In contrast to *C. multicava*, *C. streyi* is better adapted to growing in more exposed positions and will tolerate the hot midday sun. In addition, the undersides of the leaves are a purple colour and the leaves often are carried vertically, especially when stressed, to expose the colourful lower leaf surfaces. The leaves are also sessile (without leaf stalks) and more pointed than those of *C. multicava*. In common with *C. multicava*, the flowers are small, star-shaped, pinkish in colour and tend to have only four petals (and not consistently five, as is typical for *Crassula* species).

Crassula tetragona (miniature pine tree, baby pine of China)

These plants vary tremendously in growth form and other characters so that six distinct subspecies are recognised (two of which are illustrated here). The bright green leaves are borne in opposite pairs and form neat ranks along the stems. Flowers are hardly noticed, as they are very small, white and inconspicuous (the petals are less than 3 mm long). The subspecies differ markedly in the length of the flowering stalk (peduncle) and also in the shape of the flower clusters (sparse and flat-topped in some, dense and rounded in others) but the most distinctive feature is the growth form. The subsp. *acutifolia* is a plant with short, cone-shaped leaves and slender, more or less creeping, sparsely branched stems that tend to form roots at the nodes. Subsp. *tetragona* has similar leaves but the growth form is upright and more shrubby (up to 0.3 m high), with the main stems repeatedly branched. Subsp. *robusta* has a similar growth form but is taller (up to 1 m high) with flaky bark, the leaves are much larger and the stems are thick and fleshy. This South African succulent is a very popular and easy-to-grow garden plant or container plant that will also do well in indoor conditions.

Crassula streyi

Crassula streyi leaves and flowers

Crassula sarcocaulis subsp. *sarcocaulis*

Crassula sarcocaulis subsp. *rupicola*

Crassula tetragona subsp. *acutifolia*

Crassula tetragona subsp. *tetragona*

DUDLEYA

Dudleya edulis (mission lettuce, fingertips, ladies fingers)

A southern Californian species with narrow, finger-like leaves borne on branched stems. Noteworthy are the greyish green colour of the leaves and the branched clusters of cream-coloured flowers. The plant is shrubby in appearance, with the flowering branches arising from a short, thick base. Cultivation is uncomplicated but plants do best when protected from the strong afternoon sun.

Dudleya pulverulenta (chalk lettuce)

This Californian species is commonly known as chalk lettuce because of the white-powdered leaves. The plant grows as a very large solitary rosette of more than 0.5 m in diameter. The oblong leaves are silvery white in colour, contrasting beautifully with the large red flowers that hang down from stout flowering stems up to 1 m in height. These plants do very well in pots and grow well in partial shade.

Dudleya virens (alabaster plant)

The plant has narrow, pointed, greyish green leaves arranged in large rosettes. Relatively small white flowers appear in spring and are borne on flowering stems of to 0.5 m long. It occurs naturally on the coast of southern California.

ECHEVERIA

Echeveria agavoides (molded wax agave, lipstick echeveria)

Plants grow as elegant small rosettes with sharply pointed, waxy leaves – superficially resembling miniature *Agave* plants, hence the scientific name. Numerous varieties and cultivars are known, showing diverse leaf shapes and especially leaf colours (from pale green to purple-lilac). The flowers are pinkish orange outside and yellow within. The plant occurs naturally in Mexico.

Echeveria derenbergii (painted lady)

This is a clump-forming plant with short, much-branched stems bearing dense rosettes. The pale green or greyish green leaves are short and thick, with each ending in a short bristle. The leaf tips and margins are characteristically reddish in colour. Relatively small, bell-shaped flowers are borne in short clusters, with the sepals resembling the leaves and the petals bright orange and yellow.

Echeveria elegans (Mexican snow ball)

This species is widely cultivated in gardens and is commonly known as Mexican snow ball, white Mexican rose or Mexican gem. It has thick leaves that are arranged in more or less ball-shaped rosettes. The flowers are pink outside and orange-yellow inside. The plants soon form clusters and are useful as a groundcover in dry corners of the garden.

Dudleya edulis

Echeveria agavoides

Echeveria agavoides flowers

Echeveria derenbergii

Echeveria elegans

Echeveria gibbiflora (coral star)

A commonly cultivated and variable succulent with single (not branching) stems of up to 0.3 m long. The leaves are broader towards the pointed tips and are often tinged purplish, sometimes with wavy margins. Flowers are borne in branched clusters of up to 1 m long. They are bell-shaped or somewhat tubular, red on the outside and buff inside. The species grows naturally in southern Mexico but several garden forms or varieties are known. The var. *carunculata* has peculiar warty outgrowths near the leaf tips. Commonly seen in cultivation is the var. *metallica*, which has bluish grey leaves with a characteristic metallic sheen. Plants can withstand fairly cold conditions but not frost. They grow best in rich, well-drained soil and should be watered regularly during the growing season but more sparsely in winter.

Echeveria gigantea (giant echeveria)

Plants grow as single large rosettes borne on unbranched stems of up to 0.5 m high. The leaves are rounded, with purple margins and often notched at the tips. The rose red flowers are borne on branched clusters of up to 2 m high. The original species is from Mexico but some attractive cultivars have been developed, differing mainly in the shape and size of the rosettes and in the colour of the leaves.

Echeveria ×gilva (green Mexican rose, wax rosette)

This garden form originated as a hybrid between *E. agavoides* and *E. elegans*. It has short, branching stems with attractive, dense rosettes of oblong, short, pointed leaves. The single clusters of yellow and pink flowers appear in spring.

Echeveria ×imbricata (hen and chicks)

The common name of this plant reflects the numerous new rosettes that form gradually from the branching stems. It appears to have originated as a garden hybrid.

Echeveria multicaulis (copper leaf, copper roses)

The copper leaf is a popular garden succulent with much-branched stems of up to 1 m long. Blunt, bristle-tipped leaves with reddish margins are neatly arranged in dense rosettes. The small flowers are bright red on the outside and orange-yellow inside. Red sepals and orange upper bracts add to the beauty of this species.

Echeveria pringlei (Pringle's echeveria)

This is an attractive species with branching stems, relatively large rosettes, usually densely hairy leaves and bright red flowers.

Echeveria gigantea

Echeveria gibbiflora var. *crispata*

Echeveria ×*imbricata*

Echeveria pringlei

Echeveria pulvinata (plush plant, chenille plant)

This is one of the most popular and attractive of all the echeverias known to gardeners. It has a somewhat shrubby growth form, with robust branching stems up to 0.2 m long. The leaves are relatively narrow and pointed, with a characteristic dense fuzzy layer giving a velvety appearance. A cultivar known as 'Ruby' has bright red leaves, while the normal form has dull green leaves (but often with reddish leaf margins). Despite their relatively small size, the flowers are quite attractive because of their bright colours. The petals are predominantly yellow to orange, but the tips are red.

Echeveria secunda (common echeveria)

This species (and close relatives and hybrids) is perhaps the best-known member of the genus *Echeveria* because it is commonly used in public parks for live displays, to form crests, letters or floral clocks (*Sempervivum* species are often used for the same purpose in Europe). The plants proliferate to form a circle of young plants. Inflorescences are about 0.3 m high and have curling, slender tips. The flowers are dull red outside and yellow within and they all point upwards (or at least in the same direction). There are several varieties, including var. *secunda* (with relatively large, thick and silvery leaves, var. *glauca*, with large but very thin leaves that have a metallic blue colour, and var. *pumila* with small leaves that are only 15 mm wide.

Echeveria setosa (Mexican firecracker)

The common name for this attractive succulent accurately describes the bright red and yellow flowers that are borne in slender, branching clusters – resembling an exploding firecracker. All parts of the plant are covered in long hairs. This, together with the total absence of a stem, makes it an easy species to identify. Each flat-topped rosette comprises a large number of pointed, bristle-tipped leaves.

Echeveria shaviana (Mexican hens)

Mexican hens have crowded rosettes, usually without distinct stems. The plants typically have spoon-shaped, silvery grey, hairless leaves that are often slightly toothed near the tips. The pink flowers are borne in short, simple clusters. They are all arranged to one side of the stalk (second) and usually hang down (typically nodding). As with many species of *Echeveria*, there are numerous hybrids and garden clones that tend to obliterate the distinction between species. Plants are often sold under cultivar names without any attempt at making a botanical identification to the species level. One of the most popular cultivars derived from *E. shaviana* is 'Black Prince'. It is said to have originated as a hybrid between this species and *E. agavoides*.

146

Echeveria secunda

Echeveria pulvinata

Echeveria secunda flowers

Echeveria setosa

Echeveria setosa flowers

Echeveria 'Black Prince'

GRAPTOPETALUM

Graptopetalum amethystinum (jewel-leaf plant)

This Mexican species is a branching subshrub of up to 0.3 m high. The blunt, blue-green to lavender or purple leaves occur in lax rosettes. Each flower is tubular but the petals flare out in the upper half. The colour is green-yellow banded, with red dots. This attractive species is rather slow growing.

Graptopetalum bellum (=*Tacitus bellus*)

This is one of the most spectacular species of the family Crassulaceae. It has small, firm rosettes that are borne close to the ground. The bright pink flowers are borne in clusters on slender stalks. The plant was discovered in 1972 in the mountainous region between Chihuahua and Sonora in Mexico. It has become very popular in the horticultural trade and is sometimes still sold under its original name, *Tacitus bellus*. Cultivation is fairly easy, but the best results are achieved in a shady spot with some morning sun.

Graptopetalum pachyphyllum (trailing ghost plant)

Graptopetalum pachyphyllum is a very common garden succulent with trailing stems bearing small rosettes of club-shaped leaves. The leaves are typically bluish green and tinted with red towards the tips. Flowers appear in early summer. They are pale yellow and marked with red spots.

Graptopetalum paraguayense (ghost plant, mother of pearl plant)

Plants grow as small branched shrublets with compact rosettes made up of thick silver-grey and shiny leaves resembling mother of pearl. Young leaves tend to be pale mauve. The flowers are tubular with spreading lobes, resulting in a star-shaped appearance, not unlike the flowers of a *Crassula*. The colour is white to pale pink but sometimes dotted with red. *Graptopetalum paraguayense* originates from western Mexico and not from Paraguay, as the scientific name would suggest. It is easily propagated from cuttings or even from single leaves. It is one of the best-known and most popular garden succulents because it demands little attention to stay attractive.

GREENOVIA

Greenovia aurea (golden greenovia)

This beautiful small succulent from the Canary Islands forms numerous clusters of succulent rosettes. In the resting period, the rosettes look like green rose buds about to open. The leaves vary from pale green to greyish. Attractive bright yellow flowers are borne in small clusters. The flowers are very distinctive because of the unusually large number of petals (about 35!). Plants are usually grown in pots but they can be successfully grown as garden succulents in mild, temperate regions.

Graptopetalum paraguayense

Graptopetalum bellum

Graptopetalum pachyphyllum

JOVIBARBA

Jovibarba heuffelii

The rosettes closely resemble those of *Sempervivum* species but when old they multiply by division. Yellow or yellow-white bell-shaped flowers are borne in short dense clusters. The species originates from central Europe and Asia.

Jovibarba sobolifera (hen-and-chickens)

This species has small rosettes (40 mm in diameter) that multiply by suckering, hence the common name. The leaves are bright green with no hairs except along the margins. The flowers are similar to those of *J. heuffelii*. It occurs in central and southeastern Europe.

KALANCHOE

Kalanchoe beharensis (donkey's ears)

Plants are robust shrubs to small trees and may reach 6 m in height. They have very large and thick leaves that are triangular in shape, with deeply toothed margins and a thick felt-like layer of hairs on the surface. The erect flowers are urn-shaped, yellowish-green on the outside and violet within. This peculiar plant and popular garden succulent originates from Madagascar. It is propagated from cuttings and is easy to grow in warm climates. The form of the species illustrated here has oak leaf-shaped leaves.

Kalanchoe blossfeldiana (flaming Katy)

Originally from Madagascar, this is by far the best-known and most widely cultivated species of *Kalanchoe*. It is a compact perennial up to 0.4 m in height. Forms that are sold in the florist trade as potted flowers are usually hybrids with the Somalian *K. flammea* and the Madagascan *K. pumila*. The leaves have rounded teeth along the margins and are bright glossy green but turn reddish brown when the plants are stressed. Numerous flowers, each about 10 mm long, are variously coloured, including red, pink, orange, yellow or white. Flaming Katy, is a favourite houseplant and is also commonly grown in window boxes. It thrives in rich but well-drained soil and likes plenty of water.

Kalanchoe daigremontiana (flopper, devil's backbone)

An easily recognised species, *K. daigremontiana* grows up to 1 m tall and has large, broad leaves tapering to narrow, curved tips. Along the margins, numerous small plantlets are formed, one between each of the short marginal teeth. The leaf surface is beautifully decorated with purple spots and blotches. As is typical for the species that was formerly included in the genus *Bryophyllum* (now considered a group within *Kalanchoe*), the flowers are pendulous (nodding) and have an unusual violet-grey colour. The plant is indigenous to Madagascar but is grown as a pot plant or garden succulent in many parts of the world.

Kalanchoe delagoensis (chandelier plant)

This common and often weedy garden succulent is also known by older names such as *Kalanchoe tubiflora* or *Bryophyllum delagoense*. It has erect stems up to 1 m tall bearing conspicuously blotched, pencil-shaped leaves with numerous small plantlets at the tips that easily break off to form new plants. The large red flowers are nodding (pendulous) and are borne in clusters at the stem tips. The plant is indigenous to Madagascar but has become a weed in some parts of Africa and Australia.

Kalanchoe beharensis

Kalanchoe blossfeldiana

Kalanchoe blossfeldiana (double flowers)

Kalanchoe daigremontiana leaves

Kalanchoe delagoensis leaves

Kalanchoe delagoensis flowers

Kalanchoe fedtschenkoi (lavender scallops)

Plants are small dense shrublets about 0.5 m tall with distinctively toothed leaves. The leaves are smooth and usually a metallic greyish colour but variegated leaf forms are also known. The sparse, nodding flowers are an unusual purple-red colour. Plants grow very easily from cuttings. *Kalanchoe fedtschenkoi* originates from Madagascar.

Kalanchoe longiflora

The plant is a small shrub of up to 0.6 m with spreading branches. The distinctly sea-green leaves are borne on four-angled stems. They are broader above the middle and have the margins toothed towards the tips. Numerous much-branched inflorescences are formed, bearing relatively large, yellow to orange flowers. The species has a localised distribution in South Africa (KwaZulu-Natal) and is often confused with the more commonly cultivated *K. sexangularis*. It differs markedly in the distinctly turquoise leaves and longer flowers (11 to 14 mm long in *K. longiflora*, 7 to 10 mm in *K. sexangularis*).

Kalanchoe marmorata (penwiper plant)

This East African kalanchoe is a leafy succulent about 0.3 m high. The large leaves are decorated with brown or purple blotches. Plants require well-drained soil and prefer light shade (but sunlight is needed for the attractive spots on the leaves to develop fully).

Kalanchoe rotundifolia

Plants grow up to 0.5 m high and have slender perennial stems. The leaves are variable but are usually greyish green in colour, distinctly rounded (rarely three-lobed) and often have blunt marginal teeth. Tubular, erect flowers are borne in sparse clusters. They are usually orange but sometimes pink to red. This species is widely distributed in Africa, from South Africa to Socotra. It is known to be poisonous to small stock, causing a chronic form of heart glycoside poisoning in sheep and goats, known as *nenta* or *krimpsiekte*.

Kalanchoe sexangularis

Plants are erect shrublets up to 1 m in height. The leaves are large and broad, folded lengthwise and usually have numerous rounded teeth along the margins. Leaf colour is variable (green to purple) but usually dark ruby-red in cultivated forms. The flowers are greenish yellow and shorter than those of *K. longiflora*. The species is indigenous to Zimbabwe and the adjoining northern and eastern parts of South Africa. In warm regions with summer rainfall, this plant is exceptionally easy to grow. It survives mild frost. The dark leaf colour can be accentuated by grouping several specimens close together.

Kalanchoe fedtschenkoi

Kalanchoe fedtschenkoi flowers

Kalanchoe longiflora

Kalanchoe rotundifolia flowers

Kalanchoe rotundifolia

Kalanchoe sexangularis

Kalanchoe thyrsiflora (paddle plant)

This very attractive leaf succulent forms large rosettes that eventually develop into a single erect flowering stem up to 1.5 m high. After flowering, the rosette dies back but the plant increases by off-sets. The soup plate-sized leaves are often intensely tinged with broad, bright red margins. The bright yellow and sweetly scented flowers differ from the distinctly smaller and greenish yellow flowers of the similar-looking and closely related *Kalanchoe luciae*, with which this species is sometimes confused.

Kalanchoe tomentosa (panda plant)

An erect perennial herb up to 1 m in height, *K. tomentosa* has large, oblong, densely furry leaves that are grooved above. A row of very ornate red-brown spots occurs along the leaf margin in the upper third of the leaf. The flowers are yellowish green with purplish lobes and red glandular hairs. The species originally came from Madagascar and has become a popular pot plant in cold areas or an attractive garden succulent in regions with mild, frost-free climates.

Plants are propagated from stem and leaf cuttings. A single leaf stuck into the ground will soon form a new plant. Several different cultivars are available, differing in the size and shape of the leaves, as well as in the colour of the fuzz along the leaf margins (this is usual dark purple to black but can also be various shades of brown and yellow).

Kalanchoe uniflora

It is a trailing epiphytic succulent up to 0.4 m tall with dark green, elliptic leaves and bright red to pinkish red tubular flowers that typically hang down. The plant originates from mountainous areas in Madagascar, where it grows on trees (in the shade or partial shade). This species is an excellent choice for a hanging basket. Water regularly but allow the plant to dry out completely between watering. Regular feeding is important and some pruning is usually necessary after flowering. It is still often listed under the old (alternative) name, *Bryophyllum uniflorum*.

LENOPHYLLUM

Lenophyllum pusillum

This is one of six species found in the warm parts of North America. It has thick, fleshy leaves that are concave on the upper surfaces. The small yellow flowers are borne single or in branched clusters. The small, erect petals are scarcely longer than the calyx. The ten stamens are longer than the petals – five of them are fused to the petals and five are free. Plants are usually grown in pots.

Kalanchoe thyrsiflora young plants

Kalanchoe thyrsiflora flowers

Kalanchoe tomentosa

Kalanchoe tomentosa

MONANTHES

Monanthes laxiflora

The only relatively well-known species is *M. laxiflora*. It is a small, branched plant with short, thick leaves like jellybeans. The flowers are borne in few-flowered clusters but open one by one and appear to be single (hence the name *Monanthes*). The petals are variable in colour, ranging from yellow to purplish. This interesting little plant is usually grown as a curiosity in succulent collections and is not really a garden succulent.

PACHYPHYTUM

Pachyphytum glutinicaule

Plants grow as firm-leaved, clump-forming rosettes that are almost indistinguishable from *Echeveria*. The leaves are oblong, with a smooth, silvery white surface. Attractive red flowers are borne on a long, branched stalk. Plants grow well in full sun or light shade and can tolerate light frost.

Pachyphytum oviferum (moonstones)

This is the most popular and best-known species of *Pachyphytum*. The firm, stone-like, rounded to club-shaped leaves are smooth and silvery in colour. Rather inconspicuous flowers are borne between large whitish bracts on a large, drooping spike. Each flower is tubular, white on the outside and reddish inside. Cultivation requirements are similar to that of other *Pachyphytum* species. Plants should be watered regularly during the growing season but sparingly during the dormant (winter) phase.

ROSULARIA

Rosularia chrysantha

The species originates from the mountains of the eastern Mediterranean. It has bright green rosettes with leaves that are glandular-hairy along the margins. The white to pale yellow flowers are decorated with coloured veins.

Rosularia sempervivum

The plant is a small perennial herb with a short caudex and with leaves arranged in flat or rounded rosettes. The flowers are borne in much-branched clusters and are tubular or funnel-shaped, with five petals. There is much regional variation in leaf shape and flower colour, so that six subspecies are recognised. The species occurs over a wide region from the Middle East to the Himalayas.

Monanthes laxiflora

Pachyphytum glutinicaule flowers

Pachyphytum glutinicaule

Pachyphytum oviferum

Rosularia chrysantha

SEDUM

Sedum acre (common stonecrop, wall pepper)

The plant is widely distributed in Europe and North Africa and is naturalised in the eastern parts of the USA. It is a small mat-forming perennial with tiny rounded leaves and bright yellow, star-shaped flowers. Cultivars with variegated leaves (pale yellow or striped with silver) are available. The species is adapted to cold temperate regions where it is commonly found in sandy and rocky places, often growing in very shallow soil or on old walls. The species is widely known as stonecrop or wall pepper.

Sedum morganianum (donkey's tail)

The plant is a perennial leaf succulent with trailing or hanging branches. The small but thick and overlapping leaves are bluish grey and arranged in dense spirals. Small pink flowers are borne in clusters on stalks that point down. Although the exact origin of the species is unknown, it is possibly Mexican because it has been cultivated there for a long time. *Sedum morganianum* is an old favourite for hanging baskets. The drooping, tail-like stems have led to the common name donkey's tail.

Sedum nussbaumerianum

The leaves of this small shrubby species are typically yellow in colour and crowded towards the tips of the branches. Plants do not regularly flower but have fairly large white flowers borne in many-flowered clusters. The main attraction of this species is the ease with which it can be cultivated and its remarkable drought tolerance. It is an attractive garden succulent in warm climates. The plant is said to be indigenous to Mexico and Vera Cruz.

Sedum pachyphyllum

Another Mexican sedum that grows as a dwarf shrublet. *S. pachyphyllum* has short, fat leaves arranged in spirals on the erect branches. The tips of the leaves may be tinted red, especially in stressed plants. Bright yellow flowers are borne in dense, flat-topped clusters. The plant is a useful garden subject because it is exceptionally easy to grow and will thrive under almost any conditions.

Sedum prealtum

Sedum prealtum is a shrubby and bushy plant up to 0.6 m in height. It has oblong, often yellowish green leaves arranged in loose rosettes. The bright yellow flowers, up to 10 mm in diameter, are borne in large, repeatedly branched clusters on the stem tips. The species is of Mexican origin but is widely grown in gardens all over the world. It has become naturalised in the Mediterranean region and southern England. Few plants will survive the extreme conditions (drought and even frost) that this useful ornamental succulent can tolerate.

Sedum acre

Sedum morganianum

Sedum nussbaumerianum

Sedum pachyphyllum

Sedum prealtum

Sedum prealtum flowers

Sedum ×rubrotinctum (jellybean plant, pork and beans)

These low-growing miniature shrublets have been cultivated in Mexico for a long time but their exact origin is unknown. The leaves are jellybean-shaped and a combination of bright red and bluish or bright green. The reddish green leaves usually have a shiny, highly polished appearance. The bright yellow flowers are small, star-shaped and carried in sparse, rounded to elongated clusters. This is a remarkably useful groundcover as the leaves are severed easily and each of them will grow to form a perfectly shaped plant. This is yet another succulent species that is grown for its spectacular leaves rather than its flowers.

Sedum spectabile (Chinese orpine)

This species has achieved the status of "common garden plant" rather than "common garden succulent". It is extremely popular in continental Europe and some of the adjacent islands with a continental climate where the harsh environmental conditions, particularly in winter, restrict the variety of succulents that can be grown outdoors. However, *S. spectabile* easily tolerates and in fact thrives under these conditions. The flowers are usually a dull pale pink. Somewhat paradoxically, when exposed to milder climates, the plants are extremely susceptible to a variety of maladies. It is a popular border plant in Europe but originates from China and Korea. Several species with broad flat leaves not borne in rosettes are sometimes included in a separate genus *Hylotelephium*. An alternative name for this species is *Hylotelephium spectabile*.

Sedum sieboldii (Japanese orpine)

This is a low-growing perennial shrublet with spreading, often drooping branches. The flat, waxy leaves are wider than they are long and are often grouped in threes at each node. They often have a reddish hue and are toothed along the margins towards the tips. The bright pink flowers are borne in attractive rounded clusters. The species originates from Japan. Several varieties and cultivars are grown in cold regions, mostly as container plants. The plant is also known as *Hylotelephium sieboldii*.

Sedum stahlii (coral beads)

In contrast to *Sedum ×rubrotinctum*, the leaves of *S. stahlii* are shorter and more sparsely spaced along the thin wiry stems. Furthermore, the leaves have a furry rather than shiny appearance. The species originates from Mexico and is commonly cultivated in gardens.

Sedum telephium (orpine, live-forever)

The species, commonly known as orpine or live-forever, is found from Europe to Siberia. The popular garden cultivar known as 'Autumn Joy' ('Herbstfreude' in German) appears to be a hybrid between this species and the East Asian *S. spectabile*. It has large, flat leaves with toothed margins. The terminal clusters of flowers are bright salmon pink but turn bronze towards the end of summer.

Sedum spectabile

Sedum sieboldii

Sedum ×rubrotinctum

Sedum stahlii

Sedum telephium 'Autumn Joy'

Sedum telephium flowers

SEMPERVIVUM

Sempervivum arachnoideum (cobweb houseleek, spider web houseleek)

The plant forms dense clusters of rosettes, each of which is about 50 mm in diameter when fully grown. The pointed leaves are up to 12 mm long and are covered with dense cobwebby hairs. The attractive flowers are borne on erect stalks with small, often red-tipped stem leaves. Each flower is about 15 mm in diameter and has about 9 to 20 rose-red petals. Numerous varieties and cultivars have been described, differing mostly in the density of the hairs and the size and shape of the leaves and rosettes.

Sempervivum calcareum (chalky houseleek)

This species is sometimes considered to be merely a form of *S. tectorum*. However, it generally differs in having broad, bluish grey leaves with brown or purplish tips and green to white, rarely pinkish flowers (pink in *S. tectorum*). Various leaf forms are sold commercially as garden cultivars.

Sempervivum tectorum (roof houseleek, common houseleek)

The roof houseleek is an old-fashioned plant that has been grown on roofs, walls and gate pillars in Europe since ancient times. The Latin name *tectorum* means "of roofs" and refers to the common habitat of the plant. The name *Sempervivum*, which means "live forever", is equally appropriate as these plants survive extreme conditions of drought and cold despite the shallow soils (or even complete absence of soil!) where it is customarily grown. Most of the large diversity of houseleeks known in world horticulture belong to this species. There are countless forms and cultivars, many of them with fancy names. This includes a bewildering range of leaf colours and leaf forms, so that it is quite difficult to correctly identity the cultivar, variety and even the species. However, the roof houseleek is the only red-flowered species of *Sempervivum* which has completely hairless leaves, even when young.

SINOCRASSULA

Sinocrassula indica (Indian stonecrop)

The plants are small rosettes of red-blotched leaves that may be up to 60 mm long and 15 mm wide. Clusters of flowers are borne on leafy stalks about 0.3 m high. The leaves on the flowering stalks easily fall off and root to form new plants. The tiny flowers are white with red tips.

Sinocrassula yunnanensis (Chinese stonecrop)

The plant forms rosettes of 50 to 70 leaves and sporadically forms annual flowering stems about 0.3 to 0.8 m high. Each leaf is up to 25 mm long and 6 mm wide, with a tapering base and the surface covered in a dense layer of short white hairs. The small flowers are yellow-green or purplish.

Sempervivum arachnoideum

Sempervivum calcareum

Sempervivum arachnoideum flowers

Sempervivum tectorum

Sempervivum tectorum

TYLECODON

Tylecodon paniculatus (butter bush, *botterboom*)

The spirally arranged, bright green leaves are borne in clusters towards the tips of the thick, fleshy stems. With time, the main trunk becomes very thick and is characteristically greenish yellow in colour and covered with a flaky, papery bark. The attractive flowers are borne on bright red stalks, which add to the attraction this plant has for pollinating sunbirds. Flower colour varies from greenish orange through bright orange to dark red or purplish red. Plants are easily cultivated in a Mediterranean climate (wet winter and dry summer) but must be kept dry in summer rainfall regions.

Tylecodon wallichii (common *krimpsiek*)

Krimpsiek is the name given to the chronic heart glycoside poisoning that this and other species of *Tylecodon* cause in small stock (sheep and goats). The plant is a robust perennial succulent with thick, fleshy stems that bear spirally arranged clusters of slender, finger-shaped leaves. Numerous tubercles on the stems mark the spots where the leaves of previous seasons have fallen off at the start of the dry summer. The tubular flowers are similar to those of other species of *Cotyledon* and *Tylecodon* but are a dull greenish yellow colour. The stems and leaves of the common *krimpsiek* are almost identical to those of another species, *T. cacalioides* (yellow *krimpsiek*), but the flowers of the latter are bright sulphur yellow and very attractive. Both species are occasionally grown as pot plants or as garden succulents in arid regions.

UMBILICUS

Umbilicus rupestris (navelwort, pennywort)

Navelwort is a perennial herb with bright green, shield-shaped leaves borne in a basal rosette. The small tubular flowers are arranged in slender, dense clusters on a long stalk. They are greenish white or sometimes tinged with pink. The plant is commonly cultivated in Europe and Asia. It is grown from seeds or cuttings and requires well-drained soil in a sunny, sheltered spot in the garden.

VILLADIA

Villadia batesii

One can be excused for mistaking these small South American plants for members of the better-known genus *Crassula*. However, the leaves are spirally arranged, not in opposite pairs as in *Crassula*. *Villadia batesii* is a clump-forming succulent with fleshy, finger-shaped leaves and small, white to reddish, star-shaped flowers borne on the stem tips. It is very easy to propagate from stem cuttings. Another commonly cultivated species is the southern Mexican and Guatemalan species known as *V. guatemalensis*. It is a much-branched dwarf succulent with slender leaves and yellowish or greenish flowers.

Tylecodon paniculatus flower

Tylecodon paniculatus

Villadia batesii

Tylecodon wallichii in flower

Tylecodon wallichii leaves

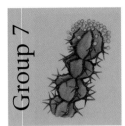

Group 7

EUPHORBIACEAE
Spurge family or Milkweed family

DISTINGUISHING FEATURES This family must rate as one of the most variable of all succulents. Species of the principal genus, *Euphorbia*, are characterised by their flowers, which are arranged into inflorescences called cyathia. However, a cyathium looks uncannily like a single flower, and not like an inflorescence. These usually rather small structures are most often conglomerates of a small number of insignificant male and female flowers, but species with separate male and female plants are also frequently encountered in this genus. Each cyathium is usually enclosed in a five-lobed leafy structure called the involucre, which often bears glands or nectaries. The cyathium may also be subtended by two or more enlarged, often brightly coloured bract-leaves. As a result of the difficulties associated with accurately observing with the naked eye the structure and composition of these tiny flowers, it only becomes apparent that a plant is female when it forms voluptuous, swollen seed capsules, or *vice versa* when it has male flowers only. *Euphorbia* flowers are not only small, but also rather dull in colour, lacking the highly coloured petals or tepals of "normal" garden flowers. If indeed colour is present, it is usually imparted by the floral bracts, as is the case with the brightly coloured "flowers" of poinsettia (*Euphorbia pulcherrima*) cultivars.

Another interesting character of the family Euphorbiaceae is that all the plant parts of its species contain milky latex. Of course, all plants that have milky latex are not euphorbias, but all euphorbias indeed have milky latex!

The African euphorbias superficially resemble the American cacti – an interesting example of convergence (where similar growth forms develop in parallel in unrelated plants). They also vary from small and barrel-shaped (such as *E. obesa*) to very large and columnar (such as *E. ingens*). On closer inspection, the differences are clear – they lack the distinctive groups of spines (areoles) of the cacti and the flowers are represented by rather inconspicuous cyathia. The milky latex is another reliable diagnostic feature.

NOTES The milky latex of most *Euphorbia* species is a virulent poison that causes irritation, or at the very least some discomfort, to exposed skin. However, getting the latex into ones eyes can be immensely painful and can lead to temporary or even permanent blindness. But the perils associated with the latex that will ooze from wounded euphorbias have not deterred the many zealous growers and collectors of these fascinating plants.

Female cyathia of *Euphorbia mauritanica*

Euphorbia cooperi

Euphorbia pulcherrima cyathia and bracts

Cyathia of *Euphorbia monteiroi*

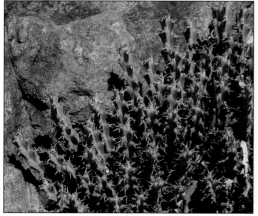

Euphorbia schinzii

Euphorbia horrida

Brief notes on genera

Euphorbia (spurge)

The spurges belong to a very large, cosmopolitan genus of some 2 000 species! Most *Euphorbia* species collected by enthusiasts have stems reminiscent of those of cacti. These could be cylindrical or globular, or any shape in between, or the species could be single- or multistemmed trees of over 20 m tall, or they could be miniatures, or even have massive underground storage organs with only the tips of the stems or branches exposed. The columnar types have become very popular as garden trees and container plants in warm regions. They combine well with other succulents and create an attractive, typically African backdrop in succulent gardens. The spines of succulent euphorbias are of two main types – either stipular (borne in opposing pairs, often on a bony ridge) or peduncular (usually single, thick, originating from the persistent remains of the flowering stalks). In a few species (*E. polygona* and *E. horrida*) the peduncular spines are not single, but two or more may arise from the same flowering eye.

Jatropha

There are about 170 species of *Jatropha*, mainly indigenous to South America. The plants are perennial herbs, shrubs or even trees. Not many species of *Jatropha* are popular in cultivation – the best-known one is the non-succulent physic nut or purging nut (*J. curcas*). The only species that is popular among succulent enthusiasts, *Jatropha podagrica*, is a fat-stemmed caudiciform, with large, umbrella-like leaves and bright red "flowers".

Monadenium

Species of *Monadenium* are herbs or stem succulents, all native to Africa. They resemble euphorbias but have bilaterally symmetrical cyathia with horseshoe-shaped glands. A commonly cultivated succulent is the southern African *M. lugardiae*.

Pedilanthus (zig-zag plant, Jacob's ladder)

In the case of *Pedilanthus*, only one species is really encountered in cultivation. This plant, *Pedilanthus tithymaloides*, has fascinating zigzag-shaped stems, sparsely covered in leaves. The genus comprises 14 shrubs indigenous to South America and the southern parts of North America.

Synadenium (dead man's tree)

The 19 known species occur naturally in southern and eastern Africa. Two species, *S. cupulare* and especially *S. grantii*, are grown in gardens. They are robust shrubs or small trees with thick fleshy stems that are marked with leaf scars and large, glossy leaves. Spines are absent. The cyathia of *Synadenium* species differ from those of *Euphorbia* in that the glands are fused to form a continuous ring. This ring is green or yellowish green in *S. cupulare* but dark red in *S. grantii*. All parts of the plant contain milky latex that is said to be extremely poisonous. Especially popular are cultivars with red leaves.

Euphorbia horrida with *E. caerulescens* (smaller plant on the right)

Euphorbia esculenta

Jatropha curcas

Monadenium lugardiae

Synadenium cupulare

Notes on species of Euphorbiaceae

EUPHORBIA

Euphorbia bupleurifolia (miniature palm tree)

This is a dwarf succulent up to 0.2 m high with rounded to elongated, usually unbranched stems. The stem is decorated with spirally arranged tubercles and a crown of narrow leaves up to 70 mm long.

Euphorbia caerulescens (*noors, sweet noors*)

The *noors* is exceedingly common in nature and forms large stands in a vegetation type called "noorsveld", which covers some 5 000 sq. km (2 000 sq. miles) in South Africa. It is an erect, multistemmed, spiny plant up to 1.5 m high. The stems are characteristically bluish in colour and become edible to small stock several days after being cut into short sections. Plants multiply by means of underground runners that form new plants at regular intervals. It is very closely related to *E. ledienii* (sour *noors*), a somewhat taller plant (1.3 to 2.0 m high) with less prominently constricted stems and a less spiny appearance. Sour *noors* is not palatable to livestock. *Euphorbia caerulescens* is commonly encountered in succulent gardens in warm regions of the world and has become a popular container plant grown under glass in Europe.

Euphorbia caput-medusae (Medusa's head, snake plant)

This euphorbia has thornless, snake-like, creeping stems radiating from a short, thick caudex. The glands in the cyathia are divided into relatively long, white, finger-like lobes. These give the individual cyathium a flower-like appearance. In order to develop the characteristic clusters of stems, the plant has to be grown from seeds (stem cuttings remain relatively unbranched). The Medusa's head is sometimes grown as a curiosity plant in succulent gardens, especially in winter-rainfall regions.

Euphorbia grandialata

Euphorbia grandialata is a thick-stemmed shrub up to 2 m high. The stems arise at ground level and gently arch upwards. They are 3–4-angled, with the angles wing-like and bearing long spines in opposite pairs. The small, yellow cymes occur in clusters of up to three along the ribs.

Euphorbia grandicornis (big horned euphorbia, cow horn)

The cow horn is a distinctive stem succulent bearing pairs of long spines along the ribs. The main stem remains at ground level and give rise to numerous side branches, which reach a height of up to 2 m. This is one of the most beautiful and popular of the so-called cactus euphorbias. It is sometimes confused with the similar-looking *E. grandialata* but the latter species has an extra pair of short spines between the long ones along the ribs and the stem segments tend to be sharply tapering towards the tips.

Euphorbia caerulescens

Euphorbia ledienii

Euphorbia grandialata

Euphorbia grandicornis

Euphorbia heptagona (milk barrel)

Plants grow as dense shrubs with numerous rather thin stems covered in thick single spines (the remains of flowering stalks). The typical form has an erect, somewhat sparse growth habit but some forms are densely much-branched and are therefore often confused with the similar-looking but much more spiny *E. ferox* (the pincushion euphorbia). Also similar is *Euphorbia pentagona* (five-angled cactus euphorbia), but this is a much taller plant (up to 3 m high), usually with a single stem at ground level and with cyathia in groups (not solitary as in *E. heptagona*).

Euphorbia horrida (African milk barrel)

This is a robust, spiny, clump-forming succulent 1 m or more in height. It is distinctly "cactus-like" in appearance due to the strongly ribbed stems (about 50 mm deep) and the long thorns (over 30 mm long). It is sometimes confused with the closely related *E. polygona* (see below). In *E. horrida*, each flowering eye may bear a single main spine up to 37 mm long (formed from a sterile flowering stalk), which may be accompanied by up to four secondary spines (formed from either sterile or fertile flowering stalks). The species is much sought after as a collector's item.

Euphorbia ingens (cactus euphorbia, *naboom*)

The *naboom* is a well-known and popular garden tree. It is about 10 m high with erect, ribbed (four or five-angled) stems. Paired thorns are absent or much reduced (up to 2 mm long). A variegated form of the species is grown as a container plant in Europe and the USA. It is very similar to the Arabian *E. ammak*. The species is widely distributed in southern Africa and is seen by many people when they visit the famous Zimbabwe Ruins. It is one of numerous tree euphorbias in Africa – others include *E. cooperi*, *E. curvirama*, *E. tetragona*, *E. tirucalli* and *E. triangularis*.

Euphorbia lactea (mottled spurge, candelabra cactus, false cactus, hat-rack cactus, dragon bones)

This is an Indian species of tree euphorbia that has become naturalised in the West Indies and in Florida in the USA. It is candelabra-shaped and grows up to 5 m high. The branches are about 50 mm in diameter and have three or four wavy ribs. The stems have a very distinctive colour – they are mottled and banded with white streaks on a green surface. A garden mutant with clustered, fan-shaped (cristate) stems has become very popular in gardens. This form is known by the common names crested euphorbia, frilled fan or elkhorn.

Euphorbia mammilaris (corn cob, corkscrew)

The corn cob is a dwarf succulent with branched and clustered stems of up to 0.2 m high. The multi-ribbed stems are decorated with angular tubercles (leaf scars), transverse lines and spines of up to 10 mm long. A variegated form with yellowish and pink markings is also commonly cultivated.

Euphorbia heptagona

Euphorbia heptagona stems

Euphorbia horrida

Euphorbia horrida with cyathia

Euphorbia ingens

Euphorbia triangularis

Euphorbia mauritanica (yellow milk bush, melkbos, jackal's food)

The yellow milk bush is a robust shrub with dense masses of thin, erect branches up to 1.5 m high. Copious amounts of milky juice oozes out when the plant is damaged. This latex is traditionally used to remove warts. The stems are characteristically yellowish green, especially when the plants are subjected to drought or heat stress. Small yellow flower clusters (cyathia) are borne at the tips of the stems.

Euphorbia meloformis (melon spurge)

In appearance, this plant is as close to a cactus as one can get! This barrel-shaped euphorbia with its smooth, ribbed stem is closely similar to some globular cacti, notably the bishop's cap (*Astrophytum myriostigma*). The species can easily be distinguished from related species by the flowering eyes that are widely spaced along the ribs and especially in the flowering stalks that tend to persist, especially in male plants.

Euphorbia meloformis may be confused with *Euphorbia valida* but the number of ribs is a useful distinguishing character: more in the former (eight to twelve), less in the latter (six only). Furthermore, *Euphorbia valida* is also a somewhat larger plant.

Euphorbia milii (crown of thorns, Christ thorn)

This Madagascan species is a scrambling spiny shrub of up to 1 m high. The relatively thin branches bear numerous green leaves and sharp spines of about 30 mm long. Attractive cyathia, each with a pair of large, brightly coloured involucral bracts, are borne on slender stalks. The most popular form of the species has brilliant red cyathia, but white, yellow and various other shades of red are also known. The crown of thorns is exceptionally common in gardens. It is drought tolerant and can withstand frost remarkably well. Plants are easily propagated from stem cuttings and will thrive in any well-drained garden soil.

Euphorbia obesa (gingham golf ball, living baseball, Zulu hut)

Succulent enthusiasts would probably agree that this is one of the most remarkable and desirable of all cultivated succulents. The rounded stems are invariably single and beautifully decorated with purple lines and rows of little round spots (the flowering eyes) on a greyish green or purplish background. Plants have a restricted distribution in the eastern Karoo in South Africa and have become quite rare as a result of illegal collecting. Fortunately it is easily propagated from seeds and there is now a large supply of plants offered by nurseries to satisfy the growing demand. As is the case with most succulents, this species requires well-drained soil but cannot withstand extreme conditions when planted in the garden. When grown under glass in a pot, it should be kept dry in winter.

Euphorbia polygona (many-angled cactus euphorbia)

This species is a close relative of the African milk barrel (*E. horrida*). The numerous cactus-like stems are often unequal in length and may reach a height of 1.7 m. Each stem has about 12 to 20 angles that are relatively shallow, protruding for about 15 mm. It differs from *E. horrida* also in the much smaller spines (only 4 to 10 mm long), which are often solitary or rarely up to five from each flowering eye. *Euphorbia polygona* is an attractive species that has been cultivated in Europe since 1790. This is an excellent accent plant that makes a beautiful display when grown in a container. The ribs are often markedly wavy and the robust, cactus-like stems are highly decorative.

Euphorbia meloformis

Euphorbia obesa

Euphorbia milii

Euphorbia milii flowering branch

Euphorbia polygona

Euphorbia polygona stem

Euphorbia pulvinata (pincushion euphorbia)

The plant is a dwarf succulent with numerous, densely crowded branches forming cushion-like masses more than 1 m in diameter. The single spines (modified flowering stalks) are 6 to 12 mm long. Rudimentary leaves occur on young stems but these soon fall off, so that the mature stems are totally leafless. The single cyathia are fairly attractive as a result of the bright purple colour of the involucre glands. This species has become a favourite amongst collectors because of the attractive growth form and the fact that it can withstand extreme conditions (it survives temperatures as low as −11°C). Two close relatives, also known as pincushion euphorbias, are *E. aggregata* and *E. ferox*. All three species are indigenous to southern Africa. All of them have leafless stems that form distinctive, dense cushions, hence the shared common name. *Euphorbia aggregata* is a dwarf succulent of only up to 80 mm high with 8–9-angled stems 30 mm in diameter. The spines are red to purple. *Euphorbia ferox* is very similar to *E. pulvinata* but is a smaller plant of only about 0.2 m in diameter. It has 9–12-angled stems (45 mm in diameter) bearing brown to greyish spines of about 30 mm long.

Euphorbia stellispina (star-spine)

The star-spine is a barrel-shaped euphorbia that ultimately forms dense clumps. The peculiar spines are solitary but have three to five spine branches at the tip. When the stalk of the spine is short or absent, the plant superficially resembles species of *Echinocactus* or *Ferocactus*. Another peculiarity is the transverse lines above the tubercles, giving the plant body the appearance of a corn cob. The star-spine is a popular curiosity plant and has been grown by succulent plant collectors for a long time. It requires fertile, well-drained soil but should be watered sparingly in the dormant season.

Euphorbia tirucalli (tiru-calli, rubber euphorbia, finger tree, pench tree)

The rubber euphorbia is a very common tree that occurs naturally over large parts of southern, central and eastern Africa. It has been introduced to Sri Lanka and numerous other warm parts of Asia by early Portuguese explorers. The plant is a spineless succulent tree up to 9 m high. The ultimate branchlets are cylindrical, pale green, jointed and about 6 mm in diameter. Female and male flowers are borne on separate trees. Plants are commonly cultivated in rural areas as living hedges and experimental plantings have been made (especially in East Africa) with the aim of producing natural rubber. Few succulents can rival this plant when it comes to ease of propagation and cultivation. It is a useful screen and hedge plant for large gardens in warm or tropical climates.

Euphorbia trigona (African milk tree)

This species is an erect shrub or small tree with erect, angular branches. The wavy white bands along the stems are characteristic of this species. Pairs of short, reddish brown thorns and small, tapering leaves are borne along the three or four ribs. Plants can be easily propagated from stem cuttings and they grow quite fast. They make a spectacular display when planted in large groups. The exact geographical origin of the species remains unknown.

Euphorbia pulvinata

Euphorbia ferox

Euphorbia stellispina

Stems and fruit of *Euphorbia tirucalli*

Tree of *Euphorbia tirucalli*

Euphorbia trigona

JATROPHA

Jatropha podagrica (gout plant, tartogo, Australian bottle plant)

The gout plant is another representative of the Euphorbiaceae with a rather exquisite, succulent stem, which is favoured by collectors of caudiciforms. But unlike most *Euphorbia* species, the stems are devoid of thorns and look a bit like those of a fat-stemmed bonsai *Ficus* tree. The shape of the stems can vary considerably, but essentially these enlarged storage organs resemble ancient wine decanters that have been stretched and twisted into beautiful elongated shapes after exposure to the intense heat of a glass-blower's flame. The stems lack spines, are an ash-grey colour and smooth when young, but will develop a typically flaky bark with age. The leaves of *Jatropha podagrica* are fairly large, umbrella-shaped and deeply incised along their edges. The cyathia of the species are quite small and bright yellow. This yellow colour is rather effectively obscured by the bright red colour of the small bracts that envelop the flowers constituting the cyathia.

Plants of *Jatropha podagrica* are perfectly suited for cultivation in containers, and because of the rather soft consistency of the stems will not damage the pots, even after many years of cultivation. The species, which occurs naturally in Guatemala and Panama, is best suited for cultivation in tropical and subtropical areas. Unfortunately it will not tolerate subzero temperatures, although it is slightly hardier than *Pedilanthus tithymaloides*. Propagation of *Jatropha* species is best from seed, which germinates very easily. Stem cuttings of *Jatropha podagrica* are very susceptible to rotting.

MONADENIUM

Monadenium lugardiae (false euphorbia)

The plant is a euphorbia-like succulent shrublet about 0.5 m high. The thick fleshy stem has prominent, broad tubercles around the leaf scars, resembling the scales on a snake. A cluster of fleshy green leaves is borne at the tip of each branch. The name *Monadenium* means "single gland" and refers to the glands that are fused into a single, pitcher-shaped structure, which is open on the one side. The flowers, although interesting, are certainly not the reason why false euphorbias are cultivated. It is rather their snake-like stems and unusual stem architecture that are the main attractions. In nature, plants growing on flat ground are usually erect, while those on rocky ledges often have the stems hanging down. The plants are fairly easily grown in warm regions provided they are kept dry in winter. It has become popular as an attractive and interesting container plant.

Of the 50 or more species of *Monadenium*, at least 17 are occasionally grown as garden succulents. Many of them are perennial herbs with succulent leaves, including *M. coccineum*, *M. echinulatum*, *M. invenustum*, *M. laeve*, *M. rhizophorum*, *M. richiei*, *M. rubellum*, *M. schubei*, *M. stapelioides* and *M. stoloniferum*. Some are spiny shrubs, such as *M. cannellii*, *M. elegans*, *M. magnificum*, *M. spectabile* and *M. torrei*. Although rarely seen in cultivation, these shrubs are likely to become increasingly popular in tropical and warm temperate regions. One species, *M. spinescens*, is an interesting and unusual tree up to 6 m high. It has warty, spiny stems and crowded flower clusters surrounded by green and pinkish bracts.

Jatropha podagrica

Jatropha podagrica flowers

Monadenium lugardiae stem

Monadenium lugardiae in flower

PEDILANTHUS

Pedilanthus tithymaloides (zig-zag plant, Jacob's ladder)

This species is a popular novelty plant in the true sense of the word. It is a stem succulent, with rather flat, thin leaves that are broadly lance-shaped. The leaves are slightly wavy along their margins and can be bright green or, more commonly, mottled with white or light yellow. However, the real fascination of the species lies in its pencil-shaped stems that lengthen in a zigzag fashion. This has given rise to its common name, Jacob's ladder. *Pedilanthus tithymaloides* will in time grow into a small shrub, and if planted close together, plants can be effectively trimmed into a neat, low hedge. The small floral bracts are a bright crimson red and resemble tiny swallows poised for flight. This species will thrive in subtropical and tropical climates and like so many other succulents, even those from rather arid areas, it prefers relatively high air humidity to look its best. Unfortunately it will not withstand any frost. Although it can be grown in a container, the species really comes into its own right when grown in the open ground.

SYNADENIUM

Synadenium cupulare (dead man's tree)

The dead man's tree is a leafy shrub to small tree about 1.5 m high. The smooth, glossy green leaves are narrowly wedge-shaped, up to 100 mm long and up to 40 mm wide. Funnel-shaped or bowl-shaped cyathia are borne in sparse clusters, each with a characteristic greenish-yellow rim-like gland. The plant has a reputation for being extremely poisonous and appears to give off poisonous fumes that can cause a burning sensation in the eyes, nose and throat. In cultivation it seems to be only moderately poisonous and many people have handled plants without feeling any effect at all. Plants require full sun and should be regularly watered in summer.

Synadenium grantii (African milk bush)

The African milk bush is a robust, leafy shrub up to 3 m high. The broad leaves are up to 175 mm long and up to 62 mm wide, with inconspicuous short hairs along the edges. Cultivated forms often have the leaves variously tinted with red, especially along the veins and midrib. This close relative of the dead man's tree is commonly encountered in tropical gardens where the cultivar 'Rubra', with its purplish red leaves, adds a touch of colour to an otherwise green landscape. The species originates from East Africa and can easily be distinguished from the less commonly cultivated southern African *S. cupulare* by the ornamental foliage (often net-veined and not uniformly glossy green) and the dark red glands on the clusters of "flowers" (cyathia), which can be quite attractive. Plants are propagated from stem cuttings and are very easy to cultivate as garden succulents or container plants in warm regions.

Pedilanthus tithymaloides (variegated form)

Pedilanthus tithymaloides flowers

Synadenium cupulare

Synadenium grantii

MESEMBRYANTHEMACEAE

Ice plant family • Mesemb family or Vygie family

DISTINGUISHING CHARACTERS Representatives of the Mesembryanthemaceae have a fascinating array of growth forms, ranging from minute button-shaped stone plants that hug the soil, through floriferous, medium-sized shrubs, to small trees. With very few exceptions, the mesembs are leaf succulents that survive the dry season through drawing on water accumulated in their leaves or in the shiny bladder-like cells on the leaf surfaces. Most species are perennial, while very few are annuals. Mesemb flowers are generally very showy and they look uncannily like daisy inflorescences. However, they are in fact true flowers and not conglomerates of disc and ray florets. The flowers of mesembs typically show diurnal movement – they open during daytime and close at night, or during inclement weather. Mesembs have intriguing fruits that have extremely fascinating shapes and microstructures. The fruits are hygroscopic, which means they react to water: they open when wet and close when dry.

NOTES The Mesembryanthemaceae is the largest family of succulent plants, although the New World Cactaceae comes a close second. It has a strong concentration in the arid winter-rainfall area of southern Africa, where it has diversified explosively. By far the most fascinating species of mesemb are those that mimic their surroundings. These plants, generally known as stone plants, liver plants or simply mimicry plants, are often difficult to find amongst the gravel stones in their habitat. In the dry season they shrivel up and enter a resting phase during which they are covered by the dry remains of the previous season's leaves, or they withdraw completely into the soil. But at the onset of the first rains their leaves start swelling, becoming fat and turgid and easier to detect in their natural surroundings. Shortly afterwards they produce delicate flowers in all shades of yellow, red, orange, purple or white.

GARDEN MESEMBS These are the shrubby and spreading species that are grown in gardens for their mass displays of brilliantly coloured flowers. Whatever your taste in horticultural objects, there will be a mesemb to suit your fancy (after all, there are more than 1 800 species to choose from!). Not surprisingly, mesembs are today some of the most popular succulent shrubs planted in garden borders and rock gardens. There is also a single annual species that has become well known as a "conventional" border plant. This is the brilliantly coloured *bokbaaivygie* or Livingstone daisy (*Dorotheanthus bellidiformis*).

MINIATURE MESEMBS Many of the curious miniature mesembs (the so-called "living stones") have become popular windowsill plants or collector's items. They are usually grown under glass in a greenhouse and often need special care to survive or look their best. Even though they would hardly qualify as garden succulents, some of them are described here simply to give a proper representation of the remarkable diversity in the family.

Unless stated otherwise, all the genera and species described below are indigenous to the dry regions of southern Africa (mainly South Africa and Namibia).

Typical mesemb flowers (*Ruschia intrusa*)

Typical mesemb fruit (*Glottiphyllum*)

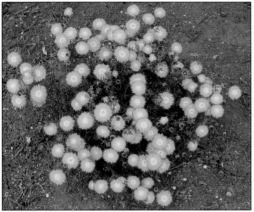

Drosanthemum bicolor shrub

Delosperma obtusa shrub

Gibbaeum heathii

Lithops pseudotruncatella

Brief notes on genera of garden mesembs

Aptenia (*brakvygies*, brack mesembs)

This small genus consists exclusively of easy-to-grow creeping succulents with broad, flat leaves, small purple or reddish flowers and soft seed capsules. Of the four species, *A. cordifolia* and *A. lancifolia* are very popular as groundcovers in rockeries and to stabilise dry, exposed slopes. These plants are undoubtedly underrated as garden plants.

Carpanthea (*vetkousie*)

The single species of this genus is an annual succulent herb with woolly stems, flat leaves and very large flowers that open in the afternoon. The large number of petals and large number of valves in the capsules (12 to 18) are also useful as diagnostic features.

Carpobrotus (pigface, sour fig)

The plants are robust succulents with long, trailing stems forming dense mats. The leaves are large, erect and sharply three-angled. Very large flowers, in various shades of purple, pink, white or yellow are followed by unusual fruits that are fleshy, without valves (and edible in some species). Most of the species occur in South Africa (seven) and Australia (five) but one (*C. chilensis*) is indigenous to the coasts of Mexico and California (USA). *Carpobrotus edulis* and *C. chilensis* have been widely used to stabilise sandy banks and road verges and have become naturalised in many parts of the world.

Delosperma (*klipvygies*, rock mesembs)

This is a large genus of some 160 species, indigenous throughout southern and eastern Africa to Arabia, Madagascar and Réunion. The plants are shrubby, with leaves that are covered in glistening water storage cells. Flower colour varies from white to various shades of pink, purple, yellow or orange. *Delosperma* means "visible seed" and refers to the seeds that are visible when the capsules open (they are not covered by membranes as in most other members of the family).

Dorotheanthus (Livingstone daisies, *bokbaaivygies*)

These are annuals and popular border plants that are well known in commercial horticulture. The plants are small and spreading, with glistening water cells on the rather non-fleshy leaves. Colourful and spectacular flowers are borne in early spring – they open in the morning and close at night. Only two of the seven species are commonly cultivated (*D. bellidiformis* and *D. gramineus*).

Drosanthemum (dewflowers, *bergvygies*)

Dewflowers are shrubby plants with glistening water cells on their leaves and large, brilliantly coloured flowers that make mass displays in spring and early summer. They can be distinguished from *Delosperma* by the seeds which are covered with membranes in the open capsules. Furthermore, the cultivated species generally have much larger and more spectacular flowers. Of the 120 known species, only about eight have become garden succulents. The spectacular *D. speciosum* (showy dewflower) is a worldwide favourite but several other species are regularly cultivated. Dewflowers tend to die after a few years, so it is important to regularly replace older plants with new seedlings or cuttings. They can be over-wintered in the greenhouse in cold regions.

Carpanthea pomeridiana

Carpobrotus dimidiatus

Dorotheanthus bellidiformis

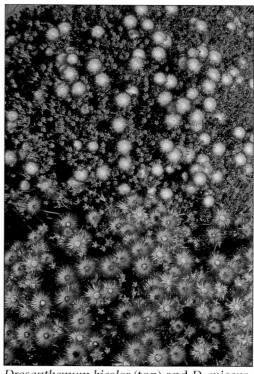

Drosanthemum bicolor (top) and *D. micans*

Lampranthus (garden *vygies,* garden mesembs)

There are few garden flowers that can match the spectacular colour intensity of a garden *vygie* in full flower. The brilliant colours are partly due to the way in which the petals of these plants reflect sunlight (the name *Lampranthus* literally means "bright flowers"). *Lampranthus* species can be distinguished by their smooth, waxy, erect stems, their diversity of flower colour (not only pink or purple as in *Ruschia* species) and technical details of their fruit capsules. There are more than 220 species of *Lampranthus*, of which about 15 are regularly grown in gardens. This is by far the most important group of garden mesembs. They are grown in most warm regions of the world and are often used for mass displays on rock gardens or as specimen plants in containers.

Malephora (finger *vygies, vingervygies*)

Finger mesembs are shrubby perennials that can be recognised by the combination of creeping stems (that sometimes root at the nodes), finger-like, distinctly waxy leaves and yellow to orange-red flowers. Other mesembs with similar-looking leaves have pink or purple flowers. Of the 13 species, about five are known in international horticulture. By far the most commonly cultivated species is the attractive *M. crocea.*

Mesembryanthemum (ice plants)

Ice plants are annuals or biennials and usually have large, flat leaves resulting in a robust, lettuce-like appearance. They are typically covered all over by very large bladder cells (water storage cells) that reflect sunlight, so that the plants look as if they are covered with ice crystals. There are about 15 species, of which all except one are found only in southern Africa. The exception is the well-known ice plant (*M. crystallinum*), which occurs along the coastal regions of most continents of the world.

Oscularia (sandstone *vygies*)

Oscularia species are shrubby plants with reddish stems bearing short, three-angled leaves that are usually covered in a grey or pale blue waxy layer. The relatively small, almond-scented flowers are white to pink in colour, with the stamens grouped together in the middle of the flower. Only one species, *O. deltoides*, is commonly grown as a garden succulent.

Ruschia (purple *vygies*)

This is a rather poorly defined group of more than 200 shrubby mesembs that typically have finger-like, often angular, leaves and small, purple or pink flowers (rarely white). More than 20 species of purple *vygies* are occasionally cultivated but these plants are less well known and less popular than the garden *vygies* (*Lampranthus*), with their much larger and more colourful flowers.

Lampranthus coralliflorus

Lampranthus comptonii

Lampranthus comptonii

Malephora crocea

Notes on species of Mesembryanthemaceae

APTENIA

Aptenia cordifolia (red aptenia, baby sun rose, *rooi brakvygie*)

Plants are typically creeping, with bright green, almost stalked, flat leaves. The leaves are well spaced on long wiry stems, with conspicuous bladder cells on the surfaces. The diurnal flowers are relatively small, reddish purple in colour and somewhat hidden by the large green sepals. This species flowers irregularly throughout the year, making it a welcome addition to any garden. The brack mesemb, as *Aptenia cordifolia* is commonly known, can be distinguished from other creeping mesembs by its consistently opposite leaves which are heart-shaped and stalked. The flower is relatively small, and the stamens are not grouped closely together as in *Delosperma*. *Aptenia cordifolia* is the most common species of the genus and occurs naturally in the Eastern Cape but it is also widely cultivated and has become naturalised in many parts of South Africa.

There is only one other *Aptenia* species grown in gardens (the lesser known *A. lancifolia*, which is found in the northern parts of South Africa). This species has narrower leaves and pinkish purple flowers and is known as purple aptenia (*pers brakvygie*). Both species are used medicinally and are reputed to have the same type of alkaloids as is found in species of *kougoed* (*Sceletium*). Unlike some other mesembs, the plants grow very easily from stem cuttings. The stems are soft and can easily be trimmed into shape in a garden bed. Seeds germinate readily and the plant has a tendency to become somewhat weedy. Garden forms with variegated foliage have become popular as groundcovers. This is an ideal plant to use on steep banks and terraced slopes, as it is evergreen and flowers almost continuously. It will tolerate both high rainfall and irregular watering, as well as very low temperatures.

CARPANTHEA

Carpanthea pomeridiana (*vetkousie*)

The *vetkousie* is an annual succulent with glistening, elongated water cells on the stems that give them a woolly appearance. The leaves are borne on long stalks and are oblong to spoon-shaped. Very large flowers with a multitude of slender, bright yellow petals are formed in the late spring and early summer. They are open during the afternoon and close at night. The capsules have numerous valves that are hygroscopic and open rapidly after rain.

This plant is one of very few mesembs that can tolerate light shade. It grows easily from seeds and has been planted in gardens throughout the world. In areas with a mild climate, seeds are sown in autumn (or early spring in very cold regions). The geographical origin is the extreme southwestern tip of the African continent, where it is commonly seen on white sand dunes. The plant is also known as an exotic in southeastern Australia. Leaves and flowers of the *vetkousie* are a traditional vegetable that makes a delicious stew when cooked with meat.

Aptenia cordifolia

Aptenia lancifolia

CARPOBROTUS

Carpobrotus acinaciformis (purple sour fig, purple pigface)

Although the use of the genus name *Carpobrotus* for the 13 angular-leaved mesembs in the group has become firmly entrenched in horticultural circles, these plants are also variously known as sour figs, creeping figs or pigface. The species perhaps most commonly grown, *Carpobrotus acinaciformis*, is a very popular groundcover that will rapidly cover denuded areas with a thick mat of robust stems and leaves. Herein lies part of the success of the species in combating soil erosion: plants grow very quickly, need the minimum of irrigation and the strong stems and leaves can be easily trimmed and kept in shape, even with an edge cutter. It has no thorns, prickles, or caustic leaf juices. Large, bright carmine-purple flowers with yellow centres are produced in profusion, another factor making the species suitable for mass planting in areas where bright, light green patches dotted with purple are required.

Carpobrotus chilensis (sea fig)

This American species, which occurs naturally on the coast of Chile, Mexico and California, is very similar *C. acinaciformis* but the flowers are magenta pink rather than purple. It rapidly forms extensive mats of 2 m or more in diameter. Although plants can easily be produced from seeds, cuttings are much better as they will cover large areas in a short time.

Carpobrotus edulis (sour fig, common sour fig)

The common sour fig is originally an inhabitant of the Cape but has become naturalised in various parts of the world, including southern Europe and California. It can easily be distinguished by the yellow flowers that turn orange and then salmon pink when they fade. Although some people would consider this an unwanted invader, the plant is loved by gardeners for its rapid growth and ability to cover large areas of bare ground. It is also much appreciated by local inhabitants of South Africa, where the edible fruits are commonly sold on street markets. The fruits are cone-shaped and fleshy, with a sweet-sour, slimy fruit pulp surrounding the numerous seeds. Unlike other mesembs, the capsules never open. The fruits can be eaten fresh by biting off the bottom end and sucking out the slimy pulp, or they may be turned into jam or added to curry dishes. A few other species, including *C. deliciosus*, are also used as a source of edible fruits. As a garden subject, the plant has few equals when it comes to tolerating drought, cold, pests and diseases.

Carpobrotus quadrifidus (*elandsvy*, large sour fig)

A form of this species with greyish blue leaves and exceptionally large flowers (up to 150 mm in diameter) was previously known as *C. sauerae* but is now included here. It deserves to be planted more often.

Carpobrotus acinaciformis

Carpobrotus edulis

Carpobrotus edulis

Carpobrotus mellei

Carpobrotus quadrifidus

DELOSPERMA

Delosperma brunthaleri (Brunthaler's rock mesemb)

This species is a shrubby perennial about 0.3 m high with large, flat leaves that are hairy and also somewhat glistening because of numerous small water cells. The flowers are violet pink and relatively large (about 30 mm in diameter). *Delosperma* species qualify as true garden succulents because they are perhaps the easiest of all mesembs to grow in the garden. Although they thrive in rich but porous garden soil, some will happily grow in heavy clayey soils. Plants should be watered freely during the growing season. Although rarely spectacular, *Delosperma* species tend to flower sporadically throughout the year. About 15 species are occasionally cultivated. They vary tremendously in growth form – from erect shrublets to creeping groundcovers.

Delosperma echinatum (prickly rock mesemb)

The distinctive leaves of this species are covered in white, hair-like water cells and have soft pointed tips, giving them a prickly appearance. It is a small, bushy species with small, white or yellow flowers.

Delosperma herbeum (white mountain mesemb, *wit bergvygie*)

White or pink flower colour forms are known and both are occasionally encountered in gardens. The plants are spreading shrublets up to about 0.5 m high that may spread up to 1 m wide. The narrowly oblong leaves are not particularly succulent and have inconspicuous water cells. Propagation is easy – either from seeds or cuttings. For best results, the soil should be rich and well drained and plants should be watered regularly.

DOROTHEANTHUS

Dorotheanthus bellidiformis (Livingstone daisy, *bokbaaivygie*)

The Livingstone daisies are perhaps the most popular and spectacular of all garden mesembs. The seven species are all annual herbs with glistening water cells on the reddish stems and leaves and large flowers in a multitude of colours. Numerous garden forms have been developed and the commercial plants are considered to be hybrids between *D. bellidiformis* and *D. gramineus*. The former is the best-known species. It has relatively broad leaves that taper towards the base. *Dorotheanthus gramineus* is very similar but has slender, narrow, bright green leaves. A wide range of flower colours are known, ranging from uniformly white, yellow, salmon, orange, pink or red to typically bicoloured, with a white or yellow centre and a halo of bright colour around the tips of the petals.

Seeds are sown in a cold frame in autumn or early spring or may be sown directly into the flowerbeds in early spring. In Mediterranean regions the plants grow during the winter and flower in early spring, but the season can be extended to early or midsummer in cold parts of the world. These plants can be grown as conventional border annuals in the garden, but they require full sun and well-drained soil. When some colour is required on an otherwise rather drab rockery, then these colourful plants are an excellent choice.

Delosperma echinatum

Delosperma herbeum

Dorotheanthus bellidiformis

DROSANTHEMUM

Drosanthemum bicolor (bicoloured dewflower)

Plants are small shrubs of about 0.3 m in height, with erect, stiff branches bearing small finger-shaped leaves covered with small, glistening water cells – hardly different from other species until in flower. Then the striking bicoloured flowers (purple and yellow) are distinctive and similar only to those of *D. micans*. As with all other species, propagation is easy from seeds or cuttings. Seeds can be sown in autumn or early summer, while cuttings are best taken after fruiting (midsummer to autumn).

Drosanthemum candens (white dewflower)

This species has long been used as a garden plant and has become naturalised in the Azores, England and Portugal. It is well known as a garden succulent in southeastern Australia. The plant is a prostrate shrub with white-hairy leaves and small, white flowers.

Drosanthemum collinum (yellow dewflower)

Although less common in cultivation, this species makes a spectacular display when in full flower. As is the case with all dewflowers, the flowers open around midday and close at night. They are bright yellow.

Drosanthemum floribundum (pink dewflower)

The pink dewflower is a well-known garden succulent with a distinctive cushion-forming growth form and slender, finger-shaped, hairy leaves. The pale pink flowers are relatively large (about 18 mm in diameter) and are borne in profusion in spring. It is well known in southern California, where is has long been used on dry slopes and sandy banks.

Drosanthemum hispidum (purple dewflower)

The plants are cushion-forming shrublets of up to 0.6 m high and 1 m wide. The finger-shaped leaves tend to become flushed with red. They are covered with large glistening water cells. The large (about 30 mm in diameter) flowers are a brilliant reddish purple.

Drosanthemum micans (haloed dewflower)

This species is easily confused with *D. bicolor* but the flowers are bright yellow and variously tinged with purple, which results in a halo of colour around the bright centres.

Drosanthemum speciosum (dewflower, showy dewflower)

The showy dewflower is an erect perennial shrublet up to 0.6 m high. It is one of the best-known species in world horticulture and can easily be distinguished by the black stamens, a character unique in the family (shared only with two close relatives, *D. bicolor* and *D. micans*). Several colour forms are known, including shades of orange and pink, but the bright orange-red "wild" form is perhaps the most striking.

Drosanthemum striatum (striped dewflower, *vleisbos, porseleinbos*)

The striped dewflower is an erect to rounded shrub (up to 0.5 m high) with pink petals, each striped with a median line of reddish purple.

Drosanthemum bicolor

Drosanthemum micans

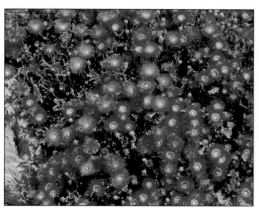

Drosanthemum speciosum

Drosanthemum speciosum

Drosanthemum hispidum

Drosanthemum striatum

LAMPRANTHUS

Lampranthus amoenus (purple garden *vygie*)

The purple *vygie* has erect, smooth stems that develop into a spreading, rounded shrub. It has bright purple flowers that make mass displays in spring and early summer. As is the case with all these popular garden *vygies* of the genus *Lampranthus*, the plant is easily propagated from seeds or from cuttings taken in late summer. Like all *vygies*, it requires full sun and good drainage but grows best when watered regularly.

Lampranthus aureus (orange garden *vygie*, golden *vygie*)

This spectacular rockery plant has erect stems of up to 0.45 m high and pale green leaves. The brilliant orange flowers are about 60 mm in diameter and have broad petals – they open in the late morning and close in the afternoon. A yellow form is also known. The orange *vygie* is an old favourite in many parts of the world and is also popular as a container plant. It survives light frost.

Lampranthus blandus (pink garden *vygie*)

This is a spreading plant of up to 0.3 m high with pale pink flowers.

Lampranthus coccineus (red garden *vygie*)

The red *vygie* has erect, smooth stems up to 0.3 m high and bears bright purplish red flowers of about 60 mm in diameter. This species is somewhat frost tender. It makes a dazzling display of colour in spring.

Lampranthus coralliflorus (mauve garden *vygie*)

The growth form of the mauve *vygie* is similar to the previous species but the flowers are a brilliant shiny mauve. It is a popular plant for rockeries and dry banks.

Lampranthus haworthii (Haworth's garden *vygie*)

This species typically has large purple flowers but a pink form is also known. It is an excellent rockery plant.

Lampranthus multiradiatus (creeping garden *vygie*)

The creeping *vygie* is a spreading plant with greyish green leaves and rose-red or pink flowers.

Lampranthus roseus (rose garden *vygie*)

The rose *vygie* is sometimes considered to be the same species as the creeping *vygie* (*L. multiradiatus*). It is very floriferous and makes a spectacular display with its pale pink, salmon, purple or rarely white flowers.

Lampranthus spectabilis (Tresco garden *vygie*)

Various cultivars of this attractive species are available, ranging from apricot orange to magenta or brilliant purplish red. It is often grown in pots or window boxes.

Lampranthus aureus

Lampranthus amoenus

Lampranthus coccineus

Lampranthus coralliflorus

Lampranthus roseus

MALEPHORA

Malephora crocea (finger *vygie, vingerkanna*)

The bright orange and yellow flowers of finger *vygies* have become a familiar sight in recent years, as the plants are quite popular amongst waterwise gardeners. It is an old favourite that has been grown in many parts of the world for at least 200 years. The plant is a creeping succulent with erect, smooth, somewhat waxy, finger-like leaves and relatively large, brightly coloured flowers. It can withstand extreme conditions but grows best in rich, well-drained soil in full sunlight.

MESEMBRYANTHEMUM

Mesembryanthemum crystallinum (ice plant)

The well-known ice plant is the only species that is commonly cultivated. It is thought to be of southern African origin but has been naturalised in California, Chile, the Mediterranean region (including the Canary Islands) and parts of Australia. The plant is a robust annual with a basal rosette of large, thick leaves that are covered in shiny water cells (the glistening cells look like ice crystals, hence the common name). Trailing, angular stems spread to a width of about 0.5 m and bear white or pink flowers. The flowers open in the morning and close at night. The large, lettuce-like leaves are edible and are cooked like spinach. Seedlings are easily grown from seed in the early spring.

OSCULARIA

Oscularia deltoides (sandstone *vygie*)

Only one species is widely grown – *Oscularia deltoides* (previously known as *Lampranthus deltoides*). The plant is a spreading perennial shrublet with decorative reddish stems and silvery grey leaves that each have a few reddish teeth along their margins. Each leaf cluster resembles a small mouth, hence the name *Oscularia*, which means "a group of small mouths". Numerous small pink or white flowers are borne from midwinter to midsummer. Propagation is mostly from cuttings, but seeds can also be used. The sandstone *vygie* prefers acid sandy soil and needs to be replaced with fresh cuttings at regular intervals, as old plants tend to become untidy.

RUSCHIA

Ruschia caroli (purple mountain *vygie*)

The purple mountain vygie is one of several species occasionally encountered in rockeries and succulent gardens. It is a small shrub with smooth stems and leaves bearing small purple flowers (much smaller than those of garden vygies (*Lampranthus* species). *Ruschia caroli* (as most other mountain *vygies*) has the stamens grouped tightly together in the middle of the flower (sometimes these are surrounded by a few rows of sterile stamens called staminodes).

Ruschia maxima (giant mountain *vygie*)

The giant mountain vygie is a large spreading shrub more than 1 m wide. It has characteristic large, half-moon-shaped leaves unlike those of any other mesemb. The flower is typical of the mountain vygies – small, purple and with a cone-shaped group of stamens in the centre.

Malephora crocea

Mesembryanthemum crystallinum

Mesembryanthemum crystallinum

Oscularia deltoides

Ruschia caroli

Ruschia maxima

Brief notes on miniature mesembs

Argyroderma (baby's bottom)

These miniature stone plants (there are 11 species) have very distinctive rounded leaf pairs with a firm, smooth texture and characteristic silvery grey colour (hence the name *Argyroderma* which means "silver skin"). The small plant bodies appear to be dead for many months and then send forth a magnificent flower, compensating for the extended "dead time". The flowers are mostly purple but rarely yellow, red or white. They are single and very large in relation to the small size of the leaf pairs. These plants are best grown in a greenhouse where the watering can be carefully regulated – water sparingly in winter (the growing season) and keep them dry in summer.

Conophytum (buttons, button plants, cone plants)

The 88 species are cushion-forming or single-bodied miniature succulents with ornate, button-like, highly fused leaf pairs. They grow in winter and become dormant during the dry summer months, when the old leaves dry out to become a papery protective layer from which the new leaf pairs (and small flowers) emerge when active growth resumes. In this genus, the petals are fused into a basal tube. These plants should be given morning sun and some afternoon shade in winter but should be kept in a cool, dry place during dormancy.

Faucaria (tiger jaws)

These curious little plants have rows of sharp teeth along the leaf margins, so that some of them appear quite similar to the Venus fly trap. Tiger jaws are very popular amongst succulent enthusiasts and have been in cultivation in Europe for more than 300 years. The best-known species amongst the 33 that have been described is the true tiger jaws, *F. tigrina*. They are easy to grow in pots but should be watered sparingly.

Fenestraria (window plant, baby's toes)

The single species of the tiny window plant can easily be recognised by the short, finger-like leaves that have translucent windows on their flat tips and by the white or yellow (never pink or purple) flowers that are borne on slender stalks. The window plant (*Fenestraria rhopalophylla*) is sometimes confused with another "window plant" of the same family (*Frithia pulchra*) but the latter (known as fairy elephant's feet) has leaves with water cells along the margins and the flowers have no stalks. Water sparingly in winter and keep completely dry in summer.

Glottiphyllum (tongue-leaved mesembs)

This group of about 17 species is easily recognised by the soft, strap-shaped leaves borne at ground level and the large yellow flowers, which have only four sepals. The leaves are easily damaged and may become unsightly but these plants are nevertheless very popular amongst succulent enthusiasts because of the relative ease with which they can be grown in rock gardens.

Argyroderma hallii

Argyroderma delaetii (yellow form)

Conophytum ficiforme

Conophytum fulleri

Faucaria tigrina

Frithia pulchra

Fenestraria rhopalophylla

Glottiphyllum regium

Lithops (stone plants)

The famous stone plants have become popular windowsill plants but can be grown outdoors in arid gardens. It is very easy to recognise these small plants by their distinctive fused leaf pairs, of which the tips are flat or rounded and beautifully marked, textured or windowed. The white, yellow or orange flowers appear from the fissure between the two leaves and are very large in relation to the small size of the plant. Old leaves form hard, papery sheaths that protect the new leaves before they emerge in the wet season. One of the secrets of growing stone plants is to only water them during the summer and autumn – they should be kept completely dry in the dormant season (winter and spring). There are about 36 species, but numerous garden forms, hybrids and cultivars have been developed.

They are best grown in a greenhouse or on a sunny windowsill. Use a mixture of gravel, sandy clay-loam and compost. Seeds are sown in the warm summer months and the small seedlings require more regular watering (from early spring until late summer). Many species are cultivated, including *L. optica*, *L. leslei*, *L. julii*, *L. schwantesii* and a German greenhouse hybrid called *L. steineckeana*.

Pleiospilos (liver plants)

These curious plants are easily recognised by their large, rock-like leaves that are decorated with numerous small dots. The large flowers are yellow to coppery orange. Of the four species, three are commonly cultivated in greenhouses and on windowsills. These are various cultivars of *P. bolusii* and *P. nelii* (both often known as "split rocks") and the true liver plant (*P. simulans*). The plants should be sparingly watered in the summer months and all except *P. nelii* should be kept dry during the winter.

Titanopsis (chalk mesembs, *kalkvygies*)

At first glance, these small succulents look exactly like pieces of limestone grouped together in a rosette. The white or greyish, spoon-shaped leaves are densely covered with large, colourful warts (that typically also occur on the sepals). The small flowers are usually yellow to amber-coloured. There are about five species but numerous varieties and colour forms, all of which are popular collector's items. Only one species, *T. calcarea*, is widely known in horticulture. It is known as tortoise feet or wart plant. *Titanopsis* species are easy to cultivate provided they are kept dry during the winter months. The soil mixture should be mineral-rich and well drained, but need not be alkaline.

Lithops leslei in nature

Lithops hallii

Lithops olivacea (flowering)

Lithops olivacea (dormant)

Pleiospilos bolusii

Titanopsis calcarea

UNUSUAL STEM SUCCULENTS (various families)

BOMBACACEAE
Baobab family

DISTINGUISHING CHARACTERS If ever there was a tree that personified the African bushveld landscape, it is *Adansonia digitata*, the baobab. This tree indeed leaves an indelible impression on anyone that lays eyes on it for the first time. Age determinations indicate that some of the oldest specimens were already 1 000 years old when Christ walked the earth some 2 000 years ago! For good reason it is often regarded as the Plant Kingdom's equivalent of the African elephant, because it is not the height of the tree that impresses the observer at first sight, but rather the immense girth and texture of the trunk. The stem resembles a giant lump of grey or copper-coloured molten wax, on top of which short, stubby-looking branches are superimposed. They shed their leaves in winter or even during times of environmental stress and then, in celebration of the new growing season, sprout a marvellous cloak of bright green foliage in spring. The leaves are followed by large, strong smelling, almost waxy, white flowers that are visited and pollinated by bats. Towards the end of summer, the flowers are replaced by large fruits containing numerous seeds which are embedded in a whitish powdery pulp.

NOTES The baobab tree is the largest of all succulents of the world. It can be grown from stem truncheons, just like any other succulent.

Adansonia

Only one species, *Adansonia digitata,* is indigenous to Africa. However, on the Red Island, Madagascar, which lies off the eastern coast of Africa, the genus *Adansonia* has diversified extensively, with seven of the nine known species having been reported from the island. Only one species, *A. gibbosa* (formerly *A. gregorii*), is indigenous to Australia.

Adansonia digitata (baobab)

All the baobab species are very similar in growth form. They invariably form massive pachycaul stems crowned with leafy branches. However, the Madagascan and Australian species bear their flowers erect, while those of the sole African species, *Adansonia digitata*, have hanging flowers.

Baobab trees, whether from Africa, Madagascar or Australia, are hardly ever encountered in domestic gardens, and once one has seen them in their habitat, the reason is immediately evident. They are enormous at maturity and few household gardens can harbour this giant! However, they are easy to grow from seed and as a novelty grown in a sawn-through wine barrel will be sure to provide an interesting point for discussion with your house guests. And of course it will take many decades for a baobab to outgrow a suburban garden.

Baobab tree (*Adansonia digitata*)

Baobab trunk

Baobab flower

DIOSCOREACAE
Wild yam family or Elephant's foot family

DISTINGUISHING CHARACTERS This small family consists of about eight genera of vines (climbers) with twining stems growing from fleshy rhizomes or tuberous roots. The leaves or leaflets are often heart-shaped and net-veined. Inconspicuous flowers are borne in elongated clusters, with the male and female ones often on separate plants. *Dioscorea* is by far the most important genus.

Dioscorea (yam)

There are more than 600 species in the yam genus, of which several are important crop plants grown for their starch-rich tubers. Cultivated yams that are predominantly grown in the tropics for their edible tubers include the white yam or water yam (*D. alata*), the Chinese yam (*D. batatas*), the air potato (*D. bulbifera*) and the cush-cush yam or yampee (*D. trifida*). Species such as the American wild yam (*D. villosa*) have been important in traditional medicine and others are a source of steroidal compounds that were once used in the synthesis of hormones and oral contraceptives. One species in particular is commonly grown as a curiosity plant by succulent enthusiasts. This is the famous elephant's foot (*D. elephantipes*). The African wild yam (*D. sylvatica*) and other species are occasionally cultivated. These two species were once included in a separate genus, *Testudinaria*.

Dioscorea elephantipes (elephant's foot)

This curious plant is indigenous to the western parts of South Africa, where it can withstand extreme drought conditions for years. It has a tuberous base that may reach 1 m in diameter in large specimens and is often borne above the ground. The thick base or bulb is fleshy inside but has numerous thick, woody protuberances on the exterior, not unlike the bark of an old pine tree or the scales on a tortoise shell. Numerous stems up to 6 m in length grow from the top of the tuber. They bear leathery heart-shaped leaves, each with seven to nine veins from the base. Small yellow flowers are borne in elongated clusters, followed (in female plants) by small fruit capsules containing winged seeds.

Plants are fairly easy to propagate from seeds which are sown in autumn. The dormant period is in summer, during which time watering should be withheld completely. A mixture of coarse river sand and clay loam is ideal. In Mediterranean gardens, the plant can be grown in a sunny, well-drained spot outside, but in other climatic conditions a succulent house is required.

Dioscorea sylvatica (African wild yam)

This species differs in the smaller tubers that are broad and flat, with a rough, corky surface, which lacks the thick surface scales of the elephant's foot. It is adapted to summer rainfall and can be grown outside in tropical and subtropical gardens, where it will thrive in partial shade. The plants should be kept quite dry during the resting period, which is in winter.

Elephant's foot (*Dioscorea elephantipes*)

Elephant's foot (leaves and flowers)

African wild yam (*Dioscorea sylvatica*)

HYACINTHACEAE

Hyacinth family

Distinguishing characters The family Hyacinthaceae is perhaps best known for its bulbous and not its succulent representatives. It is a medium-sized group of close to 30 genera and some 350 species. The family generally consists of spring- and summer-flowering bulbous plants and its flowers are mostly reminiscent of those of species of the previously rather broadly conceived Liliaceae, in which it has been included traditionally. But along with a number of other segregates, such as the asphodeloid *Aloe* and *Bulbine* groups of genera, the hyacinthoid genera are now better accommodated in a separate family.

Notes The Hyacinthaceae has given world horticulture a number of popular bulbous species of, amongst others, *Ornithogalum*, the so-called star-of-Bethlehem or chincherinchee. This family and a number of its genera are currently undergoing some major reshuffling, mainly as a result of the growing body of molecular evidence that seems to indicate that many taxa are ill-placed in their groups.

Bowiea (climbing onion)

The few species included in this genus combine above-ground bulb-like succulence with a succulent inflorescence, a rare combination found in very few other species of succulent plants.

Lachenalia (Cape cowslip, *viooltjies*)

All the species of this genus are true bulbs, but a few have also opted for leaf succulence as an additional survival mechanism. Species of *Lachenalia* are some of the most rewarding bulbs to grow in summer-dry, winter-wet Mediterranean-type climates.

Bowiea volubilis (climbing onion)

Two species are currently included in this genus. One of those, *B. gariepensis,* is still very little known in cultivation. It is restricted to South Africa where it occurs in the arid northwestern Cape. In contrast, the other species, *B. volubilis*, has a very wide distribution in southern and eastern Africa. It has fist-sized, onion-like bulbs that are partially visible above the ground. The annual branches are bright green and develop into a wiry mass of climbing, leafless stems (which is actually the inflorescence of the plant). The greenish, star-shaped flowers are followed by capsules that produce small black seeds. Plants are easily grown in warm gardens provided they can be kept quite dry during the winter months. Propagation is by seeds, which germinate readily. Bulbs of the climbing onion are very poisonous but are nevertheless popular in Zulu traditional medicine, where they are used for a wide range of ailments. The plant contains heart glycosides.

Lachenalia contaminata

This species is a pot plant with slender, succulent leaves. The flowers are white and resemble those of miniature Madagascan aloes and some grass aloes. *Lachenalia* species are not generally considered to be succulents, but they are so exquisitely beautiful that they richly deserve to be more widely cultivated by succulent plant lovers.

Climbing onion *(Bowiea volubilis)*

Climbing onion "stems" (inflorescence)

Climbing onion fruits

Lachenalia contaminata

PASSIFLORACEAE
Granadilla or Passion flower family

DISTINGUISHING CHARACTERS The passion flower family is well known for the delicious fruits produced by several species of the commercially important granadilla or passion fruit. These plants are all evergreen perennial climbers (vines) with large, lobed leaves and typical climbing tendrils, with the aid of which the stems are attached to other plants. The tendrils are straight at first but then coil tightly around thin stems or other structures. In this respect the plants are superficially similar to the grape family, where the plants also may have climbing tendrils. There are, however, three important differences. Passion flower plants are usually evergreen, not deciduous as is typical in the grape family. Passion flowers and their relatives produce attractive, often large and colourful flowers, while the flowers of the grape vines and their relatives are rather small and inconspicuous. Lastly, the fruits are single, large berries with a hard shell and numerous pips, each embedded in a fleshy, edible aril, and not clusters of small, fleshy berries as is typically the case with the grape family.

NOTES It is only *Adenia* species with their decorative, succulent stems that are of interest to the succulent enthusiast. Several species of *Passiflora*, however, have become popular garden vines (climbers) because of their evergreen, often glossy green foliage and especially their large and attractive flowers. The best-known commercial granadilla or passion fruit is the purple-fruited *P. edulis*. A yellow-fruited variety of this species, sometimes referred to as the "guavadilla", is mainly used for fruit juice. Several other species, including the sweet granadilla (*P. ligularis*), the curuba or bananadilla (*P. mollissima*) and the giant granadilla (*P. quadrangularis*) are cultivated for their delicious arillate fruit pulp. The apricot vine or maypop (*P. incarnata*) is an important medicinal plant, while the blue passion flower (*P. caerulea*) and the red passion flower (*P. coccinea*) are spectacular garden plants.

Adenia (snake vines)

This is a group of about 40 African and Asian species with climbing stems arising from a thick woody base. The leaves may be simple or hand-shaped and lobed and the climbing tendrils may be modified to form spines. The flowers are rather small and typically green, cream-coloured or yellow. The best-known cultivated species is *A. glauca*, but other less commonly cultivated species include *A. digitata*, *A. pechuelii* and *A. spinosa*.

Adenia glauca (baboon poison)

It is easy to recognise this attractive garden succulent by its bright green, bottle-shaped stem and climbing branches bearing deeply lobed leaves resembling hands with five fingers. The rather inconspicuous flowers are followed by bright red, granadilla-like fruits. As is the case with most members of the family, the leaves and stems are very poisonous. *Adenia glauca* is fairly easy to grow in well-drained but rich soil in tropical gardens, provided it can be kept dry in the winter months.

Baboon poison (*Adenia glauca*)

Baboon poison (leaves)

Baboon poison (leaf and fruit)

Adenia digitata

PEDALIACEAE
Sesame family

DISTINGUISHING CHARACTERS The sesame family is a group of about 18 genera and 95 species distributed in most parts of the world but mainly in Africa, Asia and Australia. The growth form is rather variable, as it ranges from annual herbs to spreading creepers or woody shrubs and even small trees. Distinctive features include the attractive, foxglove-like flowers in practically all the species and the peculiar fruits, which are often modified to form thorns and horn-like appendages. The best-known member of the family is the sesame plant (*Sesamum indicum*), an annual that is grown for the oil-rich, edible seeds. Another famous example is the devil's claw of the Kalahari in southern Africa. This plant bears thick tuberous roots under the ground that are widely used as a traditional remedy for arthritis and lower back pain. The flowers are typical for the family but the fruits resemble large spiders, with long thorny arms that can sometimes kill an animal if they get hooked tightly around the mouth. A well-known American member of the family is the unicorn plant or ram's horn (*Proboscidea louisianica*), sometimes also referred to as the devil's claw. It has creeping, gland-dotted stems, large speckled flowers and highly distinctive fruits, each with two very long, gracefully curved but fierce-looking spines. In southern Africa, the spectacular architecture of the sesame-bushes (*Sesamothamnus* species) makes an indelible impression on visitors. These thick-stemmed trees have small leaves but large, peculiar long tubular flowers – white in *S. lugardii*, the Limpopo sesame-bush, and yellow in the Namibian *S. guerichii*, the so-called Herero sesame-bush. Species of *Pterodiscus* are sometimes cultivated in succulent gardens for their attractive stems and colourful flowers.

Pterodiscus (wing-fruited wild sesame)

Several species of this African genus of 18 small shrubs or herbs are occasionally encountered in tropical gardens or more often in succulent plant collections. They are grown mainly for their beautiful bottle-shaped stems, which are sometimes eaten or used as a source of ferment or yeast when brewing traditional beer. Among the seven species that are cultivated, the *sandkambro* (*P. speciosus*) is particularly popular because of the attractive flowers and ease of cultivation.

Pterodiscus speciosus (*sandkambro*)

Plants have thick basal stems and a few leafy branches that bear tubular flowers closely similar to sesame flowers. The flower colour is very variable and range from bright reddish purple to almost beige. Unlike most members of the family, the fruits are not thorny or spiny but equipped with four broad wings, not unlike those of *Zygophyllum* or *Combretum* species. The fleshy stems were once used by the Koranna people of the Kalahari as a source of yeast for brewing beer. *Sandkambro* can be grown in well-drained, alkaline soil that should be kept dry during the dormant period in winter. For plants to flourish, regular watering and feeding is essential during active growth.

Pterodiscus speciosus colour variant

Pterodiscus speciosus colour variant

Pterodiscus speciosus fruiting plant

VITACEAE
Grape family

DISTINGUISHING CHARACTERS The grape family is best known for its most famous member, *Vitis vinifera*, the common grape vine. Members of the family are typically climbers (vines) with lobed and toothed leaves that fall off in winter. Stems can be woody or succulent but they usually have distinct climbing tendrils that either curl around objects or adhere to rocks or walls by means of disc-shaped suckers. The flowers are generally inconspicuous, and the fruits are small fleshy berries, borne in large bunches. Most gardeners know the non-succulent ivy creepers with their disc-shaped climbing suckers, of which two species cover the walls of many famous buildings (especially university buildings) and decorate them with brilliant colours in autumn. These are the Virginian creeper or American ivy (*Parthenocissus quinquefolia*) with its leaves divided into five separate leaflets and the Boston ivy or Japanese ivy with its simple, grape-like, three-lobed leaves. Do not confuse these ivies with the common ivy or hedera (*Hedera helix*), an evergreen climber. Only two of the 13 genera in the family contain succulents.

Cissus (African climbing cacti)

The species are all vines (climbers) with climbing tendrils and thick, angular, fleshy stems that bear lobed, somewhat succulent leaves at the nodes.

Cissus quadrangularis (edible-stemmed vine, climbing cactus)

Cissus quadrangularis is known as the edible-stemmed vine or confusingly, the climbing cactus (because the angular stems superficially resemble those of climbing cacti such as *Hylocereus* species). The climbing tendrils and grape-like leaves, however, are typical of the Vitaceae. Plants may be cultivated outside in tropical or subtropical regions where they will quickly climb into trees and add interest and diversity to the garden.

Cyphostemma (wild grapes)

Spectacular thick-stemmed members of the genus *Cyphostemma* are quite popular amongst succulent enthusiasts and are also becoming better known to regular gardeners because of the relative ease with which these striking plants can be grown in tropical and even warm temperate gardens. Plants can be propagated from seeds and require regular watering in summer, drought in winter and as much sun and heat as possible.

Cyphostemma currorii (cobas, *kobas*)

The thick stems of this striking plant may reach a height of 3 m or more. It has a yellowish brown, somewhat flaky bark and large, bright green, fleshy leaves. Inconspicuous flowers are followed by bunches of red berries that are said to be poisonous.

Cyphostemma juttae (wild grape, blue cobas, *bloukobas*)

Stems of the wild grape are 2 to 4 m high, very thick, strongly tapering, smooth and often whitish in colour. The unusual, ghost-like appearance, especially when in the leafless state, makes this species an excellent choice as accent plant. The thick, fleshy and waxy leaves have a bluish colour. Clusters of small flowers and bright red to purplish berries are borne in summer.

Wild grape (*Cyphostemma juttae*)

Wild grape (flowers and fruits)

Cissus quadrangularis

Cobas (*Cyphostemma currorii*)

UNUSUAL LEAF SUCCULENTS
(various families)

GERANIACEAE
Geranium family

Distinguishing characters This small family is characterised by the distinctive fruits, often referred to as the "stork's bill". Botanically, these are called schizocarps because they break up into smaller parts called mericarps when mature. The family has one main genus, *Pelargonium*, which contains several stem succulents and leaf succulents. One of the most popular of all succulents in the world is the so-called ivy-leaved geranium (*Pelargonium peltatum*). It makes a spectacular display in the European summer – used mainly for hanging baskets but also widely planted in containers. The zonal geranium (*Pelargonium zonale*) is equally popular for this purpose – it has slightly fleshy stems but is not really a succulent. Note that the name "geranium" is commonly used for species of *Pelargonium* despite the fact that there is also a genus called *Geranium*. True geranium (*Geranium* species) have all the petals equal in size and shape (the flowers are actinomorphic), while those of the pelargoniums (often called geraniums) have a bilateral symmetry (the flowers have a left- and a right-hand side). An interesting succulent genus of this family is *Sarcocaulon* – it has thick fleshy stems but symmetrical flowers as in *Geranium*.

Pelargonium (geraniums, *malvas*)

The genus is of considerable horticultural importance as a source of several ornamental plants, some of which are also a source of essential oil (rose geranium oil). *Pelargonium* species are perennial herbs or shrubs (rarely creepers or annuals) with bilaterally symmetrical flowers that have a nectar spur fused to the flower stalk. Most of the species are southern African, with a few spreading thinly in North Africa, Western Asia, some oceanic islands and Australia.

Pelargonium peltatum (ivy-leaved geranium, *rankmalva*)

The plant has characteristic smooth, shiny leaves that may be marked with a dark circle or blotch. Wild forms usually have single, pale pink flowers, but modern cultivars often have double flowers in a variety of colours. Popular as a hanging basket plant, the ivy-leaved geranium is also an excellent garden creeper that will scramble over bare soil or cascade from rocky banks. The succulent leaves make it remarkably drought tolerant but regular watering and feeding will ensure vigorous growth and free flowering.

Sarcocaulon (candle bushes, *kersbosse*)

The prostrate stems are often thorny and bear large, geranium-like flowers. The waxy outer layers of the stems are persistent when the plants die and are traditionally used as candles. One of the best-known species is *Sarcocaulon crassicaule*. These plants are not easy to cultivate but are sometimes seen in succulent collections.

Ivy-leaved geranium (*Pelargonium peltatum*)

Sarcocaulon crassicaule

LAMIACEAE

Mint family

Distinguishing characters A distinctive family, the Lamiaceae are easily recognised by the opposite pairs of aromatic leaves (borne on distinctly square or angled stems) combined with small, two-lipped flowers. Well-known examples are the numerous aromatic herbs that are grown in herb gardens, such as lavender, sage, mint, thyme and rosemary. These plants have oil glands on the leaf surfaces that produce aromatic essential oils. As a result, many of them are used as culinary herbs to flavour food. They are also of commercial interest in the perfume industry and are important traditional medicines. The essential oils are widely used in aromatherapy.

Only a few members of this family are succulents. One of the best-known examples is the lobster flower, *Plectranthus neochilus*. It is one of several species of *Plectranthus* that have become popular as garden plants. These include colourful and hardy perennial herbs such as *P. ecklonii*, *P. fruticosus* and *P. saccatus*.

Plectranthus neochilus (lobster flower, poor man's lavender)

The lobster flower is a hardy perennial leaf succulent with attractive light to dark purple flowers. It is indigenous to the tropical parts of southern Africa as far north as Zambia. The much-branched stems bear greyish green, sticky leaves in opposite pairs. The unusual, lobster-like flower spikes are borne high above the plants on slender stalks. They have overlapping bracts that make the cluster distinctly four-sided. The individual flowers are two-lipped and blue to purple in colour. Crushed leaves are rather smelly and are considered to be effective in keeping the neighbour's dog off your lawn – plants are sold for this purpose in some European countries!

This is an excellent choice if a colourful groundcover is required in a dry, warm region. The stems bend over and easily take root, so that plants can usually be multiplied simply by division. Regular feeding is beneficial in ensuring that that they stay vigorous and flower throughout summer. The plants are perennial but tend to become untidy, so that severe pruning in early spring is recommended. A certain amount of frost is tolerated – the stems simply grow out again. Plants prefer full sun or light shade.

Plectranthus madagascariensis (variegated plectranthus)

The leaves of this relatively poorly known leaf succulent are its main attraction, as the small white flowers are rather inconspicuous. The variegated plectranthus is a tough perennial herb that is commonly grown in hanging baskets or on rockeries for its attractive variegated leaves that sometimes are tinged with red.

Plectranthus verticillatus

This is a fast-growing groundcover for shady spots, with small rounded leaves that have toothed margins and a smooth, shiny surface. The small flowers are white with some purple lines and markings. Plant rooted cuttings or rooted runners in fertile, well-drained soil and water regularly.

Plectranthus neochilus mass display

Plectranthus madagascariensis

Plectranthus neochilus

PORTULACACEAE
Portulaca family, *Spekboom* family

DISTINGUISHING CHARACTERS The main distinguishing feature of this family is the numerous small (oblong, rounded or fat) leaves than are crowded on the often thick and fleshy stems. The flower colour is very often pink or purple. One of the best-known garden succulents is the versatile and colourful portulaca or moss rose (*Portulaca grandiflora*) – an annual that is widely grown as a border plant. It is a close relative of the equally well-known purslane (*Portulaca oleracea*), which is found as a weed in many countries. Purslane is of course also a popular salad and vegetable plant, and a form of the species is grown as a vegetable in Europe. Several species of *Anacampseros* and *Avonia* are grown by succulent collectors but are not really garden plants. *Anacampseros* species are dwarf succulents with rounded fleshy leaves and small pink flowers. *Avonia* species such as *A. papyracea* are peculiar little plants with a dense layer of white overlapping scales instead of leaves.

NOTES The family is closely related to the cactus family (Cactaceae) and also to the Didiereaceae, a small Madagascan family which includes genera such as *Alluaudia*, *Alluaudiopsis*, *Decaryia* and *Didierea*, many of which are threatened in their local habitats. These plants are often seen in succulent collections in botanical gardens but very rarely in private gardens.

Portulaca (portulaca, moss rose)

Portulaca grandiflora is an old favourite border plant that is also very useful for dry rockeries and hot windowsills. A large number of colour variants have been selected, including double and single flower forms. Seedlings are easily grown from seeds and should be planted in full sun in well-drained soil.

Portulacaria (pork bush, elephant bush, *spekboom*)

One of the succulents that dominate parts of the subtropical thickets and Karoo in South Africa is the pork bush, *Portulacaria afra*. It is an important fodder plant, not only for goats, but also for elephants! The plant is a shrub or small tree up to about 4 m tall with a thick trunk, fleshy reddish brown branches and small, rounded, highly succulent leaves. When in full flower, the small, pale pink to purple flowers can be quite attractive. The fruits are small winged capsules. The *spekboom* has become a popular garden plant and various forms with a prostrate habit or golden yellow foliage have been selected. They are ideal for mass plantings on rocky banks or steep slopes and are an excellent backdrop for other, smaller succulents. Plants are very easily grown from cuttings and tolerate high temperatures and drought but not frost. They also make excellent bonsai trees.

Amongst the numerous foliage forms and cultivars are the following: 'Tricolor' – pendulous branches and small variegated leaves (green and cream-coloured, with pink edges); 'Variegata' – dense shrubs with pale green leaves that have a broad, cream-coloured margin and thin, pinkish edge; var. *foliis-variegata* – leaves mottled yellow; var. *macrophylla* – large leaves up to 25 mm long; var. *microphylla* – small, round leaves about 6 mm long. Variegated forms have become popular as pot plants and pendulous forms are ideal for hanging baskets.

Portulaca grandiflora

Portulacaria afra (garden form)

Portulacaria afra (natural form)

Portulacaria afra flowers

WELWITSCHIACEAE
Welwitschia family

DISTINGUISHING CHARACTERS Do these paradoxical plants really require to be briefly described here? These strange, moonscape-like oddities are so distinctive and well known that it would hardly seem necessary. All students of botany are taught about these plants during their formal training and all succulentists are fascinated by their strange leaves, stems and flower-like reproductive structures.

The stem of the plant is invariably unbranched, but it could split into two lobes. Stems are mainly carried underground with up to 2 m exposed above ground in very old specimens. The terminal parts of the stems look like large, deformed, crater-like, woody corks. The plants produce two leaves, which grow and elongate from their bases. The terminal parts erode away continuously, but the leaves can reach a length of up to 9 m. As a result of the withering away of the tips of the leaves they always look rather untidy and windswept. These leaves are never shed and *Welwitschia* has been called one of the only truly evergreen plants. The reproductive structures are borne in short, branched systems. The female cones are small club-shaped structures, whereas the male cones are more cylindrical in outline. In both cases the actual reproductive structures are subtended and more or less covered and protected by leaf-like structures called bracts. This gives the cones the appearance of small species of *Crassula*, such as *C. columnaris*. The mature seeds of *Welwitschia* are rounded in outline and have distinct papery wings that facilitate wind distribution.

NOTES The genus *Welwitschia* was described as recently as 1862, about 155 years ago. It immediately caused a stir amongst botanists and for the ensuing 60 odd years they puzzled over its correct placement in a classification system. It was only in the 1920s that these bizarre plants were finally placed in their own family. In habitat, specimens of *Welwitschia* attain an estimated lifespan of between 1 500 and 2 000 years.

Welwitschia is not only a curious plant but it also has a curious distribution range in the Namib Desert on the extremely arid west coast of southern Africa. It is endemic to the Namib, meaning that it is found only here and nowhere else on earth. Why this plant should have chosen such a desolate and inhospitable area as its home range remains a mystery. Scattered individuals are encountered from the Kuiseb River in Namibia along a 100 kilometre-wide coastal strip to Moçamedes in Angola.

Welwitschia

The genus *Welwitschia* has one species only – *Welwitschia mirabilis*. Plants are either male or female, i.e. both sexes are never found on the same plant. *Welwitschia* has been doubtfully included on lists of succulent plants. Indeed, many people will regard the leaves of this extreme xerophyte as leathery rather than succulent. However, as a curiosity this plant has always fascinated succulent collectors and its inclusion here would certainly seem to be warranted. For successful cultivation it is essential that seedlings are sown in well-drained soil directly into the containers, e.g. a drainage pipe inserted vertically into the soil, in which they will grow and plants are supplied with sufficient water throughout.

Welwitschia plant in nature

Female (top) and male cones

Young female plant

ZYGOPHYLLACEAE
Devil-thorn family

DISTINGUISHING CHARACTERS Not only are the Zygophyllaceae alphabetically always the last plant family to be treated in any book on succulents, if it is treated at all, but it is also the one whose species are least considered for cultivation. Yet these plants are perfectly adapted to arid and, in some cases, milder, even subtropical growing conditions and will develop into beautiful small trees or shrubs. Furthermore, the leaves of most species are fat or at least thickened and variously beautifully wrinkled along the margins. The flowers of most species are yellow and rather small, but what they lack in size is compensated for in terms of the number produced. A *Zygophyllum* bush in full flower is indeed a magnificent sight to behold. Furthermore, the flowers have up to 10 stamens, giving them a somewhat feathery appearance. The flowers of some representatives of the Zygophyllaceae are followed by prominently angled, winged fruits.

NOTES Representatives of the Zygophyllaceae are extremely rare in succulent plant collections, and virtually impossible to come across in nurseries. Yet, many species respond well to cultivation and can be trimmed into striking shrubs or small trees. Perhaps the best-known member of the Zygophyllaceae is the creosote bush (species of the genus *Larrea*, such as *Larrea tridentata*), which is common in the deserts and other arid parts of North America and Argentina. This yellow-flowered, bushy shrub carries its flowers in spring, but rain can stimulate it to flower also at other times of the year. The smell of creosote in these deserts after rain comes from its leaves, which also have a foul taste and are never grazed by domestic livestock. These plants are certainly not the source of creosote, but on a hot summer day exude a fragrance similar to that of this timber preservative.

Augea capensis

The genus *Augea* is monotypic, i.e. it has one species only. It occurs in the southern parts of Namibia and the dry parts of South Africa. The leaves of the species are highly succulent, resembling inflated, purplish green jellybeans borne more or less erectly on a thin stem.

One could be forgiven for confusing the species *Augea capensis* with members of the Mesembryanthemaceae (*vygies*) or Crassulaceae (*plakkies*). It is truly a dead ringer for a number of representatives of both families. However, when it flowers it is immediately evident that it does not belong in either of these families that are so rich in succulent species.

Zygophyllum morgsana (tortoise bush)

The genus *Zygophyllum* has more or less 120 species that are widely distributed in the Old World. Many of the species have succulent leaves.

Z. morgsana is a large shrub with bright green, bi-lobed leaves and attractive yellow flowers. The five yellow petals and the flower shape are distinctive. *Z. foetidum* is similar but differs in the pungent smell of the leaves. Both species have large winged fruits.

Augea capensis

Zygophyllum foetidum

Zygophyllum morgsana

Further reading

Group 1. Agavaceae (Sisal family, Century plant family)

Chahinian, B.J. 2005. The Splendid *Sansevieria*. Chahinian, Buenos Aires.

Gentry, H.S. 1982. Agaves of Continental North America. University of Arizona Press, Tucson.

Hochstätter, F. 2000. Yucca I. (Agavaceae). In the Southwest and Midwest of USA and Canada. The dehiscent fruited species. Navajo Country, Mannheim.

Hochstätter, F. 2000. Yucca II. (Agavaceae). In the Southwest and Midwest of USA and Canada. Indehiscent fruited species. Navajo Country, Mannheim.

Hochstätter, F. 2004. Yucca III. (Agavaceae). Mexico. Navajo Country, Mannheim.

Irish, M. & Irish, G. 2000. Agaves, Yuccas and Related Plants. A Gardener's Guide. Timber Press, Portland.

Group 2. Apocynaceae (Carrion flower family)

Albers, F. & Meve, U. (eds). 2002. Illustrated Handbook of Succulent Plants: Asclepiadaceae. Springer, Berlin, Heidelberg, New York.

Bruyns, P.V. 2005. Stapeliads of Southern Africa and Madagascar. (2 volumes). Umdaus Press, Pretoria.

Dyer, R.A.1983. *Ceropegia, Brachystelma & Riocreuxia* in Southern Africa. A.A. Balkema, Rotterdam.

Rapanarivo, S.H., Lavranos, J.J., Leeuwenberg, A.J.M. & Roosli, W. 1999. *Pachypodium* (Apocynaceae): Taxonomy, Ecology and Cultivation. A.A. Balkema, Rotterdam.

Rowley, G. 1999. *Pachypodium & Adenium* – The Cactus File Handbook 5. Cirio Publishing Services, Southampton.

Group 3. Asphodelaceae (Aloe family)

Bayer, M.B. 1999. *Haworthia* Revisited. Umdaus Press, Pretoria.

Bayer, M.B. 2002. Haworthia Update, Essays on *Haworthia* – Volume 1. Umdaus Press, Pretoria.

Breuer, I. 1998. The World of *Haworthia*, Vol.1. Ingo Breuer.

Breuer, I. 2000. The World of *Haworthia*, Vol. 2. Ingo Breuer.

Eggli, U. (ed.) 2001. Illustrated Handbook of Succulent Plants: Monocotyledons. Springer Publishing, New York.

Pilbeam, J.W. 1983. *Haworthia and Astroloba*, A Collectors Guide. B.T. Batsford, London.

Reynolds, G.W. 1950. The Aloes of South Africa. Trustees of the Aloes of South Africa Book Fund, Johannesburg.

Reynolds, G.W. 1966. The Aloes of Tropical Africa and Madagascar. Trustees of the Aloe Book Fund, Mbabane.

Scott, C.L. 1985. The Genus *Haworthia*, A Taxonomic Revision. Aloe Books, Johannesburg.

Van Jaarsveld, E.J. 1994. Gasterias of South Africa. Fernwood Press, Cape Town.

Van Wyk, B-E. & Smith, G.F. 2003. Guide to the Aloes of South Africa. Second edition. Briza Publications, Pretoria.

Group 4. Asteraceae (Daisy family)

Eggli, U. (ed.) 2004. Illustrated Handbook of Succulent Plants: Dicotyledons. Springer Publishing, New York.

Halliday, P. 1988. Noteworthy Species of *Kleinia*. Bentham-Moxon Trust, Kew.

Rowley, G.D. 1994. Succulent Compositae: A grower's guide to succulent species of *Senecio* & *Othonna*. Strawberry Press, California.

Group 5. Cactaceae (Cactus family, Prickly pear family)

Anderson, M. 1998. The Ultimate Book of Cacti and Succulents. Lorenz Books, New York.

Anderson, E.F. 2001. The Cactus Family. Timber Press, Portland.

Cullmann, W., Götz, E. & Gröner, G. 1986. The Encyclopedia of Cacti. Alphabooks, Sherborne.

Graham, C. 2003. Cacti and Succulents: An Illustrated Guide to the Plants and Their Cultivation. The Crowood Press, Ramsbury.

Hewitt, T. 1993. The Complete Book of Cacti and Succulents. Dorling Kindersley, London.

Hunt, D. & Taylor, N. (eds) 2002. Studies in the Opuntioideae (Cactaceae). DH Books, Sherborne.

Hunt, D., Taylor, N. & Charles, G. 2006. The New Cactus Lexicon. Descriptions & Illustrations of the Cactus Family, compiled and edited by members of the International Cactaceae Systematics Group. DH Books, Sherborne.

Mace, T. & Mace, S. 1998. Cactus and Succulents. A Hamlyn Care Manual. Hamlyn, London.

McMillan, A.J.S. & Horobin, J.F. 1995. Christmas Cacti: The genus *Schlumbergera* and its hybrids. DH Books, Sherborne.

Pilbeam, J. 1999. *Mammillaria*. A Collectors Guide. Cirio Publishing Services, Southampton.

Pizzetti, M., Schuler, S. & Mazza, G. 1985. Simon & Schuster's Guide to Cacti and Succulents. Simon & Schuster, New York.

Group 6. Crassulaceae (Stonecrop family, Plakkie family)

Eggli, U. (ed.) 2003. Illustrated Handbook of Succulent Plants: Crassulaceae. Springer Publishing, New York.

Eggli, U. & 't Hart, H. 2003. Sedums of Europe: Stonecrops and Wallpeppers. A.A. Balkema, Rotterdam.

Pilbeam, J., Rodgerson C. & Tribble, D. 1998. *Adromischus* – The Cactus File Handbook 3. Cirio Publishing Services, Southampton.

Rowley, G.D. 2003. *Crassula*, a Grower's Guide. Cactus & Co. Libri.

Schulz, R. 2007. *Aeonium* in Habitat and Cultivation. Schultz Publishing, San Bruno.

Schultz, L. & Kapitany, A. 2005. *Echeveria* Cultivars. Schulz Publishing, Teesdale.

Stephensen, R. 2002. *Sedum*. Cultivated Stonecrops. Timber Press, Portland.

Van Jaarsveld, E. & Koutnik, D. 2004. *Cotyledon* and *Tylecodon*. Umdaus Press, Pretoria.

Wills, H. & Wills, S. 2004. An Introduction to *Sempervivum* and *Jovibarba* Species and Cultivars. Howard and Sally Wills, Peters Marland, Torrington, Devon.

Group 7. Euphorbiaceae (Spurge family, Milkweed family)

Eggli, U. (ed.) 2004. Illustrated Handbook of Succulent Plants: Dicotyledons. Springer Publishing, New York.

Euphorbia Society. The Euphorbia Journal (several volumes).

Turner, R. 1998. Euphorbias: A Gardener's Guide. Timber Press, Portland.

White, A., Dyer, R.A. & Sloane, B.L. 1941. The Succulent Euphorbiae (Southern Africa) Vol. 1 & 2. Abbey Garden Press, Pasadena, California.

Group 8. Mesembryanthemaceae (Ice plant family, Mesemb family)

Cole, D.T. & Cole, N.A. 2005. *Lithops* – Flowering Stones. Second Edition. Cactus & Co. Libri.

Hammer, S.A. 1993. The genus *Conophytum*. Succulent Plant Publications, Pretoria.

Hammer, S.A. 1999. *Lithops* – Treasures of the Veld. British Cactus and Succulent Society.

Hammer, S.A. 2002. Dumpling and His Wife: New Views of the Genus *Conophytum*. EAE Creative Colour Ltd, Norwich.

Hartmann, H.E.K. (ed.) 2002. Illustrated Handbook of Succulent Plants: Aizoaceae A-E. Springer Publishing, New York.

Hartmann, H.E.K. (ed.) 2002. Illustrated Handbook of Succulent Plants: Aizoaceae F-Z. Springer Publishing, New York.

Smith, G.F., Chesselet, P., Van Jaarsveld, E., Hartmann, H., Hammer, S., Van Wyk, B-E., Burgoyne, P., Klak, C. & Kurzweil, H. 1998. Mesembs of the World. Briza Publications, Pretoria.

Van Jaarsveld, E.J. & Pienaar, U. de V. 2000. *Vygies, Gems of the Veld*. Cactus & Co. Libri.

Group 9. Unusual stem succulents (various families)

De Vosjoli, P. 2004. A Guide to Growing Pachycaul and Caudiciform Plants. Advanced Visions Inc., Vista, California.

Eggli, U. (ed.) 2001. Illustrated Handbook of Succulent Plants: Monocotyledons. Springer Publishing, New York.

Eggli, U. (ed.) 2004. Illustrated Handbook of Succulent Plants: Dicotyledons. Springer Publishing, New York.

Pakenham, T. 2004. The Remarkable Baobab. Weidenfeld & Nicolson, London.

Rowley, G. 1987. Caudiciform & Pachycaul Succulents. Strawberry Press, California.

Group 10. Unusual leaf succulents (various families)

Bornmann, C.H. 1978.*Welwitschia*: paradox of a parched paradise. Struik, Cape Town.

Eggli, U. (ed.) 2004. Illustrated Handbook of Succulent Plants: Dicotyledons. Springer Publishing, New York.

General

Baldwin, D.L. 2007. Designing with Succulents. Timber Press, Portland.

Court, G.D. 2000. Succulent Flora of Southern Africa. Second Edition. A.A. Balkema, Rotterdam.

Jacobson, H. 1974. Lexicon of Succulent Plants. Blandford Press, London.

Mauseth, J. D., Kiesling, R.& Ostolaza, C. 2002. A Cactus Odyssey: Journeys in the Wilds of Bolivia, Peru, and Argentina. Timber Press, Portland.

Oliver, I. B. 1998. Grow Succulents: A Guide to the Species, Cultivation & Propagation of South African Succulents. Kirstenbosch Gardening Series. Cape Town.

Rauh, W. 1995. Succulent & Xerophytic Plants of Madagascar. Vol. 1. Strawberry Press, California.

Rauh, W. 1998. Succulent & Xerophytic Plants of Madagascar. Vol. 2. Strawberry Press, California.

Sajeva, M. & Costanzo, M. 2000. Succulents II: The New Illustrated Dictionary. Timber Press, Portland.

Smith, G.F. 2006. Cacti and Succulents. New Holland Publishers, London.

Smith, G.F., Van Jaarsveld, E.J., Arnold, T.H., Steffens, F.E., Dixon, R.D. & Retief, J.A. 1997. A List of Southern African Succulent Plants. Umdaus Press, Pretoria.

Van Jaarsveld, E., Van Wyk, B-E. & Smith, G.F. 2005. Succulents of South Africa: A Guide to Regional Diversity. Second Edition. Sunbird Publishers, Cape Town.

Van Wyk, A.E. & Smith, G.F. 2001. Regions of Floristic Endemism in Southern Africa: A Review with Emphasis on Succulents. Umdaus Press, Pretoria.

Quick guide to garden succulents of the world

Regions of origin: Africa (Afr); Asia (As); Australia (Aus); Europe (Eu); North America (NAm); Central America [including Mexico] (CAm); South America (SAm); garden origin (Cult).

Treated and illustrated species are printed ***bold and underlined***; illustrated species are printed **bold only**.

Unfortunately, there are alternative classification systems, and therefore alternative names for many of the common garden succulents. Name changes are often due to new insights resulting from modern DNA analyses. The list below is a quick name guide for gardeners and non-specialist readers – the specialists are advised to consult the latest technical publications and revisions. The list is not comprehensive but includes only commonly cultivated succulents. Some genera (especially of the families Mesembryanthemaceae and Apocynaceae) are incompletely listed because the species are not really garden succulents and are grown as potted plants or as curiosities by specialist growers.

Genera and Species	Common name(s)	Origin
Acanthocereus ■ CACTACEAE		
Acanthocereus colombianus		CAm
Acanthocereus horridus		CAm
Acanthocereus occidentalis		CAm
Acanthocereus subinermis		CAm
Acanthocereus tetragonus		CAm
Acrodon ■ MESEMBRYANTHEMACEAE		
Acrodon bellidiflorus		Afr
Adansonia ■ BOMBACACEAE		
Adansonia digitata	baobab	Afr
Adenia ■ PASSIFLORACEAE		
Adenia digitata	wild granadilla, baboon poison, *bobbejaangif*	Afr
Adenia fruticosa		Afr
Adenia glauca	baboon poison	Afr
Adenia pechuelii	elephant's foot	Afr
Adenia spinosa		Afr
Adenium ■ APOCYNACEAE		
Adenium boehmianum	pink impala lily	Afr
Adenium multiflorum	impala lily	Afr
Adenium obesum	desert rose	Afr
Adenium oleifolia		Afr
Adenium socotranum		Afr
Adenium somalense		Afr
Adenium swazicum	large-leaf impala lily	Afr
Adromischus ■ CRASSULACEAE		
Adromischus alstonii		Afr

Adromischus caryophyllaceus		Afr
Adromischus cooperi	plover eggs	Afr
Adromischus cristatus	crinkle-leaf plant	Afr
Adromischus filicaulis		Afr
Adromischus hemisphaericus		Afr
Adromischus maculatus		Afr
Adromischus mammillaris		Afr
Adromischus marianae	*brosplakkie*	Afr
Adromischus maximus		Afr
Adromischus roaneanus		Afr
Adromischus schuldtianus		Afr
Adromischus sphenophyllus		Afr
Adromischus triflorus		Afr
Adromischus trigynus	calico hearts	Afr
Adromischus umbraticola		Afr
Aeonium ■ CRASSULACEAE		
Aeonium arboreum	tree aeonium, velvet rose	Afr
Aeonium balsamiferum		Afr
Aeonium canariense	Canary Island aeonium, velvet rose, giant velvet rose	Afr
Aeonium castello-paive		Afr
Aeonium ciliatum		Afr
Aeonium cuneatum		Afr
Aeonium decorum		Afr
Aeonium glandulosum		Afr
Aeonium glutinosum		Afr
Aeonium gomerense		Afr
Aeonium goochiae	pinwheel	Afr
Aeonium haworthii		Afr
Aeonium hierrense		Afr
Aeonium lancerottense		Afr
Aeonium lindleyi		Afr
Aeonium nobile		Afr
Aeonium percarneum		Afr
Aeonium saundersii		Afr
Aeonium sedifolium		Afr
Aeonium simsii		Afr
Aeonium smithii		Afr
Aeonium spathulatum		Afr
Aeonium tabuliforme		Afr
Aeonium undulatum	saucer plant	Afr
Aeonium urbicum		Afr
Aeonium valverdense		Afr
Aeonium ×hybridum		Cult
Agave ■ AGAVACEAE		
Agave albomarginata		CAm
Agave americana var. **americana**	century plant, maguey, American aloe	CAm

Agave americana var. *marginata*	century plant, maguey, American aloe	CAm
Agave americana var. **mediopicta alba**	variegated century plant, variegated maguey, American aloe	CAm
Agave angustifolia	maguey lechugilla, narrow-leaf century plant	SAm, CAm
Agave applanata		CAm
Agave atrovirens	maguey	CAm
Agave attenuata	elephant's trunk, fox tail agave	CAm
Agave aurea		NAm
Agave bourgaei		CAm
Agave bovicornuta	cow horn agave, lechuguilla verde	CAm
Agave bracteosa	squid agave	CAm
Agave brevispina		CAm
Agave cantala	cantala	SAm, CAm
Agave celsii		CAm
Agave chrysantha	golden-flowered agave	NAm
Agave colimana		CAm
Agave colorata	mescal ceniza	CAm
Agave cupreata		CAm
Agave decipiens	false agave	NAm
Agave deserti	desert agave	NAm
Agave desmettiana	smooth agave	CAm
Agave difformis		CAm
Agave ellemeetiana		CAm
Agave fenzliana		CAm
Agave ferox		CAm
Agave filifera	thread-leaf agave	CAm
Agave fourcroydes	henequen	CAm
Agave franzosinii		CAm
Agave funkiana	ixtle de jaumave	CAm
Agave ghiesbreghtii		CAm
Agave guadalajarana	maguey chato	CAm
Agave guiengola		CAm
Agave gypsophila		CAm
Agave horrida		CAm
Agave karwinskii		CAm
Agave kewensis		CAm
Agave lechuguilla		CAm
Agave lophantha	thorncrest century plant	CAm
Agave lurida		CAm
Agave macroacantha		CAm
Agave marmorata		CAm
Agave missionum	Eggers' century plant	CAm
Agave multifilifera	chahuiqui	CAm
Agave murpheyi	Murphey's agave, hohokam agave	CAm, NAm
Agave neomexicana	mescale	NAm
Agave nizandensis		CAm
Agave ocahui		CAm

Agave palmeri	Palmer's agave	CAm, NAm
Agave parrasana		CAm
Agave parryi	mescal, Parry's agave	CAm, NAm
Agave parviflora	small-flower agave	CAm, NAm
Agave peacockii		CAm
Agave pedunculifera		CAm
Agave pendula		CAm
Agave polyacantha		CAm
Agave potatorum		CAm
Agave pumila		CAm
Agave salmiana	pulque agave	CAm
Agave scabra		CAm, NAm
Agave schidigera		CAm
Agave schottii	Schott's century plant, shindagger	CAm, NAm
Agave seemanniana		CAm
Agave shawii	coastal century plant	CAm, NAm
Agave sisalana	sisal, sisal plant	CAm
Agave sobria		NAm
Agave striata	espadin	CAm
Agave stricta	hedgehog agave	CAm
Agave tequilana	tequila plant, blue agave, agave azul	CAm
Agave toumeyana	Toumey's century plant	NAm
Agave triangularis		CAm
Agave utahensis	Utah agave	NAm
Agave victoriae-reginae	Queen Victoria agave, queen agave	CAm
Agave vilmoriniana	octopus agave	CAm
Agave warelliniana		CAm
Agave weberi	Weber agave	CAm
Agave wercklei		CAm
Agave xylonacantha		CAm
Agave yuccaefolia		CAm
Aichryson ■ CRASSULACEAE		
Aichryson bethencoutianum		Afr
Aichryson bollei		Afr
Aichryson divaricatum		Afr
Aichryson ×domesticum	youth-and-old-age	Afr
Aichryson laxum		Afr
Aichryson palmense		Afr
Aichryson porphyrogennetos		Afr
Aichryson tortuosum	gouty houseleek	Afr
Aichryson villosum		Afr
Alluaudia ■ DIDIEREACEAE		
Alluaudia ascendens		Afr
Alluaudia comosa		Afr
Alluaudia dumosa		Afr
Alluaudia humbertii		Afr
Alluaudia montagnacii		Afr

Alluaudia procera	Madagascar ocotillo	Afr
Alluaudiopsis ■ Dᴵᴰᴵᴱᴿᴱᴬᴄᴱᴬᴱ		
Alluaudiopsis fiherensis		Afr
Alluaudiopsis marnieriana		Afr
Aloe ■ Aѕᴘʜᴏᴅᴇʟᴀᴄᴇᴀᴇ		
Aloe aculeata	red hot poker aloe	Afr
Aloe africana		Afr
Aloe albida		Afr
Aloe albiflora		Afr
Aloe alooides		Afr
Aloe andringitrensis		Afr
Aloe arborescens	kranz aloe, candelabra aloe, octopus plant, torch plant, "Japan aloe"	Afr
Aloe arenicola		Afr
Aloe aristata	torch plant, lace aloe	Afr
Aloe audhalica		Afr
Aloe bainesii (=A. barberae)		
Aloe bakeri		Afr
Aloe barbadensis (=Aloe vera)		
Aloe barberae	tree aloe	Afr
Aloe barbertoniae		Afr
Aloe bellatula		Afr
Aloe branddraaiensis		Afr
Aloe brevifolia	short-leaf aloe, blue aloe	Afr
Aloe broomii	bergaalwyn	Afr
Aloe buettneri		Afr
Aloe bulbilifera		Afr
Aloe cameronii		Afr
Aloe camperi	East African aloe, *groenaalwyn*	Afr
Aloe candelabrum (=A. ferox)		
Aloe capitata		Afr
Aloe castanea	cat's tail aloe	Afr
Aloe chabaudii		Afr
Aloe ciliaris	climbing aloe, fringed climbing aloe, *rankaalwyn*	Afr
Aloe comosa		Afr
Aloe cooperi		Afr
Aloe cremnophila		Afr
Aloe cryptopoda		Afr
Aloe davyana (=A. greatheadii var. davyana)		
Aloe descoingsii		Afr
Aloe dichotoma	quiver tree, common quiver tree	Afr
Aloe dinteri	Namibian partridge breast aloe	Afr
Aloe distans	jeweled aloe	Afr
Aloe divaricata		Afr
Aloe doei		Afr
Aloe dorotheae		Afr

Aloe ecklonis		Afr
Aloe erinacea		Afr
Aloe esculenta		Afr
Aloe excelsa	Zimbabwe aloe, noble aloe	Afr
Aloe ferox	Cape aloe, bitter aloe, tap aloe	Afr
Aloe fosteri		Afr
Aloe gariepensis		Afr
Aloe glauca	blue aloe	Afr
Aloe globuligemma		Afr
Aloe grandidentata	*bontaalwyn*	Afr
Aloe greenii		Afr
Aloe harlana		Afr
Aloe haworthioides		Afr
Aloe hereroensis		Afr
Aloe humilis	spider aloe, hedgehog aloe, crocodile-jaws	Afr
Aloe inermis		Afr
Aloe jacksonii		Afr
Aloe jucunda		Afr
Aloe juvenna		Afr
Aloe karasbergensis		Afr
Aloe krapohliana	dwarf aloe	Afr
Aloe lineata	lined aloe	Afr
Aloe littoralis	spotted mountain aloe, Windhoek aloe	Afr
Aloe longistyla	karoo aloe, *ramenas*	Afr
Aloe lutescens		Afr
Aloe macroclada		Afr
Aloe maculata	soap aloe, zebra aloe	Afr
Aloe marlothii	mountain aloe, common mountain aloe	Afr
Aloe melanacantha		Afr
Aloe microstigma	speckled aloe, *gevlekte aalwyn*	Afr
Aloe millottii		Afr
Aloe mitriformis (see *A. perfoliata*)		
Aloe myriacantha		Afr
Aloe niebuhriana		Afr
Aloe ortholopha		Afr
Aloe pachygaster		Afr
Aloe parvibracteata		Afr
Aloe parvula		Afr
Aloe pearsonii		Afr
Aloe peglerae		Afr
Aloe perfoliata	gold tooth aloe	Afr
Aloe perryi	Socotrine aloe, Perry's aloe	Afr
Aloe petricola		Afr
Aloe pillansii	giant quiver tree	Afr
Aloe plicatilis	fan aloe	Afr
Aloe pluridens		Afr
Aloe polyphylla		Afr

234

Aloe pratensis	rosette aloe	Afr
Aloe pretoriensis		Afr
Aloe ramosissima	maiden quiver tree	Afr
Aloe rauhii		Afr
Aloe reitzii		Afr
Aloe rigens		Afr
Aloe rubroviolacea		Afr
Aloe rupestris	bottlebrush aloe	Afr
Aloe saponaria (see *A. maculata*)		
Aloe secundiflora		Afr
Aloe simii		Afr
Aloe sinkatana		Afr
Aloe sladeniana		Afr
Aloe somaliensis		Afr
Aloe speciosa	showy aloe, tilt-head aloe	Afr
Aloe spectabilis (see *A. marlothii*)		
Aloe squarrosa		Afr
Aloe steudneri		Afr
Aloe striata	coral aloe	Afr
Aloe striata × *A. maculata*	garden aloe	Afr
Aloe striatula		Afr
Aloe succotrina	fynbos aloe	Afr
Aloe suprafoliata		Afr
Aloe suzannae		Afr
Aloe swynnertonii		Afr
Aloe tenuior	climbing aloe	Afr
Aloe thorncroftii		Afr
Aloe thraskii	dune aloe, beach aloe	Afr
Aloe turkanensis		Afr
Aloe vaombe		Afr
Aloe vaotsanda		Afr
Aloe variegata	partridge-breasted aloe, falcon feather, *kanniedood* aloe, tiger aloe	Afr
Aloe vera (=*A. barbadensis*)	Barbados aloe, medicinal aloe	Afr
Aloe wickensii		Afr
Aloe wildii		Afr
Aloe zebrina	zebra leaf aloe	Afr
Aloinopsis ■ MESEMBRYANTHEMACEAE		
Aloinopsis hilmarii		Afr
Aloinopsis jamesii		Afr
Aloinopsis lodewykii		Afr
Aloinopsis luckhoffii		Afr
Aloinopsis malherbei	giant jewel plant	Afr
Aloinopsis orpenii		Afr
Aloinopsis peersii (see *Deilanthe peersii*)		
Aloinopsis rosulata		Afr

Aloinopsis rubrolineata		Afr
Aloinopsis schooneesii		Afr
Aloinopsis setifera		Afr
Aloinopsis spathulata		Afr
Aloinopsis villetii		Afr
×*Alworthia* ■ ASPHODELACEAE		
×*Alworthia* 'Black Gem' (*Haworthia cymbiformis* × *Aloe* sp.)		Afr
Anacampseros ■ PORTULACACEAE		
Anacampseros species		Afr
Anredera ■ BASELLACEAE		
Anredera cordifolia	Madeira vine, mignonette vine	SAm
Aporocactus flagelliformis (see *Disocactus flagelliformis*)		
Aporocactus martianus (see *Disocactus martianus*)		
Aptenia ■ MESEMBRYANTHEMACEAE		
Aptenia cordifolia	red aptenia, baby sun rose, ice plant, *rooi brakvygie*	Afr
Aptenia lancifolia	purple aptenia, *pers brakvygie*	Afr
Argyroderma ■ MESEMBRYANTHEMACEAE		
Argyroderma congregatum		Afr
Argyroderma crateriforme		Afr
Argyroderma delaetii		Afr
Argyroderma fissum		Afr
Argyroderma framesii		Afr
Argyroderma hallii		Afr
Argyroderma ×*kleijnhansii*		Afr
Argyroderma patens		Afr
Argyroderma pearsonii		Afr
Argyroderma ringens		Afr
Argyroderma subalbum		Afr
Argyroderma testiculare		Afr
×*Argyrops* ■ MESEMBRYANTHEMACEAE		
×*Argyrops* 'Moonstones' (*Argyroderma* × *Lithops*)		Cult
Aridaria ■ MESEMBRYANTHEMACEAE		
Aridaria noctiflora		Afr
Ariocarpus ■ CACTACEAE		
Ariocarpus agavoides	living rock	CAm
Ariocarpus fissuratus	living rock, Chautle living rock, false peyote	CAm
Ariocarpus kotschoubeyanus	living rock	CAm
Ariocarpus retusus	living rock, seven stars	CAm
Ariocarpus scaphirostris	living rock	CAm
Ariocarpus trigonus	living rock	CAm
Armatocereus ■ CACTACEAE		
Armatocereus cartwrightianus		CAm
Armatocereus godingianus		CAm

Armatocereus laetus		CAm
Armatocereus mutacanensis		CAm
Arrojadoa ■ CACTACEAE		
Arrojadoa penicillata		CAm
Arrojadoa rhodantha		Cam
Arthrocereus ■ CACTACEAE		
Arthrocereus glaziovii		CAm
Arthrocereus melanurus		CAm
Arthrocereus rondonianus		Cam
Astridia ■ MESEMBRYANTHEMACEAE		
Astridia species		Afr
Astroloba ■ ASPHODELACEAE		
Astroloba bullulata		Afr
Astroloba foliolosa		Afr
Astroloba herrei		Afr
Astroloba muricata		Afr
Astroloba rubriflora		Afr
Astroloba spiralis		Afr
Astrophytum ■ CACTACEAE		
Astrophytum asterias	sea urchin, silver dollar cactus	CAm, NAm
Astrophytum capricorne	goat's horns cactus	CAm
Astrophytum myriostigma	bishop's cap, bishop's hat	CAm
Astrophytum ornatum	monk's hood	Cam
×*Astroworthia* ■ ASPHODELACEAE		
×*Astroworthia skinneri* (*Astroloba muricata* × *Haworthia maxima*)		Afr
Augea ■ ZYGOPHYLLACEAE		
Augea capensis		Afr
Austrocactus ■ CACTACEAE		
Austrocactus hibernus		SAm
Austrocactus patagonicus		SAm
Austrocactus spiniflorus		SAm
Aztekium ■ CACTACEAE		
Aztekium ritterii		CAm
Basella ■ BASELLACEAE		
Basella alba	Indian spinach, Malabar spinach	Afr, As
Beaucarnia ■ AGAVACEAE / NOLINACEAE		
Beaucarnia recurvata	ponytail, ponytail palm, bottle palm, bottle ponytail, elephant's foot tree	NAm, CAm
Beaucarnia stricta	ponytail palm, bottle palm	CAm
Bergeranthus ■ MESEMBRYANTHEMACEAE		
Bergeranthus artus		Afr
Bergeranthus glenensis (see *Hereroa glenensis*)		
Bergeranthus multiceps		Afr
Bergeranthus scapiger		Afr

237

Bergeranthus vespertinus		Afr
Bergerocactus ■ CACTACEAE		
Bergerocactus emoryi	golden cactus	NAm
Beschorneria ■ AGAVACEAE		
Beschorneria bracteata	green-flowered beschorneria	CAm
Beschorneria decosteriana		CAm
Beschorneria toneliana		CAm
Beschorneria tubiflora		CAm
Beschorneria wrightii		CAm
Beschorneria yuccoides	Mexican lily, false red yucca	CAm
Bijlia ■ MESEMBRYANTHEMACEAE		
Bijlia cana (see *B. dilatata*)		
Bijlia dilatata	Prince Albert *vygie*	Afr
Blossfeldia ■ CACTACEAE		
Blossfeldia liliputana		SAm
Bowiea ■ HYACINTHACEAE		
Bowiea volubilis	climbing onion	Afr
Brachycereus ■ CACTACEAE		
Brachycereus nesioticus	lava cactus	CAm
Brachystelma ■ APOCYNACEAE		
Brachystelma species		Afr
Brasilicereus ■ CACTACEAE		
Brasilicereus phaeacanthus		SAm
Braunsia ■ MESEMBRYANTHEMACEAE		
Braunsia apiculata		Afr
Braunsia geminata		Afr
Browningia ■ CACTACEAE		
Browningia candelaris		SAm
Browningia chlorocarpa		SAm
Browningia hertlingiana		SAm
Browningia microsperma		SAm
Browningia viridis		SAm
Bryophyllum species (see *Kalanchoe*)		
Bulbine ■ ASPHODELACEAE		
Bulbine alooides		Afr
Bulbine annua		Afr
Bulbine diphylla		Afr
Bulbine frutescens	burn jelly plant, stalked bulbine, *rankkopieva*	Afr
Bulbine haworthioides		Afr
Bulbine latifolia	*rooiwortel*	Afr
Bulbine mesembryanthoides		Afr
Bulbine natalensis		Afr
Bulbine succulenta		Afr
Bulbine triebneri		Afr
Calymmanthium ■ CACTACEAE		

238

Calymmanthium substerile		SAm
Caralluma ■ Apocynaceae		
Caralluma species		Eu, Afr, As
Carnegiea ■ Cactaceae		
Carnegiea gigantea	cowboy cactus, saguaro cactus, sahuaro	Cam, NAm
Carpanthea ■ Mesembryanthemaceae		
Carpanthea pomeridiana	*vetkousie*	Afr
Carpobrotus ■ Mesembryanthemaceae		
Carpobrotus acinaciformis	purple pigface, purple sour fig	Afr
Carpobrotus aequilaterus	angular pigface	Aus
Carpobrotus chilensis	sea fig	SAm, CAm
Carpobrotus deliciosus	*gaukum*	Afr
Carpobrotus dimidiatus	east coast sour fig	Afr
Carpobrotus edulis	sour fig, common sour fig, hottentot fig	Afr
Carpobrotus glaucescens		Aus
Carpobrotus mellei		Afr
Carpobrotus modestus	inland pigface	Aus
Carpobrotus muirii		Afr
Carpobrotus quadrifidus	large sour fig, *elandsvy*	Afr
Carpobrotus rossii		Aus
Carpobrotus sauerae (see *C. quadrifidus*)		
Carpobrotus virescens		Aus
Carruanthus ■ Mesembryanthemaceae		
Carruanthus peersii	*tierbekvygie*	Afr
Carruanthus ringens	*tierbekvygie*	Afr
Cephalocereus ■ Cactaceae		
Cephalocereus apicicephalium		CAm
Cephalocereus columna-trajani	organo	CAm
Cephalocereus senilis	old man cactus, old man of Mexico	CAm
Cephalophyllum ■ Mesembryanthemaceae		
Cephalophyllum alstonii	*rankvygie*	Afr
Cephalophyllum caespitosum		Afr
Cephalophyllum diversiphyllum		Afr
Cephalophyllum pillansii		Afr
Cephalophyllum subulatoides		Afr
Cephalophyllum tricolorum		Afr
Ceraria ■ Portulacaceae		
Ceraria fruticulosa		Afr
Ceraria namaquensis		Afr
Ceraria pygmaea		Afr
Cereus ■ Cactaceae		
Cereus aethiops		SAm
Cereus alacriportanus		SAm
Cereus argentinensis		SAm
Cereus azureus		SAm
Cereus campinensis		SAm
Cereus chalybaeus		SAm

239

Cereus dayami		SAm
Cereus diffusus		SAm
Cereus fernambucensis		SAm
Cereus glaucus		SAm
Cereus haageana		SAm
Cereus hexagonus	lady of the night cactus	CAm, SAm
Cereus hildmannianus	queen of the night	SAm
Cereus huntingtonianus		unknown
Cereus insularis		SAm
Cereus jamacaru	pitaya, queen of the night, pleated cereus	SAm
Cereus pachyrrhizus		SAm
Cereus peruvianus	pitaya	SAm
Cereus pseudocaesius		unknown
Cereus repandus	hedge cactus, Peruvian apple cactus	SAm
Cereus saxicola		SAm
Cereus smithianus		SAm
Cereus spegazzinii		SAm
Cereus stenogonus		SAm
Cereus trigonodendron		SAm
Cereus uruguayanus		SAm
Cereus validus		SAm
Cereus xanthocarpus		SAm
Cerochlamys ■ MESEMBRYANTHEMACEAE		
Cerochlamys pachyphylla	*pronkvingertjies*, showy vingers	Afr
Ceropegia ■ APOCYNACEAE		
Ceropegia sandersonii	parachute plant, umbrella plant	Afr
Ceropegia woodii	hearts on a string, sweetheart vine, hearts entangled, rosary vine	Afr
Chasmatophyllum ■ MESEMBRYANTHEMACEAE		
Chasmatophyllum musculinum	*geelbergvygie*, yellow mountain mesemb, yellow swallowtail mesemb	Afr
Cheiridopsis ■ MESEMBRYANTHEMACEAE		
Cheiridopsis acuminata		Afr
Cheiridopsis aspera		Afr
Cheiridopsis caroli-schmidtii		Afr
Cheiridopsis cigarettifera	cigarette holder	Afr
Cheiridopsis denticulata		Afr
Cheiridopsis derenbergiana		Afr
Cheiridopsis herrei		Afr
Cheiridopsis peculiaris	donkey ear	Afr
Cheiridopsis pillansii		Afr
Cheiridopsis purpurea		Afr
Cheiridopsis robusta	clock plant	Afr
Cheiridopsis rostrata		Afr
Cheiridopsis speciosa		Afr
Cheiridopsis turbinata		Afr
Cheiridopsis vanzylii		Afr
Cheiridopsis verrucosa		Afr

Chiastophyllum ■ Crassulaceae		
Chiastophyllum oppositifolium	lamb's tail	As
Chortolirion ■ Asphodelaceae		
Chortolirion angolense	onion aloe	Afr
Cipocereus ■ Cactaceae		
Cipocereus pleurocarpus		SAm
Cissus ■ Vitaceae		
Cissus cactiformis		Afr
Cissus quadrangularis	edible-stemmed vine, climbing cactus	Afr, As
Cissus tuberosa		CAm
Claytonia ■ Portulacaceae		
Claytonia australasica	white purslane	Aus
Claytonia caroliniana		NAm
Claytonia lanceolata		NAm
Claytonia megarhiza		NAm
Claytonia parvifolia		NAm
Claytonia rosea		NAm
Claytonia virginica	spring beauty	NAm
Cleistocactus ■ Cactaceae		
Cleistocactus acanthurus		SAm
Cleistocactus anguinus		SAm
Cleistocactus baumannii	scarlet bugler, firecracker cactus	SAm
Cleistocactus brookei		SAm
Cleistocactus candelilla		SAm
Cleistocactus dependens		SAm
Cleistocactus fieldianus		SAm
Cleistocactus fusiflorus		SAm
Cleistocactus hyalacanthus		SAm
Cleistocactus icosagonus		SAm
Cleistocactus laniceps		SAm
Cleistocactus luribayensis		SAm
Cleistocactus morawetzianus		SAm
Cleistocactus parviflorus		SAm
Cleistocactus ritteri		SAm
Cleistocactus roezlii		SAm
Cleistocactus samaipatanus		SAm
Cleistocactus sepium		SAm
Cleistocactus serpens		SAm
Cleistocactus sextonianus		SAm
Cleistocactus smaragdiflorus		SAm
Cleistocactus strausii	silver torch cactus	SAm
Cleistocactus tenuiserpens		SAm
Cleistocactus tominensis		SAm
Cleistocactus tupizensis		SAm
Cleistocactus varispinus		SAm
Cleistocactus vulpis-cauda		SAm
Cleistocactus winteri	golden rat's tail cactus	Sam

Coleocephalocereus ■ CACTACEAE		
Coleocephalocereus aureus		SAm
Coleocephalocereus fluminensis		SAm
Coleocephalocereus goebelianus		SAm
Conicosia ■ MESEMBRYANTHEMACEAE		
Conicosia pugioniformis	pig salad, goslings	Afr
Conophytum ■ MESEMBRYANTHEMACEAE		
Conophytum species		Afr
Copiapoa ■ CACTACEAE		
Copiapoa bridgesii		SAm
Copiapoa calderana		SAm
Copiapoa cinerascens		SAm
Copiapoa cinerea		SAm
Copiapoa coquimbana		SAm
Copiapoa echinoides		SAm
Copiapoa humulis		SAm
Copiapoa hypogaea		SAm
Copiapoa krainziana		SAm
Copiapoa malletiana		SAm
Copiapoa marginata		SAm
Copiapoa megarhiza		SAm
Copiapoa montana		SAm
Copiapoa solaris		SAm
Copiapoa tenuissima		Sam
Corryocactus ■ CACTACEAE		
Corryocactus aureus		SAm
Corryocactus brachypetalus		SAm
Corryocactus brevistylus	guacalla	SAm
Corryocactus erectus		SAm
Corryocactus melanotrichus		SAm
Corryocactus pulquinensis		SAm
Corryocactus squarrosus		SAm
Coryphantha ■ CACTACEAE		
Coryphantha bergeriana		CAm
Coryphantha bumamma		CAm
Coryphantha clavata		CAm
Coryphantha compacta		CAm
Coryphantha cornifera	rhinoceros cactus	CAm
Coryphantha delaetiana		CAm
Coryphantha difficilis		CAm
Coryphantha durangensis		CAm
Coryphantha echinus	prickly beehive cactus	CAm
Coryphantha elephantidens	elephant's tooth	CAm
Coryphantha erecta		CAm
Coryphantha glanduligera		CAm
Coryphantha guerkeana		CAm
Coryphantha macromeris	nipple beehive cactus	CAm
Coryphantha maiz-tablasensis		CAm

Coryphantha nickelsiae		CAm
Coryphantha octacantha		CAm
Coryphantha odorata		CAm
Coryphantha ottonis	Indian head	CAm
Coryphantha pallida		CAm
Coryphantha poselgeriana		CAm
Coryphantha pseudoechinus		CAm
Coryphantha pycnacantha		CAm
Coryphantha radians		CAm
Coryphantha ramillosa	big bend cory cactus	CAm
Coryphantha recurvata	golden chested beehive cactus, Santa Cruz beehive	CAm
Coryphantha retusa		CAm
Coryphantha salm-dyckiana		CAm
Coryphantha scheeri		CAm
Coryphantha scolymoides		CAm
Coryphantha sulcata	finger cactus, nipple cactus	CAm
Coryphantha sulcolanata		CAm
Coryphantha unicornis		CAm
Coryphantha vaupeliana		CAm
Coryphantha wedermannii		CAm
Cotyledon ■ CRASSULACEAE		
Cotyledon adscendens		Afr
Cotyledon barbeyi	hoary navelwort	Afr
Cotyledon campanulata		Afr
Cotyledon cuneata		Afr
Cotyledon macrantha	pig's ears	Afr
Cotyledon orbiculata	pig's ears, *plakkie*	Afr
Cotyledon papillaris		Afr
Cotyledon tomentosa subsp. ladismithiensis	bear's paw, kitten paws	Afr
Cotyledon tomentosa subsp. *tomentosa*	bear's paw, kitten paws	Afr
Cotyledon undulata	silver crown, silver ruflles	Afr
Cotyledon velutina		Afr
Cotyledon woodii		Afr
Crassula ■ CRASSULACEAE		
Crassula alba		Afr
Crassula alstonii		Afr
Crassula aquatica		Eu, As, NAm
Crassula arborescens	silver jade plant, silver dollar, Chinese jade	Afr
Crassula argyrophylla		Afr
Crassula atropurpurea		Afr
Crassula barbata		Afr
Crassula barkleyi	rattlesnake crassula, *wurmplakkie*	Afr
Crassula brevifolia		Afr
Crassula capensis		Afr
Crassula capitella		Afr

Crassula coccinea	rock flower	Afr
Crassula columella		Afr
Crassula columnaris	*koesnaatjie*	Afr
Crassula congesta		Afr
Crassula corallina		Afr
Crassula cordata		Afr
Crassula cultrata	airplane propeller plant, propeller plant	Afr
Crassula deceptor		Afr
Crassula dejecta		Afr
Crassula deltoidea	silver beads	Afr
Crassula dentata		Afr
Crassula dependus		Afr
Crassula dichotoma		Afr
Crassula elegans	elegant crassula	Afr
Crassula ericoides		Afr
Crassula excilis		Afr
Crassula fascicularis		Afr
Crassula fusca		Afr
Crassula globularioides		Afr
Crassula helmsii		Afr
Crassula hemisphaerica	arab's turban	Afr
Crassula justi-corderoyi		Cult
Crassula lactea	flowering crassula, tailor's patch	Afr
Crassula lanuginosa		Afr
Crassula macowaniana		Afr
Crassula mesembryanthemopsis		Afr
Crassula montana		Afr
Crassula multicava	fairy crassula	Afr
Crassula muscosa	shoe-lace plant, moss cypress, princess pine, rattail cypress, toy cypress, watch-chain cypress	Afr
Crassula namaquensis		Afr
Crassula nemorosa		Afr
Crassula nudicaulis		Afr
Crassula obovata		Afr
Crassula obtusa		Afr
Crassula orbicularis		Afr
Crassula ovata	dollar plant, jade plant, jade tree	Afr
Crassula pellucida	pink buttons, trailing crassula	Afr
Crassula perfoliata var. *falcata*	airplane plant, airplane propellers, propeller plant, scarlet paint brush, sickle plant	Afr
Crassula perfoliata var. *perfoliata*		Afr
Crassula perforata	string of buttons, skewer plant	Afr
Crassula phlegmatoides		Afr
Crassula pubescens		Afr
Crassula pyramidalis		Afr
Crassula rubricaulis		Afr

Crassula rupestris	bead vine, buttons on a string, necklace vine, rosary vine	Afr
Crassula sarcocaulis	bonsai crassula	Afr
Crassula sarmentosa		Afr
Crassula schmidtii		Afr
Crassula sericea		Afr
Crassula setulosa		Afr
Crassula socialis		Afr
Crassula spathulata		Afr
Crassula streyi	purple-leaved fairy crassula	Afr
Crassula susannae		Afr
Crassula tecta		Afr
Crassula tetragona	baby pine of China, miniature pine tree	Afr
Crassula tomentosa		Afr
Crassula vaginata		Afr, As

×Cremneria ■ Crassulaceae		
×Cremneria expatriata (Cremnophila liguifolia × Echeveria microcalyx)		Cult
×Cremneria mutabilis (Cremnophila liguifolia × Echeveria carnicolor)		Cult
×Cremneria scaphylla		Cult

Cremnophila ■ Crassulaceae		
Cremnophila linguifolia		CAm
Cremnophila nutans		CAm

Cylindrophyllum ■ Mesembryanthemaceae		
Cylindrophyllum calamiforme		Afr
Cylindrophyllum comptonii		Afr
Cylindrophyllum dyeri		Afr

Cylindropuntia (see Opuntia)		

Cyphostemma ■ Vitaceae		
Cyphostemma bainesii	gouty vine	Afr
Cyphostemma cirrhosum		Afr
Cyphostemma cornigera		Afr
Cyphostemma currorii	cobas, *kobas*	Afr
Cyphostemma hereroensis		Afr
Cyphostemma juttae	wild grape, blue cobas, *bloukobas*	Afr
Cyphostemma laza		Afr
Cyphostemma uter		Afr

Dactylopsis digitata (see Phyllobolus digitatus)		

Dasylirion ■ Agavaceae		
Dasylirion longissimum	Mexican grass tree	CAm
Dasylirion wheeleri	common sotol, desert spoon	NAm

Decaryia ■ DIDIEREACEAE		
Decaryia madagascariensis		Afr
Deilanthe ■ MESEMBRYANTHEMACEAE		
Deilanthe peersii		Afr
Delosperma ■ MESEMBRYANTHEMACEAE		
Delosperma aberdeenense		Afr
Delosperma abyssinicum		Afr
Delosperma brunthaleri	Brunthaler's rock mesemb	Afr
Delosperma cooperi	hardy pink ice plant	Afr
Delosperma echinatum	prickly rock mesemb	Afr
Delosperma ecklonis		Afr
Delosperma expersum		Afr
Delosperma grandiflorum		Afr
Delosperma hallii		Afr
Delosperma herbeum	*wit bergvygie* (white mountain mesemb)	Afr
Delosperma lehmannii		Afr
Delosperma lineare		Afr
Delosperma lydenburgense		Afr
Delosperma nubigenum	hardy yellow ice plant	Afr
Delosperma obtusa		Afr
Delosperma pruinosum		Afr
Delosperma sutherlandii		Afr
Delosperma tadescantioides		Afr
Delosperma taylorii		Afr
Denmoza ■ CACTACEAE		
Denmoza erythrocephala		SAm
Denmoza rhodacantha		SAm
Didierea ■ DIDIEREACEAE		
Didierea madagascariensis	octopus tree	Afr
Didierea trollii	octopus tree	Afr
Didymaotus ■ MESEMBRYANTHEMACEAE		
Didymaotus lapidiformis	*tweelingvygie* (twin mesemb)	Afr
Dinteranthus ■ MESEMBRYANTHEMACEAE		
Dinteranthus inexpectatus		Afr
Dinteranthus microspermus		Afr
Dinteranthus pole-evansii	vegetable golf ball	Afr
Dinteranthus puberulus		Afr
Dinteranthus vanzylii		Afr
Dinteranthus wilmotianus		Afr
Dioscorea ■ DIOSCOREACEAE		
Dioscorea alata	white yam, water yam	Afr
Dioscorea amarantoides		SAm
Dioscorea balcanica		Eu
Dioscorea batatas	Chinese yam, cinnamon vine	As
Dioscorea bulbifera	air potato	Afr, As
Dioscorea cotinifolia		Afr
Dioscorea discolor		SAm

Dioscorea elephantipes	elephant's foot	Afr
Dioscorea hastifolia		Aus
Dioscorea macrostachya	yam	CAm
Dioscorea sylvatica	African wild yam	Afr
Dioscorea trifida	cush-cush, yampee	SAm, CAm
Diplosoma ■ Mesembryanthemaceae		
Diplosoma luckhoffii		Afr
Diplosoma retroversum	*eendvoetvygie* (duck foot mesemb)	Afr
Discocactus ■ Cactaceae		
Discocactus hartmannii		SAm
Discocactus heptacanthus		SAm
Discocactus horstii		SAm
Discocactus placentiformis		SAm
Discocactus pseudoinsignis		SAm
Discocactus subviridigriseus		SAm
Discocactus zehntneri		SAm
Disocactus ■ Cactaceae		
Disocactus ackermannii	red Christmas cactus	CAm
Disocactus alatus		CAm
Disocactus biformis		CAm
Disocactus eichlamii		CAm
Disocactus flagelliformis (=*Aporocactus flagelliformis*)	rat's tail cactus	CAm
Disocactus himantocladus		CAm
Disocactus ×*hybridus* (=*Epiphyllum* cultivars)	orchid cactus, Christmas cactus, epiphyllum, epi	CAm
Disocactus macranthus		CAm
Disocactus martianus		CAm
Disocactus nelsonii		CAm
Disocactus quezaltecus		CAm
Disocactus ramulosus		CAm
Disphyma ■ Mesembryanthemaceae		
Disphyma australe		Afr, Aus
Disphyma crassifolium	wishbone plant	Afr
Dorotheanthus ■ Mesembryanthemaceae		
Dorotheanthus bellidiformis	Livingstone daisy, *bokbaaivygie*	Afr
Dorotheanthus gramineus	narrow-leaved Livingstone daisy	Afr
Dracaena ■ Dracaenaceae / Agavaceae		
Dracaena aletriformis	African dracaena	Afr
Dracaena americana		CAm
Dracaena arborea	tree dracaena	Afr
Dracaena bicolor		Afr
Dracaena cincta		unknown
Dracaena concinna		Afr
Dracaena deremensis		Afr
Dracaena draco	dragon tree, dragon's blood tree	Afr
Dracaena elliptica		Afr
Dracaena fragrans	fragrant dracaena, corn plant	Afr

Dracaena goldieana		Afr
Dracaena hookeriana		Afr
Dracaena marmorata		As
Dracaena pearsonii		Afr
Dracaena phrynioides		Afr
Dracaena reflexa	pleomele, song of India	Afr
Dracaena sanderiana	Belgian evergreen	Afr
Dracaena surculosa	gold dust dracaena, spotted dracaena	Afr
Dracaena thalioides		Afr
Dracaena transvaalensis	curley-leaved dracaena	Afr
Dracaena umbraculifera		Afr
Dracophilus ■ MESEMBRYANTHEMACEAE		
Dracophilus species		Afr
Dregea ■ APOCYNACEAE		
Dregea sinensis		As
Drosanthemum ■ MESEMBRYANTHEMACEAE		
Drosanthemum bicolor	bicoloured dewflower	Afr
Drosanthemum candens	white dewflower	Afr
Drosanthemum collinum	yellow dewflower	Afr
Drosanthemum floribundum	pink dewflower	Afr
Drosanthemum hispidum	purple dewflower	Afr
Drosanthemum micans	haloed dewflower	Afr
Drosanthemum paxianum		Afr
Drosanthemum speciosum	dewflower, showy dewflower	Afr
Drosanthemum stokoei		Afr
Drosanthemum striatum	striped dewflower, *vleisbos, porseleinbos*	Afr
Dudleya ■ CRASSULACEAE		
Dudleya abramsii		NAm
Dudleya albiflora		NAm
Dudleya arizonica		NAm, CAm
Dudleya attenuata	Orcutt's liveforever, tapertip liveforever	NAm
Dudleya brittonii		NAm
Dudleya caespitosa	sea lettuce	NAm
Dudleya candelabrum		NAm
Dudleya candida		NAm
Dudleya cultrata		NAm
Dudleya cymosa		NAm
Dudleya densiflora		NAm
Dudleya edulis	mission lettuce, fingertips, ladies fingers	NAm
Dudleya farinosa		NAm
Dudleya greenei		NAm
Dudleya lanceolata		NAm
Dudleya linearis		NAm
Dudleya pulverulenta	chalk lettuce, chalk dudleya	NAm
Dudleya rigida		NAm
Dudleya saxosa		NAm
Dudleya stolonifera		NAm

Dudleya virens	alabaster plant	NAm
Dudleya viscida		NAm
Duvalia ■ APOCYNACEAE		
Duvalia species		Afr
Duvaliandra ■ APOCYNACEAE		
Duvaliandra dioscoridis		As
Ebracteola ■ MESEMBRYANTHEMACEAE		
Ebracteola derenbergiana		Afr
Ebracteola montis-moltkei		Afr
Ebracteola wilmaniae		Afr
Echeveria ■ CRASSULACEAE		
Echeveria acutifolia		CAm
Echeveria affinis		CAm
Echeveria agavoides	lipstick echeveria, molded wax agave	CAm
Echeveria albicans		CAm
Echeveria amoena		CAm
Echeveria amphoralis		CAm
Echeveria atropurpurea		CAm
Echeveria australis		CAm
Echeveria bella		CAm
Echeveria bicolor		SAm
Echeveria bifida		CAm
Echeveria carnicolor	coral echeveria	CAm
Echeveria chiapensis		CAm
Echeveria chihuahuaensis		CAm
Echeveria chilonensis		SAm
Echeveria ciliata		CAm
Echeveria coccinea		CAm
Echeveria craigii		CAm
Echeveria crenulata		CAm
Echeveria cuspidata		CAm
Echeveria dactylifera		CAm
Echeveria derenbergii	painted lady	CAm
Echeveria elegans	Mexican snow ball, white Mexican rose, Mexican gem	CAm
Echeveria fimbriata		CAm
Echeveria fulgens		CAm
Echeveria gibbiflora	coral star	CAm
Echeveria gigantea	giant echeveria	CAm
Echeveria ×gilva	green Mexican rose, wax rosette	Cult
Echeveria goldiana		CAm
Echeveria gracilis		CAm
Echeveria ×graessneri		Cult
Echeveria grandifolia		CAm
Echeveria halbingeri		CAm
Echeveria harmsii		CAm
Echeveria heterosepala		CAm

Echeveria humilis		CAm
Echeveria hyalina		CAm
Echeveria ×imbricata	hen and chickens	CAm
Echeveria johnsonii		SAm
Echeveria laui		CAm
Echeveria leucotricha	chenille plant	CAm
Echeveria lindsayana		CAm
Echeveria longissima		CAm
Echeveria lozanii		CAm
Echeveria lutea		CAm
Echeveria macdougallii		CAm
Echeveria maculata		CAm
Echeveria maxonii		CAm
Echeveria megacalyx		CAm
Echeveria minima		CAm
Echeveria montana		CAm
Echeveria moranii		CAm
Echeveria mucronata		CAm
Echeveria multicaulis	copper leaf, copper roses	CAm
Echeveria nodulosa		CAm
Echeveria nuda		CAm
Echeveria obtusifolia		CAm
Echeveria paniculata		CAm
Echeveria peacockii	peacock echeveria	CAm
Echeveria pilosa		CAm
Echeveria pinetorum		CAm
Echeveria pittieri		CAm
Echeveria platyphylla		CAm
Echeveria potosina		CAm
Echeveria pringlei	Pringle's echeveria	CAm
Echeveria prolifica		CAm
Echeveria pulchella		CAm
Echeveria pulidonis		CAm
Echeveria pulvinata	plush plant, chenille plant	CAm
Echeveria purpusorum		CAm
Echeveria quitensis		CAm
Echeveria racemosa		CAm
Echeveria rauschii		SAm
Echeveria recurvata		CAm
Echeveria rosea		CAm
Echeveria rubromarginata		CAm
Echeveria runyonii		CAm
Echeveria sanchez-mejoradae		CAm
Echeveria sayulensis		CAm
Echeveria schaffneri		CAm
Echeveria scheerii		CAm
Echeveria secunda	common echeveria	CAm

Echeveria semivestita		CAm
Echeveria sessiliflora		CAm
Echeveria setosa	Mexican firecracker	CAm
Echeveria shaviana	Mexican hens	CAm
Echeveria simulans		CAm
Echeveria skinneri		CAm
Echeveria spectabilis		CAm
Echeveria stolonifera		CAm
Echeveria strictiflora		CAm, NAm
Echeveria subrigida		CAm
Echeveria turgida		CAm
Echeveria vanvlietii		SAm
Echeveria venezuelensis		CAm
Echeveria walpoleana		CAm
Echeveria waltheri		CAm
Echeveria whitei		SAm
Echidnopsis ■ Apocynaceae		
Echidnopsis species		Afr, As
Echinocactus ■ Cactaceae		
Echinocactus grusonii	golden barrel cactus, mother-in-law's cushion	CAm
Echinocactus horizonthalonius	devil's head cactus	CAm
Echinocactus platyacanthus	giant barrel cactus	CAm
Echinocactus polycephalus	cottontop cactus	CAm
Echinocactus texensis	horse crippler, candy cactus	CAm
Echinocereus ■ Cactaceae		
Echinocereus adustus		CAm
Echinocereus barthelowanus		CAm
Echinocereus berlandieri	Berlandier's hedgehog cactus	CAm
Echinocereus brandegeei	strawberry cactus	CAm
Echinocereus chisoensis	Chisos Mountain hedgehog cactus	CAm
Echinocereus chloranthus		CAm
Echinocereus cinerascens		CAm
Echinocereus coccineus	Mexican claret cup	CAm
Echinocereus delaetii		CAm
Echinocereus engelmannii	dagger-spine hedgehog	CAm
Echinocereus enneacanthus	cob cactus	CAm
Echinocereus fendleri		CAm
Echinocereus ferreirianus	pinkflower hedgehog cactus	CAm
Echinocereus grandis		CAm
Echinocereus knippelianus		CAm
Echinocereus laui		CAm
Echinocereus leucanthus		CAm
Echinocereus longisetus		CAm
Echinocereus maritimus		CAm
Echinocereus octacanthus		CAm
Echinocereus palmeri		CAm
Echinocereus papillosus		CAm
Echinocereus pectinatus	comb hedgehog	CAm

Echinocereus pensilis	snake cactus	CAm
Echinocereus pentalophus	lady finger cactus	CAm
Echinocereus polyacanthus	Mojave mound cactus	CAm
Echinocereus poselgeri	sacasil	CAm
Echinocereus pseudopectinatus		CAm
Echinocereus pulchellus		CAm
Echinocereus reichenbachii		CAm
Echinocereus rigidissimus	Arizona rainbow hedgehog cactus	CAm
Echinocereus scheeri	Choyita	CAm
Echinocereus schmollii		CAm
Echinocereus sciurus		CAm
Echinocereus scopulorum	Sonoran rainbow cactus	CAm
Echinocereus stoloniferus		CAm
Echinocereus stramineus	straw-coloured hedgehog	CAm
Echinocereus subinermis		CAm
Echinocereus triglochidiatus	claret cup, strawberry cactus	CAm
Echinocereus viridiflorus	nylon hedgehog cactus	CAm
Echinocereus websterianus		CAm
Echinopsis ■ CACTACEAE		
Echinopsis ancistrophora		SAm
Echinopsis arachnacantha		SAm
Echinopsis aurea	golden easter lily cactus	SAm
Echinopsis backebergii		SAm
Echinopsis bertramiana		SAm
Echinopsis bruchii		SAm
Echinopsis calochlora		SAm
Echinopsis calorubra		SAm
Echinopsis camarguensis		SAm
Echinopsis candicans		SAm
Echinopsis chalaensis		SAm
Echinopsis chamaecereus	peanut cactus	SAm
Echinopsis chilensis		SAm
Echinopsis chrysantha		SAm
Echinopsis chrysochete		SAm
Echinopsis cinnabarina		SAm
Echinopsis comarapana		SAm
Echinopsis coquimbana		SAm
Echinopsis cuzcoensis		SAm
Echinopsis deserticola		SAm
Echinopsis eyriesii	pink Easter lily cactus	SAm
Echinopsis ferox		SAm
Echinopsis formosa		SAm
Echinopsis haematanha		SAm
Echinopsis hamatacantha		SAm
Echinopsis hertrichiana		SAm
Echinopsis herzogiana		SAm
Echinopsis huascha	red torch cactus	SAm
Echinopsis knuthiana		SAm

Echinopsis kratochviliana		SAm
Echinopsis kuehnrichii		SAm
Echinopsis lageniformis		SAm
Echinopsis lamprochlorus		SAm
Echinopsis laterita		SAm
Echinopsis leucantha		SAm
Echinopsis litoralis		SAm
Echinopsis longispina		SAm
Echinopsis macrogona		SAm
Echinopsis mamillosa		SAm
Echinopsis marsoneri		SAm
Echinopsis maximiliana		SAm
Echinopsis mirabilis		SAm
Echinopsis multiplex (see *E. oxygona*)		
Echinopsis obrepanda	violet easter lily cactus	SAm
Echinopsis oxygona (=*E. multiplex*)	Easter lily cactus, sea urchin cactus	SAm
Echinopsis pachanoi	San Pedro cactus	SAm
Echinopsis pampana		SAm
Echinopsis pasacana		SAm
Echinopsis pentlandii		SAm
Echinopsis peruvianus	San Pedro macho	SAm
Echinopsis polyancistra		SAm
Echinopsis pugionacantha		SAm
Echinopsis purpureopilosa		SAm
Echinopsis rhodotricha		SAm
Echinopsis saltensis		SAm
Echinopsis sanguiniflora		SAm
Echinopsis schickendantzii		SAm
Echinopsis schieliana		SAm
Echinopsis schreiteri		SAm
Echinopsis silvestrii		SAm
Echinopsis smrziana		SAm
Echinopsis spachiana	torch cactus, golden torch cactus	SAm
Echinopsis spiniflora		SAm
Echinopsis strigosa		SAm
Echinopsis taquimbalensis		SAm
Echinopsis tarijensis		SAm
Echinopsis tegeleriana		SAm
Echinopsis terscheckii		SAm
Echinopsis thelegona		SAm
Echinopsis thelegonoides		SAm
Echinopsis thionantha		SAm
Echinopsis tiegeliana		SAm
Echinopsis toralapana		SAm
Echinopsis torrecillasensis		SAm
Echinopsis trichosa		SAm

Echinopsis tubiflora		SAm
Echinopsis uyupampensis		SAm
Echinopsis volliana		SAm
Echinopsis walteri		SAm
Epiphyllum ■ Cactaceae		
Epiphyllum anguliger	fishbone cactus	CAm
Epiphyllum caudatum		CAm
Epiphyllum chrysocardium		CAm
Epiphyllum crenatum		CAm
Epiphyllum cultivars (see *Disocactus hybridus*)		
Epiphyllum hookeri		CAm
Epiphyllum lepidocarpum		CAm
Epiphyllum oxypetalum	white orchid cactus, night blooming cactus	CAm
Epiphyllum phyllanthus		CAm
Epiphyllum pumilum		CAm
Epiphyllum thomasianum		CAm
Epithelantha ■ Cactaceae		
Epithelantha micromeres	button cactus	NAm, CAm
Erepsia ■ Mesembryanthemaceae		
Erepsia aperta		Afr
Erepsia gracilis		Afr
Erepsia heteropetala		Afr
Erepsia inclaudens		Afr
Erepsia lacera		Afr
Erepsia mutabilis		Afr
Erepsia pillansii (=*Kensitia pillansii*)		Afr
Eriosyce ■ Cactaceae		
Eriosyce sandillon		SAm
Escobaria ■ Cactaceae		
Escobaria aguirreana		CAm
Escobaria albicolumnaria	silver lace cob cactus	NAm
Escobaria chihuahuensis		CAm
Escobaria dasyacantha	cob cactus	NAm, CAm
Escobaria emskoetteriana		CAm
Escobaria henricksonii		CAm
Escobaria hesteri		NAm
Escobaria lloydii		CAm
Escobaria minima		NAm
Escobaria missouriensis	Missouri foxtail cactus	NAm, CAm
Escobaria roseana		CAm
Escobaria sneedii	carpet foxtail cactus	NAm
Escobaria tuberculosa		NAm, CAm
Escobaria vivipara	beehive cactus	NAm, CAm
Escobaria zilziana		CAm
Escontria ■ Cactaceae		
Escontria chiotilla	chiotilla, jiotilla	CAm
Espostoa ■ Cactaceae		

Espostoa blossfeldiorum		SAm
Espostoa lanata	Peruvian old man cactus	SAm
Espostoa melanostele		SAm
Espostoa ritteri	Peruvian old man	SAm
Espostoa senilis	Peruvian old man	SAm
Espostoopsis ■ Cactaceae		
Espostoopsis dybowskii		SAm
Eulychnia ■ Cactaceae		
Eulychnia acida	copao	SAm
Eulychnia breviflora		SAm
Eulychnia castanea		SAm
Eulychnia iquiquensis		SAm
Eulychnia ritteri		SAm
Eulychnia saint-pieana		SAm
Euphorbia ■ Euphorbiaceae		
Euphorbia abyssinica		Afr
Euphorbia actinoclada		Afr
Euphorbia aeruginosa		Afr
Euphorbia aggregata	pincushion euphorbia	Afr
Euphorbia albertensis		Afr
Euphorbia alluaudii		Afr
Euphorbia ammak 'Variegata'		As
Euphorbia ampliphylla		Afr
Euphorbia anoplia		Afr
Euphorbia antiquorum		As
Euphorbia antisyphilitica		NAm
Euphorbia aphylla		Afr
Euphorbia arida		Afr
Euphorbia atrispina		Afr
Euphorbia atropurpurea		Afr
Euphorbia avasmontana		Afr
Euphorbia baioensis		Afr
Euphorbia ballyana		Afr
Euphorbia barnhartii		As
Euphorbia baylissii		Afr
Euphorbia beaumeriana		Afr
Euphorbia beharensis		Afr
Euphorbia bergeri		Afr
Euphorbia bougheyi		Afr
Euphorbia bravoana		Afr
Euphorbia breviarticulata		Afr
Euphorbia brevitorta		Afr
Euphorbia bubalina	buffalo euphorbia	Afr
Euphorbia bupleurifolia	miniature palm tree, miniature cycad	Afr
Euphorbia burmannii		Afr
Euphorbia buruana		Afr
Euphorbia bussei		Afr

Euphorbia cactus		Afr, As
Euphorbia caerulescens	*noors*, sweet *noors*	Afr
Euphorbia canariensis	Canary Island spurge	Afr
Euphorbia candelabrum		Afr
Euphorbia cap-saintemeniensis		Afr
Euphorbia caput-medusae	medusa's head, snake plant	Afr
Euphorbia cereiformis	milk barrel	Cult
Euphorbia clandestina	the soldier	Afr
Euphorbia classenii		Afr
Euphorbia clava		Afr
Euphorbia clavarioides	lion's spoor	Afr
Euphorbia clivicola		Afr
Euphorbia colliculina		Afr
Euphorbia columnaris		Afr
Euphorbia confinalis		Afr
Euphorbia cooperi	lesser candelabra tree	Afr
Euphorbia cryptospinosa		Afr
Euphorbia curvirama		Afr
Euphorbia cylindrifolia		Afr
Euphorbia davyi		Afr
Euphorbia dawei		Afr
Euphorbia decaryi		Afr
Euphorbia decepta		Afr
Euphorbia decidua		Afr
Euphorbia decipiens		Afr
Euphorbia deightonii		Afr
Euphorbia delphinensis		Afr
Euphorbia desmondii		Afr
Euphorbia dregeana		Afr
Euphorbia echinus		Afr
Euphorbia enopla		Afr
Euphorbia enormis		Afr
Euphorbia ephedroides		Afr
Euphorbia esculenta		Afr
Euphorbia evansii		Afr
Euphorbia excelsa		Afr
Euphorbia fasciculata		Afr
Euphorbia ferox	pincushion euphorbia	Afr
Euphorbia filiflora		Afr
Euphorbia fimbriata		Afr
Euphorbia flanaganii		Afr
Euphorbia fluminis		Afr
Euphorbia fortissima		Afr
Euphorbia franckiana		Afr
Euphorbia francoisii		Afr
Euphorbia franksiae		Afr
Euphorbia fruticosa		Afr

256

Euphorbia fusca		Afr
Euphorbia gemmea		Afr
Euphorbia globosa	globose spurge	Afr
Euphorbia gorgonis		Afr
Euphorbia graciliramea		Afr
Euphorbia grandialata		Afr
Euphorbia grandicornis	big horned euphorbia, cow horn	Afr
Euphorbia grandidens	big tooth euphorbia, naboom	Afr
Euphorbia grantii		Afr
Euphorbia greenwayi		Afr
Euphorbia griseola		Afr
Euphorbia groenewaldii		Afr
Euphorbia hadramautica		As
Euphorbia halipedicola		Afr
Euphorbia hamata	elephant's milk bush	Afr
Euphorbia handiensis		Afr
Euphorbia heptagona	milk barrel	Afr
Euphorbia heterochroma		Afr
Euphorbia hislopii		Afr
Euphorbia horrida	African milk barrel	Afr
Euphorbia hottentota		Afr
Euphorbia inconstantia		Afr
Euphorbia inermis		Afr
Euphorbia ingens	*naboom*, cactus euphorbia, candelabra tree	Afr
Euphorbia inornata		Afr
Euphorbia isacantha		Afr
Euphorbia jansenvillensis		Afr
Euphorbia kamerunica		Afr
Euphorbia knuthii		Afr
Euphorbia lactea	candelabra plant, mottled spurge, false cactus, hat-rack cactus, dragon bones	As
Euphorbia lactea 'Cristata'	crested euphorbia, frilled fan, elkhorn	As
Euphorbia lateriflora		Afr
Euphorbia ledienii	sour *noors*	Afr
Euphorbia lignosa		Afr
Euphorbia ×*lomii*	giant crown of thorns	Afr
Euphorbia longituberculosa		Afr
Euphorbia lophogona		Afr
Euphorbia loricata		Afr
Euphorbia malevola		Afr
Euphorbia mammilaris	corn cob, corkscrew	Afr
Euphorbia marlothiana		Afr
Euphorbia mauritanica	yellow milk bush, *melkbos*, jackal's food	Afr
Euphorbia meloformis	melon spurge	Afr
Euphorbia memoralis		Afr
Euphorbia meridionalis		Afr
Euphorbia micracantha		Afr
Euphorbia milii	crown of thorns, Christ thorn	Afr

Euphorbia mlanjeana		Afr
Euphorbia monteroi		Afr
Euphorbia muirii		Afr
Euphorbia multiceps		Afr
Euphorbia multiramosa		Afr
Euphorbia namibensis		Afr
Euphorbia neriifolia	hedge euphorbia, oleander spurge	CAm, SAm, As
Euphorbia nesemannii		Afr
Euphorbia nigrispina		Afr
Euphorbia nivulia		As
Euphorbia nubica		Afr
Euphorbia nubigens		Afr
Euphorbia obesa	Gingham golf ball, living baseball, Zulu hut, baseball plant	Afr
Euphorbia obtusifolia		Afr
Euphorbia officinarum		Afr
Euphorbia ornithopus	bird's foot euphorbia	Afr
Euphorbia pentagona		Afr
Euphorbia persistens		Afr
Euphorbia persistentifolia		Afr
Euphorbia petraea		Afr
Euphorbia pillansii		Afr
Euphorbia piscidermis	fish skin euphorbia	Afr
Euphorbia platyclada		Afr
Euphorbia poissonii		Afr
Euphorbia polyacantha	fishbone	Afr
Euphorbia polycephala		Afr
Euphorbia polygona	many-angled cactus euphorbia	Afr
Euphorbia pseudocactus		Afr
Euphorbia pseudoglobosa		Afr
Euphorbia pteroneura		CAm
Euphorbia pubiglans		Afr
Euphorbia pugniformis		Afr
Euphorbia pulvinata	pincushion euphorbia	Afr
Euphorbia punicea		CAm
Euphorbia ramipressa		Cult
Euphorbia regis-jubae		Afr
Euphorbia resinifera	official spurge	Afr
Euphorbia restituta		Afr
Euphorbia restricta		Afr
Euphorbia robecchii		Afr
Euphorbia royleana		As
Euphorbia samburensis		Afr
Euphorbia saxorum		Afr
Euphorbia schinzii		Afr
Euphorbia schoenlandii		Afr

258

Euphorbia sekukuniensis		Afr
Euphorbia septentrionalis		Afr
Euphorbia silenifolia		Afr
Euphorbia similiramea		Afr
Euphorbia sipolisii		SAm
Euphorbia squarrosa		Afr
Euphorbia stapfii		Afr
Euphorbia stellispina	star-spine	Afr
Euphorbia stellata		Afr
Euphorbia stenoclada	silver thicket	Afr
Euphorbia stolonifera		Afr
Euphorbia submammillaris		Afr
Euphorbia subsalsa		Afr
Euphorbia susannae		Afr
Euphorbia symmetrica		Afr
Euphorbia taruensis		Afr
Euphorbia tenuirama		Afr
Euphorbia tetragona	naboom	Afr
Euphorbia tirucalli	tiru-calli, pencil bush, rubber euphorbia, finger tree, pencil tree	Afr, As
Euphorbia tirucalli 'Sticks on Fire'	red pencil bush, red pencil tree	Cult
Euphorbia tortirama		Afr
Euphorbia trapifolia		Afr
Euphorbia triaculeata		Afr, As
Euphorbia triangularis	river euphorbia, chandelier tree	Afr
Euphorbia tridentata		Afr
Euphorbia trigona	African milk tree	unknown
Euphorbia tuberculata		Afr
Euphorbia tuberculatoides		Afr
Euphorbia tubiglans		Afr
Euphorbia turbiniformis		Afr
Euphorbia undulatifolia		Cult
Euphorbia valida		Afr
Euphorbia vallaris		Afr
Euphorbia vandermerwei		Afr
Euphorbia viguieri		Afr
Euphorbia virosa		Afr
Euphorbia wakefieldii		Afr
Euphorbia waterbergensis		Afr
Euphorbia wildii		Afr
Euphorbia wilmaniae		Afr
Euphorbia woodii		Afr
Euphorbia xantii		NAm
Euphorbia xylophylloides		Afr
Facheiroa ■ CACTACEAE		
Facheiroa ulei		SAm

259

Faucaria ■ Mesembryanthemaceae		
Faucaria albidens		Afr
Faucaria boscheana		Afr
Faucaria britteniae		Afr
Faucaria candida		Afr
Faucaria felina	tiger-jaw(s)	Afr
Faucaria lupina		Afr
Faucaria peersii		Afr
Faucaria subintegra		Afr
Faucaria tigrina	tiger-jaw(s)	Afr
Faucaria tuberculosa		Afr
Fenestraria ■ Mesembryanthemaceae		
Fenestraria aurantiaca	baby's toes, baby toes, window plant	Afr
Fenestraria rhopalophylla	baby's toes, baby toes, window plant	Afr
Ferocactus ■ Cactaceae		
Ferocactus chrysacanthus		CAm
Ferocactus cylindraceus	desert barrel cactus, compass barrel cactus	NAm, CAm
Ferocactus diguetii		CAm
Ferocactus echidne		CAm
Ferocactus emoryi		NAm, CAm
Ferocactus flavovirens		CAm
Ferocactus fordii		NAm
Ferocactus glaucescens	blue barrel cactus	CAm
Ferocactus gracilis		NAm
Ferocactus haematacanthus		CAm
Ferocactus hamatacanthus	Turk's head	NAm, CAm
Ferocactus histrix	porcupine barrel cactus, electrode cactus	CAm
Ferocactus latispinus	broad-spined barrel cactus, crow's claw cactus	CAm
Ferocactus macrodiscus		CAm
Ferocactus peninsulae		NAm
Ferocactus pilosus	red-spined barrel cactus, Mexican fire barrel cactus	CAm
Ferocactus potsii		CAm
Ferocactus reppenhagenii		CAm
Ferocactus robustus		CAm
Ferocactus schwarzii		CAm
Ferocactus viridescens	San Diego barrel cactus	NAm
Ferocactus wislizeni	fishhook barrel cactus	CAm
Fockea ■ Apocynaceae		
Fockea angustifolia	Kalahari kambro	Afr
Fockea crispa	mountain kambro, *bergkambro*	Afr
Fockea dammarana		Afr
Fockea edulis	kambro, common kambro	Afr
Fockea multiflora		Afr
Frailea ■ Cactaceae		
Frailea albicolumnaris		SAm
Frailea castanea		SAm
Frailea cataphracta		SAm

Frailea chiquitana		SAm
Frailea colombiana		SAm
Frailea curvispina		SAm
Frailea gracillima		SAm
Frailea grahliana		SAm
Frailea horstii		SAm
Frailea ignacionensis		SAm
Frailea knippeliana		SAm
Frailea lepida		SAm
Frailea mammifera		SAm
Frailea moseriana		SAm
Frailea perumbilicata		SAm
Frailea phaeodisca		SAm
Frailea pumila		SAm
Frailea pygmaea		SAm
Frailea schilinzkyana		SAm
Frithia ■ MESEMBRYANTHEMACEAE		
Frithia pulchra	fairy elephant's feet	Afr
Furcraea ■ AGAVACEAE		
Furcraea albispina		CAm
Furcraea bedinghausii		CAm
Furcraea cabuya	cabuya	CAm
Furcraea elegans		CAm
Furcraea flavoviridis		CAm
Furcraea foetida	Mauritius hemp, green aloe	CAm
Furcraea foetida var. mediopicta	variegated Mauritius hemp	
Furcraea hexapetala	Cuba hemp	CAm
Furcraea longaeva		CAm
Furcraea macdougalii		CAm
Furcraea pubescens		CAm
Furcraea selloa	false agave	CAm
Furcraea stricta		CAm
Furcraea tuberosa		CAm
×Gasteraloe ■ ASPHODELACEAE		
×Gasteraloe beguinii (Aloe aristata × Gasteria carinata var. verrucosa)		Afr
×Gasteraloe pethamensis (Aloe variegata × Gasteria carinata var. verrucosa)		Afr
×Gasterhaworthia ■ ASPHODELACEAE		
×Gasterhaworthia 'Royal Highness'		Afr
×Gasterhaworthia bayfieldii		Afr
×Gasterhaworthia holtzei		Afr
×Gasterhaworthia squarrosa		Afr

Gasteria ■ Asphodelaceae		
Gasteria acinacifolia		Afr
Gasteria angustiarum var. angustiarum		Afr
Gasteria angustiarum var. bayeri		Afr
Gasteria batesiana		Afr
Gasteria baylissiana		Afr
Gasteria bicolor var. bicolor		Afr
Gasteria bicolor var. liliputana		Afr
Gasteria carinata var. carinata		Afr
Gasteria carinata var. retusa		Afr
Gasteria carinata var. verrucosa		Afr
Gasteria ×cheilophylla		Afr
Gasteria croucheri		Afr
Gasteria disticha		Afr
Gasteria excelsa		Afr
Gasteria nitida var. armstrongii		Afr
Gasteria nitida var. nitida		Afr
Gasteria obliqua		Afr
Gasteria pillansii		Afr
Gasteria rawlinsonii		Afr
Gasteria vlokii		Afr
×Gastroloba ■ Asphodelaceae		
×Gastroloba apicroides		Afr
Gibbaeum ■ Mesembryanthemaceae		
Gibbaeum album		Afr
Gibbaeum angulipes		Afr
Gibbaeum cryptopodium		Afr
Gibbaeum dispar		Afr
Gibbaeum fissoides		Afr
Gibbaeum geminum		Afr
Gibbaeum gibbosum		Afr
Gibbaeum haagei		Afr
Gibbaeum heathii		Afr
Gibbaeum nebrownii		Afr
Gibbaeum pachypodium		Afr
Gibbaeum petrense		Afr
Gibbaeum pilosulum		Afr
Gibbaeum pubescens		Afr
Gibbaeum schwantesii		Afr
Gibbaeum velutinum		Afr
Glottiphyllum ■ Mesembryanthemaceae		
Glottiphyllum depressum	tortoise food	Afr
Glottiphyllum fragrans		Afr
Glottiphyllum latum		Afr
Glottiphyllum linguiforme	tongue-leaved mesemb	Afr
Glottiphyllum longum	tortoise food	Afr

Glottiphyllum nelii		Afr
Glottiphyllum oligocarpum		Afr
Glottiphyllum parvifolium		Afr
Glottiphyllum regium		Afr
Glottiphyllum semicylindricum		Afr
Graptopetalum ▪ CRASSULACEAE		
Graptopetalum amethystinum	jewel-leaf plant, lavender pebbles	CAm
Graptopetalum bellum (=*Tacitus bellus*)	*Tacitus bellus*	CAm
Graptopetalum filiferum		CAm
Graptopetalum grande		CAm
Graptopetalum macdougalii		NAm
Graptopetalum pachyphyllum	trailing ghost plant	CAm
Graptopetalum paraguayense	ghost plant, mother of pearl plant	CAm
Graptopetalum rusbyi		CAm, NAm
×*Graptophytum* ▪ CRASSULACEAE		
Graptophytum 'Anita' (*Graptopetalum filiferum* × *Pachyphytum oviferum*)		Cult
×*Graptosedum* ▪ CRASSULACEAE		
×*Graptosedum* 'Heswall' (*Graptopetalum bellum* × *Sedum suaveolens*)		Cult
×*Graptoveria* ▪ CRASSULACEAE		
×*Graptoveria* hybrids		Cult
Greenovia ▪ CRASSULACEAE		
Greenovia aizoon		Afr
Greenovia aurea	golden greenovia, green rose buds	Afr
Gymnocalycium ▪ CACTACEAE		
Gymnocalycium albiareolatum		SAm
Gymnocalycium andreae		SAm
Gymnocalycium anisitsii		SAm
Gymnocalycium baldianum	dwarf chin	SAm
Gymnocalycium bruchii		SAm
Gymnocalycium buenekeri		SAm
Gymnocalycium calochlorum		SAm
Gymnocalycium capillaense		SAm
Gymnocalycium cardenasianum		SAm
Gymnocalycium castellanosii		SAm
Gymnocalycium chiquitanum		SAm
Gymnocalycium denudatum	spider cactus	SAm
Gymnocalycium fleischerianum		SAm
Gymnocalycium gibbosum		SAm
Gymnocalycium horstii		SAm
Gymnocalycium hybopleurum		SAm
Gymnocalycium leeanum		SAm
Gymnocalycium marsoneri		SAm

Gymnocalycium mazanense		SAm
Gymnocalycium megalothelos		SAm
Gymnocalycium mesopotamicum		SAm
Gymnocalycium mihanovichii var. *friedrichii*		SAm
Gymnocalycium mihanovichii var. mihanovichii	red cap, plaid cactus, moon cactus, ruby ball	SAm
Gymnocalycium monvillei		SAm
Gymnocalycium moserianum		SAm
Gymnocalycium mostii		SAm
Gymnocalycium multiflorum		SAm
Gymnocalycium paraguayense		SAm
Gymnocalycium pflanzii		SAm
Gymnocalycium platense		SAm
Gymnocalycium quehlianum	rose plaid cactus	SAm
Gymnocalycium ragonesei		SAm
Gymnocalycium saglionis	giant chin cactus	SAm
Gymnocalycium schickendantzii		SAm
Gymnocalycium schroederianum		SAm
Gymnocalycium spegazzinii		SAm
Gymnocalycium stellatum		SAm
Gymnocalycium tillianum		SAm
Gymnocalycium uruguayense		SAm
Gymnocalycium vatteri		SAm
Haageocereus ■ Cactaceae		
Haageocereus decumbens		SAm
Haageocereus limensis		SAm
Haageocereus multangularis		SAm
Haageocereus versicolor		SAm
Haageocereus weberbaueri		SAm
Harrisia ■ Cactaceae		
Harrisia adscendens		SAm
Harrisia earlei		CAm
Harrisia eriophora		CAm, NAm
Harrisia gracilis		CAm, NAm
Harrisia guelichii		SAm
Harrisia jusbertii		Cult
Harrisia martinii	moon cactus	SAm
Harrisia nashii		CAm
Harrisia pomanensis	apple cactus	SAm
Harrisia portoricensis	Porto Rico apple cactus	CAm
Harrisia regelii		SAm
Harrisia tetracantha		SAm
Harrisia tortuosa		SAm
Hatiora ■ Cactaceae		
Hatiora rosea	pink Easter cactus	SAm

Hatiora salicornioides	bottle cactus, bottle plant, drunkard's dream, spice cactus	SAm
Hatiora* ×*gaertneri	red Easter cactus	SAm
Hatiora ×*graeseri* (*H. rosea* × *H. gaertneri*)		Cult
Haworthia ■ ASPHODELACEAE		
Haworthia 'Kuentzii'		Cult
Haworthia 'Ollasonii'		Cult
Haworthia altilinea		Afr
Haworthia angustifolia		Afr
Haworthia arachnoidea	cobweb aloe	Afr
Haworthia aranea		Afr
Haworthia archeri		Afr
Haworthia aristata		Afr
Haworthia armstrongii		Afr
Haworthia asperula		Afr
Haworthia attenuata		Afr
Haworthia batesiana		Afr
Haworthia blackburniae		Afr
Haworthia bolusii		Afr
Haworthia bruynsii		Afr
Haworthia chloracantha		Afr
Haworthia coarctata		Afr
Haworthia ×*coarctatoides*		Afr
Haworthia comptoniana		Afr
Haworthia cooperi* var. *dielsiana		Afr
Haworthia curta		Afr
Haworthia ×*cuspidata*	star window plant	Afr
Haworthia cymbiformis		Afr
Haworthia emelyae		Afr
Haworthia fasciata	zebra haworthia	Afr
Haworthia floribunda		Afr
Haworthia glabrata		Afr
Haworthia glauca		Afr
Haworthia graminifolia	grass haworthia	Afr
Haworthia heidelbergensis		Afr
Haworthia integra		Afr
Haworthia kewensis		Afr
Haworthia kingiana		Afr
Haworthia koelmaniorum		Afr
Haworthia limifolia	fairy washboard	Afr
Haworthia lockwoodii		Afr
Haworthia longiana		Afr
Haworthia magnifica		Afr
Haworthia ×*mantelii* (*H. cuspidata* × *H. truncata*)		Afr
Haworthia marginata		Afr
Haworthia marumiana		Afr

Haworthia maughanii		Afr
Haworthia maxima (= *H. pumila; H. margaritifera*)	pearl haworthia	Afr
Haworthia mclarenii		Afr
Haworthia minima		Afr
Haworthia mirabilis		Afr
Haworthia mucronata		Afr
Haworthia mutica		Afr
Haworthia nigra		Afr
Haworthia nortieri		Afr
Haworthia notabilis		Afr
Haworthia parksiana		Afr
Haworthia pearsonii		Afr
Haworthia pehlemanniae		Afr
Haworthia ×perplexa		Afr
Haworthia poellnitziana		Afr
Haworthia pulchella		Afr
Haworthia pumila (see *H. maxima*)		
Haworthia radula		Afr
Haworthia recurva		Afr
Haworthia reinwardtii		Afr
Haworthia reticulata		Afr
Haworthia retusa		Afr
Haworthia ×rigida		Cult
Haworthia rubrobrunnea		Afr
Haworthia rycroftiana		Afr
Haworthia scabra		Afr
Haworthia semiviva		Afr
Haworthia smitii		Afr
Haworthia sordida		Afr
Haworthia springbokvlakensis		Afr
Haworthia starkiana		Afr
Haworthia ×tauteae		Afr
Haworthia tessellata subsp. **tessellata**		Afr
Haworthia tortuosa		Afr
Haworthia translucens		Afr
Haworthia truncata	horse teeth	Afr
Haworthia turgida		Afr
Haworthia variegata		Afr
Haworthia venosa		Afr
Haworthia viscosa		Afr
Haworthia wittebergensis		Afr
Haworthia woolleyi		Afr
Haworthia xiphiophylla		Afr
Haworthia zantneriana		Afr
Heliocereus ■ Cᴀᴄᴛᴀᴄᴇᴀᴇ		

266

Heliocereus aurantiacus (=*Disocactus aurantiacus*)		CAm
Heliocereus cinnabarinus (=*Disocactus cinnabarinus*)		CAm
Heliocereus schrankii (=*Disocactus schrankii*)		CAm
Heliocereus speciosus (=*Disocactus speciosus*)		CAm
Hereroa ■ MESEMBRYANTHEMACEAE		
Hereroa calycina		Afr
Hereroa carinans		Afr
Hereroa dyeri (=*Rhombophyllum dolabriforme*)		
Hereroa granulata		Afr
Hereroa herrei		Afr
Hereroa hesperanthera		Afr
Hereroa incurva		Afr
Hereroa muirii		Afr
Hereroa puttkameriana	clock plant	Afr
Hereroa uncipetala		Afr
Herrea ■ MESEMBRYANTHEMACEAE		
Herrea elongata		Afr
Herreanthus ■ MESEMBRYANTHEMACEAE		
Herreanthus meyeri		Afr
Hesperaloe ■ AGAVACEAE		
Hesperaloe campanulata	bell flower hesperaloe	CAm
Hesperaloe funifera	giant hesperaloe	CAm
Hesperaloe parviflora	red yucca	CAm
Hoodia ■ APOCYNACEAE		
Hoodia alstonii		Afr
Hoodia currorii subsp. *currorii*		Afr
Hoodia currorii subsp. *lugardii*		Afr
Hoodia dregei		Afr
Hoodia flava	yellow *ghaap*	Afr
Hoodia gordonii	common *ghaap*, bitter *ghaap*	Afr
Hoodia grandis		Afr
Hoodia juttae		Afr
Hoodia officinalis subsp. *delaetiana*		Afr
Hoodia officinalis subsp. *officinalis*		Afr
Hoodia parviflora		Afr
Hoodia pedicellata		Afr
Hoodia pilifera subsp. annulata	purple *ghaap*	Afr
Hoodia pilifera subsp. pilifera		Afr
Hoodia ruschii	queen of the Namib	Afr
Hoodia triebneri		Afr

Hoodiopsis triebneri (see *Hoodia triebneri*)		

Hoya ■ APOCYNACEAE		
Hoya australis		Aus
Hoya carnosa	wax plant, wax flower, porcelain flower	As
Hoya lanceolata subsp. *bella*	miniature wax plant	As
Hoya lanceolata subsp. *lanceolata*		As
Huernia ■ APOCYNACEAE		
Huernia hystrix	toad plant	Afr
Huernia keniensis	Kenyan dragon flower	Afr
Huernia pillansii	cocklebur	Afr
Huernia schneideriana	red dragon flower	Afr
Huernia zebrina	toad plant, owl-eyes, little owl	Afr
Huerniopsis ■ APOCYNACEAE		
Huerniopsis atrosanguinea		Afr
Huerniopsis decipiens		Afr
Hylocereus ■ CACTACEAE		
Hylocereus calcaratus		CAm
Hylocereus costaricensis	Costa Rica night-blooming cactus	CAm
Hylocereus escuintlensis		CAm
Hylocereus extensus		CAm
Hylocereus guatemalensis		CAm
Hylocereus lemairei		CAm
Hylocereus minutiflorus		CAm
Hylocereus monacanthus		CAm
Hylocereus ocamponis		CAm
Hylocereus polyrhizus	pitajaya	CAm
Hylocereus stenopterus		CAm
Hylocereus triangularis		CAm
Hylocereus trigonus	strawberry pear	CAm
Hylocereus undatus	dragon fruit, night-blooming cactus	CAm
Hylotelephium ■ CRASSULACEAE		
Hylotelephium 'Autumn Joy' (*H. telephium* × *H. spectabile*)		Cult
Hylotelephium anacampseros	love-restorer	Eu, As
Hylotelephium caucasicum		Eu, As
Hylotelephium cauticolum		As
Hylotelephium cyaneum		As
Hylotelephium erythrostictum		As
Hylotelephium ewersii		Eu, As
Hylotelephium hybrids		Cult
Hylotelephium pallescens		As
Hylotelephium pluricaule		As
Hylotelephium populifolium		As
Hylotelephium sieboldii		As
Hylotelephium sordidum		As
Hylotelephium spectabile	ice plant, orpine, live-forever	As

Hylotelephium tatorinowii		As
Hylotelephium telephioides		NAm
Hylotelephium telephium	orpine, live-forever	Eu, As
Hylotelephium ussuriense		As
Hylotelephium verticillatum		As

Jacobsenia ■ MESEMBRYANTHEMACEAE		
Jacobsenia hallii		Afr
Jacobsenia kolbei		Afr
Jasminocereus ■ CACTACEAE		
Jasminocereus thouarsii		CAm
Jatropha ■ EUPHORBIACEAE		
Jatropha podagrica	gout plant, tartoga, Australian bottle tree, spicy jatropha	CAm
Jensenobotrya ■ MESEMBRYANTHEMACEAE		
Jensenobotrya lossowiana	bunch-of-grapes	Afr
Jordaaniella ■ MESEMBRYANTHEMACEAE		
Jordaaniella clavifolia		Afr
Jordaaniella cuprea		Afr
Jordaaniella dubia	beach mesemb, creeping mesemb	Afr
Jordaaniella uniflora		Afr
Jovibarba ■ CRASSULACEAE		
Jovibarba heuffelii		Eu
Jovibarba hirta		Eu
Jovibarba sobolifera	hen-and-chickens	Eu
Jovibarba velenovskyi		Eu
Juttadinteria ■ MESEMBRYANTHEMACEAE		
Juttadinteria albata		Afr
Juttadinteria decumbens		Afr
Juttadinteria deserticola		Afr
Juttadinteria kovismontana		Afr
Juttadinteria longipetala		Afr
Juttadinteria simpsonii		Afr
Juttadinteria suavissima		Afr

Kalanchoe ■ CRASSULACEAE		
Kalanchoe beauverdii	sotre-sotry	Afr
Kalanchoe beharensis	donkey's ears, felt plant, felt bush	Afr
Kalanchoe bentii		Afr
Kalanchoe blossfeldiana	flaming Katy, florist kalanchoe	Afr
Kalanchoe crenata		Afr, SAm
Kalanchoe daigremontiana	devil's backbone, flopper	Afr
Kalanchoe delagonensis	chandelier plant	Afr
Kalanchoe eriophylla		Afr
Kalanchoe farinacea		Afr
Kalanchoe fedtschenkoi	kalanchoe stonecrop, lavender scallops	Afr
Kalanchoe flammea		Afr
Kalanchoe gastonis-bonnieri	donkey's ears, life plant	Afr

Kalanchoe glaucescens		Afr
Kalanchoe gracilipes		Afr
Kalanchoe gracilipes × *K. manginii*		Cult
Kalanchoe grandiflora		Afr
Kalanchoe hildbrandtii		Afr
Kalanchoe jongmansii		Afr
Kalanchoe ×kewensis (*K. flammea* × *K. bentii*)		Cult
Kalanchoe laciniata	Christmas tree kalanchoe, fir tree kalanchoe	Afr
Kalanchoe lateritia		Afr
Kalanchoe laxiflora		Afr
Kalanchoe longiflora		Afr
Kalanchoe manginii		Afr
Kalanchoe marmorata	penwiper plant	Afr
Kalanchoe millottii		Afr
Kalanchoe miniata		Afr
Kalanchoe nyikae		Afr
Kalanchoe orgyalis		Afr
Kalanchoe peltata		Afr
Kalanchoe petitiana		Afr
Kalanchoe pinnata		Afr
Kalanchoe porphyrocalyx		Afr
Kalanchoe prolifera	blooming boxes	Afr
Kalanchoe pumila		Afr
Kalanchoe quartiniana		Afr
Kalanchoe rhombopilosa		Afr
Kalanchoe rotundifolia		Afr
Kalanchoe schizophylla		Afr
Kalanchoe sexangularis		Afr
Kalanchoe synsepala	cup kalanchoe, walking kalanchoe	Afr
Kalanchoe thyrsiflora	paddle plant	Afr
Kalanchoe tomentosa	panda plant, pussy ears	Afr
Kalanchoe tubiflora (see *K. delagonensis*)		
Kalanchoe uniflora		Afr
Kalanchoe 'Wendy' (*K. miniata* × *K. porphyrocalyx*)		Cult
Kensitia pillansii (see *Erepsia pillansii*)		
Kleinia ■ ASTERACEAE		
Kleinia abyssinica		Afr
Kleinia amaniensis		Afr
Kleinia anteuphorbium		Afr
Kleinia fulgens	scarlet kleinia	Afr
Kleinia galpinii		Afr
Kleinia grandiflora		As
Kleinia grantii		Afr

Kleinia gregorii	peppermint stick	Afr
Kleinia implexa		Afr
Kleinia leptophylla		Afr, As
Kleinia longiflora	sjambok bush	Afr
Kleinia madagascarensis		Afr
Kleinia mweroensis		Afr
Kleinia neriifolia		Afr
Kleinia odora		Afr, As
Kleinia pendula		Afr, As
Kleinia petraea		Afr
Kleinia picticaulis		Afr
Kleinia polytoma		Afr
Kleinia saginata		Afr
Kleinia scottii		Afr
Kleinia squarrosa		Afr
Kleinia stapeliiformis		Afr
Kleinia subulifolia		Afr

Lachenalia ■ HYACINTHACEAE		
Lachenalia contaminata	Cape cowslip, *viooltjie*	
Lampranthus ■ MESEMBRYANTHEMACEAE		
Lampranthus amoenus	purple garden vygie, midday flower	
Lampranthus aurantiacus		Afr
Lampranthus aureus	orange garden vygie, golden vygie	Afr
Lampranthus bicolor		Afr
Lampranthus blandus	pink garden vygie	Afr
Lampranthus coccineus	red garden vygie	Afr
Lampranthus comptonii		Afr
Lampranthus conspicuus		Afr
Lampranthus copiosus	ice plant	Afr
Lampranthus coralliflorus	mauve garden vygie	Afr
Lampranthus deltoides (see *Oscularia deltoides*)		Afr
Lampranthus emarginatus		Afr
Lampranthus falcatus		Afr
Lampranthus haworthii	Haworth's garden vygie	Afr
Lampranthus multiradiatus	creeping garden vygie, ice plant	Afr
Lampranthus primivernus	ice plant	Afr
Lampranthus promontorii		Afr
Lampranthus roseus	rose garden vygie	Afr
Lampranthus spectabilis	Tresco garden vygie, trailing ice plant	Afr
Lapidaria ■ MESEMBRYANTHEMACEAE		
Lapidaria margaretae	rock mesemb, karoo rose	Afr
Larryleachia ■ APOCYNACEAE		
Larryleachia cactiformis var. *cactiformis*		Afr
Larryleachia cactiformis var. *felina*		Afr

Larryleachia marlothii		Afr
Larryleachia perlata		Afr
Larryleachia picta		Afr
Lavrania ■ APOCYNACEAE		
Lavrania haagnerae		Afr
Ledebourea ■ HYACINTHACEAE		
Ledebourea socialis	silver squill	Afr
Leipoldtia ■ MESEMBRYANTHEMACEAE		
Leipoldtia species		Afr
Lenophyllum ■ CRASSULACEAE		
Lenophyllum acutifolium		CAm
Lenophyllum guttatum		CAm
Lenophyllum pusillum		CAm, NAm
Lenophyllum texanum		NAm
Lenophyllum weinbergii		CAm
Leocereus ■ CACTACEAE		
Leocereus bahiensis		SAm
Lepismium ■ CACTACEAE		
Lepismium cruciforme		SAm
Lepismium houlletianum		SAm
Lepismium ianthothele		SAm
Lepismium lumbricoides		SAm
Lepismium micranthum		SAm
Lepismium monacantha		SAm
Lepismium warmingianum		SAm
Leptocereus ■ CACTACEAE		
Leptocereus weingartianus		CAm
Leuchtenbergia ■ CACTACEAE		
Leuchtenbergia principis	agave cactus	CAm
Lewisia ■ PORTULACACEAE		
Lewisia brachycalyx		NAm
Lewisia cantelovii		NAm
Lewisia columbiana		NAm
Lewisia congdonii		NAm
Lewisia cotyledon		NAm
Lewisia disepala		NAm
Lewisia kelloggii		NAm
Lewisia leana		NAm
Lewisia nevadensis		NAm
Lewisia oppositifolia		NAm
Lewisia pygmaea		NAm
Lewisia rediviva	bitterroot	NAm
Lewisia triphylla		NAm
Lewisia tweedyi		NAm
Lewisia ×*whiteae* (*L. cotyledon* × *L. leana*)		NAm
Lithops ■ MESEMBRYANTHEMACEAE		
Lithops species	stone plants	Afr

Lophophora ■ Cactaceae		
Lophophora diffusa	peyote	CAm
Lophophora williamsii	mescal, peyote	CAm, NAm
Machairophyllum ■ Mesembryanthemaceae		
Machairophyllum acuminatum	large-leaved dagger plant	Afr
Machairophyllum albidum		Afr
Machairophyllum cookii		Afr
Maihuenia ■ Cactaceae		
Maihuenia patagonica		SAm
Maihuenia poeppigii	chupa sangre	SAm
Malephora ■ Mesembryanthemaceae		
Malephora crocea var. crocea	finger vygie, *vingerkanna*, ice plant, coppery mesemb	Afr
Malephora crocea var. purpureo-crocea		Afr
Malephora engleriana		Afr
Malephora herrei		Afr
Malephora lutea		Afr
Malephora thunbergii		Afr
Mammillaria ■ Cactaceae		
Mammillaria albescens		CAm
Mammillaria albicans		CAm
Mammillaria albicoma		CAm
Mammillaria albilanata		CAm
Mammillaria anniana		CAm
Mammillaria arida		CAm
Mammillaria armillata		NAm
Mammillaria aureilanata		CAm
Mammillaria aurihamata		CAm
Mammillaria backebergiana		CAm
Mammillaria barbata		CAm
Mammillaria baumii		CAm
Mammillaria baxteriana		CAm
Mammillaria bella		CAm
Mammillaria beneckei		CAm
Mammillaria blossfeldiana		NAm
Mammillaria bocasana	powder puff cactus	CAm
Mammillaria bocensis		CAm
Mammillaria bombycina	silken pincushion	CAm
Mammillaria boolii		CAm
Mammillaria brandegeei		CAm
Mammillaria brauneana		CAm
Mammillaria bravoae		CAm
Mammillaria calacantha		CAm
Mammillaria camptotricha	bird's nest cactus	CAm
Mammillaria candida		CAm
Mammillaria canelensis		CAm

273

Mammillaria capensis		NAm
Mammillaria carmenae		CAm
Mammillaria carnea		CAm
Mammillaria carretii		CAm
Mammillaria chionocephala		CAm
Mammillaria coahuilensis		CAm
Mammillaria columbiana		CAm
Mammillaria compressa	mother of hundreds	CAm
Mammillaria craigii		CAm
Mammillaria crucigera		CAm
Mammillaria decipiens		CAm
Mammillaria deherdtiana		CAm
Mammillaria densispina		CAm
Mammillaria dioica	strawberry cactus	NAm
Mammillaria discolor		CAm
Mammillaria dixanthocentron		CAm
Mammillaria dodsonii		CAm
Mammillaria dumetorum		CAm
Mammillaria duoformis		CAm
Mammillaria eichlamii		CAm
Mammillaria elongata	golden stars, lady finger cactus	CAm
Mammillaria eriacantha		CAm
Mammillaria erythrosperma		CAm
Mammillaria fera-rubra		CAm
Mammillaria formosa		CAm
Mammillaria fraileana		CAm
Mammillaria gaumeri		CAm
Mammillaria geminispina	whitey	CAm
Mammillaria gigantea		CAm
Mammillaria glassii		CAm
Mammillaria goldii		CAm
Mammillaria goodridgei		CAm
Mammillaria gracilis	thimble cactus	CAm
Mammillaria grahamii	fishhook cactus	NAm
Mammillaria grusonii		CAm
Mammillaria guelzowiana		CAm
Mammillaria guerreronis		CAm
Mammillaria gummifera		CAm
Mammillaria haageana		CAm
Mammillaria hahniana	old lady cactus	CAm
Mammillaria halei		CAm
Mammillaria hamata		CAm
Mammillaria heidiae		CAm
Mammillaria herrerae		CAm
Mammillaria heyderi	little nipple cactus	CAm, NAm
Mammillaria humboldtii		CAm
Mammillaria hutchisoniana		NAm

Mammillaria insularis		CAm
Mammillaria jaliscana		CAm
Mammillaria johnstonii		CAm
Mammillaria karwinskiana		CAm
Mammillaria kewensis		CAm
Mammillaria klissingiana		CAm
Mammillaria kraehenbuehlii		CAm
Mammillaria lasiacantha	lacespine nipple cactus	CAm, NAm
Mammillaria laui		CAm
Mammillaria lenta		CAm
Mammillaria leucantha		CAm
Mammillaria leucocentra		CAm
Mammillaria lloydii		CAm
Mammillaria longicoma		CAm
Mammillaria longiflora		CAm
Mammillaria longimamma		CAm
Mammillaria magallanii		CAm
Mammillaria magnifica		CAm
Mammillaria magnimamma	nipple cactus	CAm
Mammillaria mainiae	counter-clockwise fishhook	CAm, NAm
Mammillaria mammilaris		CAm
Mammillaria maritima		NAm
Mammillaria marksiana		CAm
Mammillaria matudae		CAm
Mammillaria mazatlanensis		CAm
Mammillaria meiacantha		CAm, NAm
Mammillaria melaleuca		CAm
Mammillaria melanocentra		CAm
Mammillaria mendeliana		CAm
Mammillaria mercadensis		CAm
Mammillaria meyranii		CAm
Mammillaria microhelia		CAm
Mammillaria mieheana		CAm
Mammillaria milleri		CAm, NAm
Mammillaria moelleriana		CAm
Mammillaria mollendorffiana		CAm
Mammillaria morganiana		CAm
Mammillaria muehlenpfordtii		CAm
Mammillaria multidigitata		CAm
Mammillaria mundtii		CAm
Mammillaria mystax		CAm
Mammillaria napina		CAm
Mammillaria nejapensis		CAm
Mammillaria neopalmeri		CAm
Mammillaria nivosa	woolly nipple cactus	CAm
Mammillaria nunezii		CAm
Mammillaria painteri		CAm

Mammillaria parkinsonii	owl's eyes	CAm
Mammillaria pectinifera		CAm
Mammillaria peninsularis		NAm
Mammillaria pennispinosa		CAm
Mammillaria perbella		CAm
Mammillaria petrophila		CAm
Mammillaria petterssonii		CAm
Mammillaria phitauiana		CAm
Mammillaria picta		CAm
Mammillaria pilcayensis		CAm
Mammillaria pilispina		CAm
Mammillaria plumosa	feather cactus	CAm
Mammillaria polyedra		CAm
Mammillaria polythele		CAm
Mammillaria pondii		CAm
Mammillaria poselgeri		CAm
Mammillaria pottsii	rattail cactus	CAm, NAm
Mammillaria pringlei		CAm
Mammillaria prolifera	Texas nipple cactus	CAm, NAm
Mammillaria pseudoperbella		CAm
Mammillaria pubispina		CAm
Mammillaria pygmaea		CAm
Mammillaria rekoi		CAm
Mammillaria rettigiana		CAm
Mammillaria rhodantha		CAm
Mammillaria roseoalba		CAm
Mammillaria rubida		CAm
Mammillaria saboae		CAm
Mammillaria sartorii		CAm
Mammillaria schiedeana		CAm
Mammillaria schumannii		CAm
Mammillaria scrippsiana		CAm
Mammillaria sempervivi		CAm
Mammillaria senilis		CAm
Mammillaria setispina		NAm
Mammillaria sheldonii	Sheldon's pincushion	CAm
Mammillaria sinistrohamata		CAm
Mammillaria sonorensis		CAm
Mammillaria sphacelata	longmamma nipple cactus	CAm
Mammillaria sphaerica		CAm, NAm
Mammillaria spinosissima		CAm
Mammillaria standleyi		CAm
Mammillaria stella-de-tacubaya		CAm
Mammillaria supertexta		CAm
Mammillaria surculosa		CAm
Mammillaria swinglei		CAm
Mammillaria tesopacensis		CAm

Mammillaria tetrancistra	California pincushion	CAm, NAm
Mammillaria theresae		CAm
Mammillaria thornberi	clustered fishhook pincushion	CAm, NAm
Mammillaria uncinata		CAm
Mammillaria vetula		CAm
Mammillaria viperiana		CAm
Mammillaria viridiflora		CAm, NAm
Mammillaria voburnensis		CAm
Mammillaria wiesingeri		CAm
Mammillaria wildii		CAm
Mammillaria winterae		CAm
Mammillaria woodsii		CAm
Mammillaria wrightii	Wright's nipple cactus	CAm, NAm
Mammillaria yaquensis		CAm
Mammillaria zahniana		CAm
Mammillaria zeilmanniana		CAm
Mammillaria zephyranthoides		CAm
Mammillaria zeyeriana		CAm
Matucana ■ CACTACEAE		
Matucana aurantiaca		SAm
Matucana aureiflora		SAm
Matucana haynei		SAm
Matucana madisoniorum		SAm
Matucana myriacantha		SAm
Matucana oreodoxa		SAm
Matucana paucicostata		SAm
Matucana ritteri		SAm
Matucana weberbaueri		SAm
Melocactus ■ CACTACEAE		
Melocactus ×albicephalus		SAm
Melocactus azureus	Turk's cap cactus	SAm
Melocactus bahiensis		SAm
Melocactus broadwayi		CAm
Melocactus concinnus		SAm
Melocactus conoideus		SAm
Melocactus curvispinus		CAm, SAm
Melocactus ernestii		SAm
Melocactus glaucescens		SAm
Melocactus harlowii		CAm
Melocactus intortus		CAm
Melocactus levitestatus		SAm
Melocactus macracanthos		CAm
Melocactus matanzanus	dwarf Turk's cap cactus	CAm
Melocactus neryi		SAm
Melocactus oreas		SAm
Melocactus peruvianus		SAm
Melocactus salvadorensis		SAm

Melocactus violaceus		SAm
Melocactus zehntneri		SAm
Mesembryanthemum ■ Mᴇꜱᴇᴍʙʀʏᴀɴᴛʜᴇᴍᴀᴄᴇᴀᴇ		
Mesembryanthemum crystallinum	ice plant	Afr
Mestoklema ■ Mᴇꜱᴇᴍʙʀʏᴀɴᴛʜᴇᴍᴀᴄᴇᴀᴇ		
Mestoklema species		Afr
Meyerophytum ■ Mᴇꜱᴇᴍʙʀʏᴀɴᴛʜᴇᴍᴀᴄᴇᴀᴇ		
Meyerophytum meyeri var. *holgatense*		Afr
Meyerophytum meyeri var. *meyeri*		Afr
Micranthocereus ■ Cᴀᴄᴛᴀᴄᴇᴀᴇ		
Micranthocereus polyanthus		SAm
Mila ■ Cᴀᴄᴛᴀᴄᴇᴀᴇ		
Mila caespitosa		SAm
Mitrophyllum ■ Mᴇꜱᴇᴍʙʀʏᴀɴᴛʜᴇᴍᴀᴄᴇᴀᴇ		
Mitrophyllum mitratum	clock plant, calendar plant, bishop's cap mesemb	Afr
Monadenium ■ Eᴜᴘʜᴏʀʙɪᴀᴄᴇᴀᴇ		
Monadenium cannellii		Afr
Monadenium coccineum		Afr
Monadenium echinulatum		Afr
Monadenium elegans		Afr
Monadenium invenustum		Afr
Monadenium laeve		Afr
Monadenium lugardiae	false euphorbia	Afr
Monadenium magnificum		Afr
Monadenium rhizophorum		Afr
Monadenium ritchiei		Afr
Monadenium rubellum		Afr
Monadenium schubei		Afr
Monadenium spectabile		Afr
Monadenium spinescens		Afr
Monadenium stapelioides		Afr
Monadenium stoloniferum		Afr
Monadenium torrei		Afr
Monanthes ■ Cʀᴀꜱꜱᴜʟᴀᴄᴇᴀᴇ		
Monanthes anagensis		Afr
Monanthes brachycaulon		Afr
Monanthes laxiflora		Afr
Monanthes muralis		Afr
Monanthes pallens		Afr
Monanthes polyphylla		Afr
Monanthes subcrassicaulis		Afr
Monilaria ■ Mᴇꜱᴇᴍʙʀʏᴀɴᴛʜᴇᴍᴀᴄᴇᴀᴇ		
Monilaria chrysoleuca		Afr
Monilaria moniliformis		Afr
Monilaria pisiformis		Afr

Montia ■ Portulacaceae		
Montia chamissoi		NAm
Montia perfoliata	miner's lettuce, winter purslane, Cuban spinach	NAm
Montia sibirica	Siberian purslane	NAm
Muiria ■ Mesembryanthemaceae		
Muiria hortenseae	schmoo plant	Afr
Myrtillocactus ■ Cactaceae		
Myrtillocactus cochal		NAm
Myrtillocactus geometrizans	myrtle cactus, raisin cactus, blue candle	CAm
Myrtillocactus schenckii	garambullo, whortleberry cactus	CAm
Namibia ■ Mesembryanthemaceae		
Namibia cinerea		Afr
Namibia pomonae		Afr
Nananthus ■ Mesembryanthemaceae		
Nananthus aloides		Afr
Nananthus transvaalensis		Afr
Nananthus vittatus		Afr
Nananthus wilmaniae		Afr
Neobuxbaumia ■ Cactaceae		
Neobuxbaumia euphorbioides		CAm
Neobuxbaumia macrocephala		CAm
Neobuxbaumia mezcalaensis		CAm
Neobuxbaumia polylopha	cone cactus	CAm
Neobuxbaumia tetetzo	tetetzo	CAm
Neohenricia ■ Mesembryanthemaceae		
Neohenricia sibbettii	coral plant	Afr
Neolloydia ■ Cactaceae		
Neolloydia conoidea	Chihuahuan beehive	CAm, NAm
Neolloydia gielsdorfiana		CAm
Neolloydia horripila		CAm
Neolloydia knuthiana		CAm
Neolloydia laui		CAm
Neolloydia lophophoroides		CAm
Neolloydia mandragora		CAm
Neolloydia pseudomacrochele		CAm
Neolloydia pseudopectinata		CAm
Neolloydia saueri		CAm
Neolloydia schmiedickeana		CAm
Neolloydia smithii		CAm
Neolloydia valdeziana		CAm
Neolloydia viereckii		CAm
Neoporteria ■ Cactaceae		
Neoporteria aricensis		SAm
Neoporteria bulbocalyx		SAm
Neoporteria chilensis		SAm
Neoporteria clavata		SAm

Neoporteria confinis		SAm
Neoporteria curvispina		SAm
Neoporteria horrida		SAm
Neoporteria islayensis		SAm
Neoporteria jussieui		SAm
Neoporteria napina		SAm
Neoporteria nidus		SAm
Neoporteria occulta		SAm
Neoporteria odieri		SAm
Neoporteria paucicostata		SAm
Neoporteria reichei		SAm
Neoporteria strausiana		SAm
Neoporteria subgibbosa		SAm
Neoporteria taltalensis		SAm
Neoporteria umadeave		SAm
Neoporteria villosa		SAm
Neoporteria wagenknechtii		SAm
Neoraimondia ■ CACTACEAE		
Neoraimondia arequipensis		SAm
Neoraimondia herzogiana	caripari	SAm
Neowerdermannia ■ CACTACEAE		
Neowerdermannia chilensis		SAm
Neowerdermannia vorwerkii		SAm
Nolina recurvata (see *Beaucarnia*)		
Nopalxochia (see *Epiphyllum, Disocactus*)		
Notocactus leninghausii (see *Parodia leninghausii*)		
Obregonia ■ CACTACEAE		
Obregonia denegrii	artichoke cactus	CAm
Odontophorus ■ MESEMBRYANTHEMACEAE		
Odontophorus angustifolius		Afr
Odontophorus marlothii		Afr
Odontophorus nanus		Afr
Oophytum ■ MESEMBRYANTHEMACEAE		
Oophytum nanum		Afr
Oophytum oviforme		Afr
Opuntia ■ CACTACEAE		
Opuntia acanthocarpa		CAm, NAm
Opuntia alexanderi		SAm
Opuntia aoracantha		SAm
Opuntia arbuscula		CAm, NAm
Opuntia arenaria		CAm, NAm
Opuntia articulata	paper-spined cactus	SAm
Opuntia atrispina	dark-spined prickly pear	CAm
Opuntia auberi		CAm
Opuntia aurantiaca	tiger-pear	SAm
Opuntia austrina		NAm

Opuntia azurea	coyotillo	CAm
Opuntia basilaris	beavertail cactus	CAm, NAm
Opuntia beckeriana		unknown
Opuntia bergeriana		unknown
Opuntia bigelovii	teddy-bear cholla	CAm, NAm
Opuntia boliviana		SAm
Opuntia bradtiana		CAm
Opuntia brasiliensis		SAm
Opuntia bravoana		CAm
Opuntia bulbispina		CAm
Opuntia burrageana		CAm
Opuntia cantabrigiensis		unknown
Opuntia chlorotica		CAm, NAm
Opuntia cholla	chain-link cholla	NAm
Opuntia clavarioides		SAm
Opuntia clavata		NAm
Opuntia cochenillifera		CAm
Opuntia compressa		NAm
Opuntia corrugata		SAm
Opuntia crassa		unknown
Opuntia curassavica		CAm
Opuntia cylindrica		SAm
Opuntia decumbens		CAm
Opuntia dejecta	spiny nopal	CAm
Opuntia echinocarpa		CAm, NAm
Opuntia erinacea		NAm
Opuntia exaltata		SAm
Opuntia falcata		CAm
Opuntia ficus-indica	prickly pear, Indian fig, barbary fig	CAm
Opuntia floccosa		SAm
Opuntia fragilis	brittle cactus, fragile prickly pear	NAm
Opuntia fulgida	chain-fruit cholla	CAm, NAm
Opuntia glomerata		SAm
Opuntia hyptiacantha		CAm
Opuntia imbricata	chain-link cactus, chain cholla	CAm, NAm
Opuntia invicta		NAm
Opuntia kleiniae		CAm, NAm
Opuntia kuehnrichiana		NAm
Opuntia lagopus		SAm
Opuntia lanceolata		unknown
Opuntia leptocaulis		CAm, NAm
Opuntia leucotricha		CAm
Opuntia lindheimeri		CAm
Opuntia littoralis	coastal prickly pear	CAm, NAm
Opuntia macracantha		CAm
Opuntia macrocentra	black-spine prickly pear	CAm, NAm
Opuntia macrorhiza	plains prickly pear	CAm, NAm

Opuntia marenae		CAm
Opuntia marnieriana		CAm
Opuntia maxima		Cult
Opuntia microdasys	rabbit-ears, bunny-ears, polka dot cactus	CAm
Opuntia mieckleyi		SAm
Opuntia miquelii		SAm
Opuntia moelleri		CAm
Opuntia molinensis		NAm
Opuntia monacantha	common prickly pear	SAm
Opuntia moniliformis		CAm
Opuntia munzii		NAm
Opuntia nigrispina		SAm
Opuntia ovata		SAm
Opuntia pachypus		SAm
Opuntia pailana		CAm
Opuntia paraguayensis		SAm
Opuntia parishii		CAm, NAm
Opuntia parryi		CAm, NAm
Opuntia pentlandii		SAm
Opuntia phaeacantha	Mojave prickly pear	CAm, NAm
Opuntia picardoi		NAm
Opuntia pilifera		CAm
Opuntia platyacantha		SAm
Opuntia polyacantha		CAm, NAm
Opuntia prolifera		CAm, NAm
Opuntia puberula		CAm
Opuntia pubescens		CAm, SAm
Opuntia pycnantha		CAm
Opuntia quimilo		SAm
Opuntia ramosissima		CAm, NAm
Opuntia repens	roving prickly pear	CAm
Opuntia retrorsa		SAm
Opuntia robusta	silver dollar	CAm
Opuntia rosarica		NAm
Opuntia rosea		CAm
Opuntia rubescens		CAm
Opuntia rufida	cow blinder	CAm, NAm
Opuntia salmiana		SAm
Opuntia santamaria		CAm
Opuntia santa-rita	purple prickly pear, Santa Rita prickly pear	CAm, NAm
Opuntia scheeri		CAm
Opuntia schickendantzii		NAm
Opuntia schottii		CAm, NAm
Opuntia soehrensii		SAm
Opuntia sphaerica		SAm
Opuntia spinosior		CAm, NAm
Opuntia spinosissima		CAm

Opuntia stenarthra		SAm
Opuntia stenopetala		CAm
Opuntia streptacantha		CAm
Opuntia stricta	Australian pest pear, coastal prickly pear	CAm, NAm
Opuntia strigil	marble fruit prickly pear	CAm, NAm
Opuntia subulata		SAm
Opuntia sulphurea		SAm
Opuntia tesajo		NAm
Opuntia tomentosa	woolly-joint prickly pear	CAm
Opuntia tuna	elephant ear prickly pear, tuna prickly pear	CAm
Opuntia tunicata	sheathed cholla	CAm, NAm
Opuntia velutina		CAm
Opuntia verschaffeltii		SAm
Opuntia versicolor		CAm, NAm
Opuntia vestita		SAm
Opuntia vilis		CAm
Opuntia whipplei		NAm
Orbea ■ Apocynaceae		
Orbea lutea subsp. lutea	yellow carrion flower	Afr
Orbea variegata	common carrion flower, Cape fritillary, toad cactus, starfish cactus	Afr
Orbeanthus ■ Apocynaceae		
Orbeanthus conjunctus		Afr
Orbeanthus hardyi		Afr
Orbeopsis ■ Apocynaceae		
Orbeopsis species		Afr
Oreocereus ■ Cactaceae		
Oreocereus celsianus	old man of the Andes	SAm
Oreocereus doelzianus	old man of the Andes	SAm
Oreocereus hempelianus		SAm
Oreocereus leucotrichus		SAm
Oreocereus pseudofossulatus		SAm
Oreocereus trollii	old man of the mountain	SAm
Orostachys ■ Crassulaceae		
Orostachys aggregata		As
Orostachys chanetii		As
Orostachys erubescens		As
Orostachys fimbriata		As
Orostachys furusei		As
Orostachys iwarenge		As
Orostachys malacophylla		As
Orostachys spinosa		As
Oroya ■ Cactaceae		
Oroya borchersii		SAm
Oroya peruviana		SAm
Ortegocactus ■ Cactaceae		
Ortegocactus macdougallii		CAm

283

Oscularia ■ MESEMBRYANTHEMACEAE		
Oscularia deltoides	sandstone *vygie*	Afr

Othonna ■ ASTERACEAE		
Othonna arborescens		Afr
Othonna capensis	little-pickles	Afr
Othonna dentata		Afr
Othonna euphorbioides		Afr
Othonna quercifolia		Afr
Othonna retrofracta		Afr
Othonna triplinervia		Afr

Pachycereus ■ CACTACEAE		
Pachycereus grandis		CAm
Pachycereus hollianus		CAm
Pachycereus marginatus	organ-pipe cactus, Mexican fence cactus	CAm
Pachycereus militaris		CAm
Pachycereus pectin-aboriginum		CAm
Pachycereus pringlei	giant Mexican cereus, Mexican giant	CAm
Pachycereus schottii	whisker cactus	CAm
Pachycereus weberi		CAm

Pachycymbium ■ APOCYNACEAE		
Pachycymbium species		Afr, As

Pachyphytum ■ CRASSULACEAE		
Pachyphytum bracteosum		NAm
Pachyphytum compactum		NAm
Pachyphytum fittkaui		NAm
Pachyphytum glutinicaule		NAm
Pachyphytum hookeri		NAm
Pachyphytum longifolium		NAm
Pachyphytum oviferum	moonstones	NAm
Pachyphytum viride		NAm
Pachyphytum werdermanii		NAm

Pachypodium ■ APOCYNACEAE		
Pachypodium baronii		Afr
Pachypodium bispinosum		Afr
Pachypodium brevicaule		Afr
Pachypodium decaryi		Afr
Pachypodium densiflorum		Afr
Pachypodium geayi	hairy-leaf pachypodium	Afr
Pachypodium horombense		Afr
Pachypodium lamerei	smooth-leaf pachypodium, Madagascar bottle tree	Afr
Pachypodium lealii		Afr
Pachypodium namaquanum	Namaqualand pachypodium, elephant's trunk, *halfmens*	Afr
Pachypodium rosulatum		Afr
Pachypodium rutenbergianum		Afr
Pachypodium saundersii	bottle tree	Afr

Pachypodium succulentum		Afr
×*Pachyveria* ■ Crassulaceae		
×*Pachyveria clavata* (*Echeveria* sp. × *Pachyphytum bracteosum*) ×		Cult
×*Pachyveria clevelandii* (*Echeveria* sp. × *Pachyphytum bracteosum*) ×		Cult
×*Pachyveria glauca* (*Pachyphytum compactum* × *Echeveria* sp.)		Cult
×*Pachyveria mirabilis* (*Echeveria scheeri* × *Pachyphytum bracteosum*)		Cult
×*Pachyveria pachyphytoides* (*Echeveria gibbiflora* 'Metallica' × *Pachyphytum bracteosum*)		Cult
×*Pachyveria scheideckeri* (*Echeveria secunda* × *Pachyphytum bracteosum*)		Cult
×*Pachyveria sobrina*		Cult
×*Pachyveria sodalis*		Cult
Parodia ■ Cactaceae		
Parodia alacriportana		SAm
Parodia allosiphon		SAm
Parodia aureicentra		SAm
Parodia ayopayana		SAm
Parodia brevihamata		SAm
Parodia buenekeri		SAm
Parodia buiningii		SAm
Parodia caespitosa		SAm
Parodia chrysacanthion	golden powder puff	SAm
Parodia claviceps		SAm
Parodia comarapana		SAm
Parodia concinna		SAm
Parodia crassigibba		SAm
Parodia erinacea		SAm
Parodia erythrantha		SAm
Parodia faustiana		SAm
Parodia formosa		SAm
Parodia gibbulosa		SAm
Parodia gracilis		SAm
Parodia graessneri		SAm
Parodia haselbergii	scarlet ball cactus	SAm
Parodia herteri		SAm
Parodia heteracantha		SAm
Parodia horstii		SAm
Parodia leninghausii	golden ball cactus, yellow tower	SAm
Parodia maassii		SAm
Parodia magnifica	yellow ball cactus	SAm

Parodia mairanana		SAm
Parodia mammulosa	Tom Thumb cactus	SAm
Parodia microsperma		SAm
Parodia miguillensis		SAm
Parodia mueller-melchersii		SAm
Parodia mutabilis		SAm
Parodia neohorstii		SAm
Parodia nivosa		SAm
Parodia ocampoi		SAm
Parodia ottonis		SAm
Parodia penicillata		SAm
Parodia procera		SAm
Parodia rigidispina		SAm
Parodia rutilans		SAm
Parodia schuetziana		SAm
Parodia schumanniana		SAm
Parodia schwebsiana		SAm
Parodia scopa	silver ball cactus	SAm
Parodia stuemeri		SAm
Parodia succinea		SAm
Parodia tuberculata		SAm
Parodia warasii		SAm
Parodia wedermanniana		SAm
Pectinaria ■ APOCYNACEAE		
Pectinaria species		Afr
Pedilanthus ■ EUPHORBIACEAE		
Pedilanthus bracteatus	candellila	NAm, CAm
Pedilanthus cymbiferus		CAm
Pedilanthus macrocarpus	slipper plant	CAm
Pedilanthus tithymaloides	zig-zag plant, Jacob's ladder, devil's backbone, ribbon cactus	NAm, CAm
Pediocactus ■ CACTACEAE		
Pediocactus bradyi	Marble Canyon cactus	NAm
Pediocactus knowltonii	Knowlton's cactus	NAm
Pediocactus paradinei	kaibab pincushion cactus	NAm
Pediocactus peeblesianus	Peeble's Navajo cactus	NAm
Pediocactus sileri	Siler pincushion cactus	NAm
Pediocactus simpsonii	mountain cactus	NAm
Pelargonium ■ GERANIACEAE		
Pelargonium carnosum		Afr
Pelargonium ceratophyllum		Afr
Pelargonium cotyledonis		Afr
Pelargonium crithmifolium	samphire-leaved geranium	Afr
Pelargonium echinatum	cactus geranium, sweetheart geranium	Afr
Pelargonium fulgidum		Afr
Pelargonium gibbosum	gouty geranium, knotted geranium	Afr
Pelargonium peltatum	ivy geranium, hanging geranium	Afr

Pelargonium tetragonum	square-stack cranesbill	Afr
Pelecyphora ■ CACTACEAE		
Pelecyphora aselliformis		CAm
Pelecyphora strobiliformis	pinecone cactus	CAm
Peniocereus ■ CACTACEAE		
Peniocereus greggii	night-blooming cereus	CAm, NAm
Peniocereus johnstonii		NAm
Peniocereus maculatus		CAm
Peniocereus serpentinus		CAm
Peniocereus striatus	dahlia-rooted cereus	CAm, NAm
Peniocereus viperinus		CAm
Pereskia ■ CACTACEAE		
Pereskia aculeata	Barbados gooseberry, West Indian gooseberry	CAm, SAm
Pereskia bleo		CAm
Pereskia grandifolia	rose cactus	SAm
Pereskia lychnidiflora		CAm
Pereskia nemorosa		SAm
Pereskia sacharosa		SAm
Pereskia weberiana		SAm
Pereskiopsis ■ CACTACEAE		
Pereskiopsis aquosa	tasajillo	CAm
Pereskiopsis diguetii		CAm
Pereskiopsis gatesii		NAm
Pereskiopsis porteri		CAm
Pereskiopsis rotundifolia		CAm
Phyllobolus ■ MESEMBRYANTHEMACEAE		
Phyllobolus digitatus subsp. *digitatus*	hitchhiker plant, *vingertjie-en-duimpie* (finger and thumb)	Afr
Phyllobolus digitatus subsp. *littlewoodii*		Afr
Piaranthus ■ APOCYNACEAE		
Piaranthus species		Afr
Pilosocereus ■ CACTACEAE		
Pilosocereus alensis		CAm
Pilosocereus arrabidae		SAm
Pilosocereus catingicola		SAm
Pilosocereus chrysacanthus		CAm
Pilosocereus chrysostele		SAm
Pilosocereus coerulescens		SAm
Pilosocereus collinsii		CAm
Pilosocereus glaucochrous		SAm
Pilosocereus gounellei		SAm
Pilosocereus hapalacanthus		SAm
Pilosocereus lanuginosus		SAm
Pilosocereus leucocephalus	woolley torch	CAm
Pilosocereus moritzianus		SAm
Pilosocereus pentaedrophorus		SAm

Pilosocereus piauhyensis		SAm
Pilosocereus purpusii		CAm
Pilosocereus royenii	Royen's tree cactus	CAm
Plectranthus ■ LAMIACEAE		
Plectranthus madagascariensis	variegated plectranthus	Afr
Plectranthus neochilus	lobster flower, poor man's lavender	Afr
Plectranthus oertendahlii		Afr
Plectranthus saccatus		Afr
Plectranthus verticillatus		Afr
Pleiospilos ■ MESEMBRYANTHEMACEAE		
Pleiospilos bolusii	split rock, mimicry plant, living rock cactus	Afr
Pleiospilos compactus		Afr
Pleiospilos nelii	split rock, splitrock, cleftstone, mimicry plant	Afr
Pleiospilos simulans	liver plant	Afr
Plumeria ■ APOCYNACEAE		
Plumeria alba	white frangipani, West Indian jasmine	CAm
Plumeria obtusa	frangipani	CAm
Plumeria pudica	frangipani	CAm
Plumeria rubra	red frangipani	CAm
Polaskia ■ CACTACEAE		
Polaskia chende		CAm
Polaskia chichipe		CAm
Portulaca ■ PORTULACACEAE		
Portulaca grandiflora	moss rose, rose moss, portulaca, sun plant, eleven-o'clock	SAm
Portulaca oleracea	purslane, pussley, kitchen-garden purslane	Cosm
Portulaca pilosa	shaggy garden purslane	
Portulacaria ■ PORTULACACEAE		
Portulacaria afra var. afra	pork bush, elephant bush, *spekboom*	Afr
Portulacaria afra var. *foliis-variegatis*	variegated elephant bush	Afr
Portulacaria afra var. *macrophylla*	large-leaved elephant bush	Afr
Portulacaria afra var. *microphylla*	small-leaved elephant bush	Afr
Psammophora ■ MESEMBRYANTHEMACEAE		
Psammophora species	glue plant	Afr
Psilocaulon ■ MESEMBRYANTHEMACEAE		
Psilocaulon arenosum		Afr
Psilocaulon ciliatum		Afr
Psilocaulon dinteri	scorpion plant	Afr
Psilocaulon marlothii		Afr
Pterocactus ■ CACTACEAE		
Pterocactus fischeri		SAm
Pterocactus kuntzei		SAm
Pterocactus valentinii		SAm
Pterodiscus ■ PEDALIACEAE		

Pterodiscus angustifolius		Afr
Pterodiscus aurantiacus		Afr
Pterodiscus coeruleus		Afr
Pterodiscus kellerianus		Afr
Pterodiscus luridus		Afr
Pterodiscus ruspolii		Afr
Pterodiscus speciosus	*sandkambro*	Afr
Quaqua ■ APOCYNACEAE		
Quaqua incarnata		Afr
Quiabentia ■ CACTACEAE		
Quiabentia zehntneri		SAm
Rabiea ■ MESEMBRYANTHEMACEAE		
Rabiea lesliei		Afr
Rabiea albinota		Afr
Rabiea albipuncta		Afr
Raphionacme ■ APOCYNACEAE		
Raphionacme brownii		Afr
Raphionacme burkei		Afr
Raphionacme daronii		Afr
Raphionacme elata		Afr
Raphionacme hirsuta		Afr
Raphionacme keayi		Afr
Rathbunia alamosensis (see *Stenocereus alamosensis*)		CAm
Rebutia ■ CACTACEAE		
Rebutia albiflora		SAm
Rebutia albopectinata		SAm
Rebutia arenacea		SAm
Rebutia aureiflora		SAm
Rebutia candiae		SAm
Rebutia canigueralii		SAm
Rebutia cylindrica		SAm
Rebutia deminuta		SAm
Rebutia einsteinii		SAm
Rebutia famatinensis		SAm
Rebutia fidaiana		SAm
Rebutia fiebrigii		SAm
Rebutia glomeriseta		SAm
Rebutia heliosa		SAm
Rebutia krainziana		SAm
Rebutia krugeri		SAm
Rebutia kupperiana		SAm
Rebutia margarethae		SAm
Rebutia marsoneri		SAm

Rebutia mentosa		SAm
Rebutia minuscula	red crown cactus	SAm
Rebutia neocumingii		SAm
Rebutia neumanniana		SAm
Rebutia pseudodeminuta		SAm
Rebutia pulchra		SAm
Rebutia pygmaea		SAm
Rebutia senilis		SAm
Rebutia spegazziniana		SAm
Rebutia spinosissima		SAm
Rebutia steinbachii		SAm
Rebutia steinmannii		SAm
Rebutia taratensis		SAm
Rebutia tiraquensis		SAm
Rebutia vizcarrae		SAm
Rebutia wessneriana		SAm
Rebutia xanthocarpa		SAm
Rhinephyllum ■ MESEMBRYANTHEMACEAE		
Rhinephyllum species		Afr
Rhipsalis ■ CACTACEAE		
Rhipsalis baccifera	rope cactus, mistletoe cactus	SAm,CAm, Afr, As
Rhipsalis cereoides		SAm
Rhipsalis cereuscula		SAm
Rhipsalis clavata		SAm
Rhipsalis crispata		SAm
Rhipsalis dissimilis		SAm
Rhipsalis elliptica		SAm
Rhipsalis floccosa		SAm
Rhipsalis gracilis		SAm
Rhipsalis hadrosoma		SAm
Rhipsalis megalantha		SAm
Rhipsalis mesembryanthoides	mesemb cactus	SAm
Rhipsalis micrantha		SAm
Rhipsalis oblonga		SAm
Rhipsalis pachyptera		SAm
Rhipsalis paradoxa	chain rhipsalis	SAm
Rhipsalis pentaptera		SAm
Rhipsalis pilocarpa		SAm
Rhipsalis pulvinigera		SAm
Rhipsalis puniceodiscus		SAm
Rhipsalis trigona		SAm
Rhodiola ■ CRASSULACEAE		
Rhodiola atropurpurea		As
Rhodiola bupleuroides		As
Rhodiola dumulosa		As
Rhodiola fastigiata		As
Rhodiola heterodonta		As

Rhodiola himalensis		As
Rhodiola hobsonii		As
Rhodiola integrifolia		As, NAm
Rhodiola kirilowii		As
Rhodiola primuloides		As
Rhodiola purpureoviridis		As
Rhodiola quadrifida		As
Rhodiola rhodantha		NAm
Rhodiola rosea	roseroot, rose-root	As
Rhodiola semenowii		As
Rhodiola sinuata		As
Rhodiola stephanii		As
Rhodiola tibetica		As
Rhodiola wallichiana		As
Rhodiola yunnanensis		As
Rhombophyllum ■ Mesembryanthemaceae		
Rhombophyllum dolabriforme		Afr
Rhombophyllum nelii		Afr
Rhombophyllum rhomboideum		Afr
Rhytidocaulon ■ Apocynaceae		
Rhytidocaulon fulleri		As
Rhytidocaulon macrolobum		As
Rhytidocaulon paradoxum		Afr
Rhytidocaulon piliferum		Afr
Rhytidocaulon sheilae		As
Rhytidocaulon subscandens		Afr
Rosularia ■ Crassulaceae		
Rosularia adenotricha		As
Rosularia aizoon		As
Rosularia chrysantha		Eu
Rosularia globulariifolia		Eu
Rosularia haussknechtii		As
Rosularia lineata		As
Rosularia rechingeri		As
Rosularia sedoides		As
Rosularia sempervivum		As
Rosularia serpentinica		Eu
Rosularia serrata		Eu
Ruschia ■ Mesembryanthemaceae		
Ruschia acuminata		Afr
Ruschia caroli	purple mountain mesemb	Afr
Ruschia crassa		Afr
Ruschia dualis		Afr
Ruschia evoluta		Afr
Ruschia granitica		Afr
Ruschia karrooica		Afr
Ruschia macowanii		Afr

Ruschia maxima	giant mountain mesemb	Afr
Ruschia mollis		Afr
Ruschia mucronata		Afr
Ruschia multiflora		Afr
Ruschia odontocalyx		Afr
Ruschia pygmaea		Afr
Ruschia rostella		Afr
Ruschia rubricaulis		Afr
Ruschia schollii		Afr
Ruschia semidentata		Afr
Ruschia stenophylla		Afr
Ruschia strubeniae		Afr
Ruschia tumidula		Afr
Ruschia umbellata		Afr
Ruschia uncinata		Afr
Ruschia vulvaria		Afr
Ruschianthus ■ MESEMBRYANTHEMACEAE		
Ruschianthus falcatus		Afr
Samaipaticereus ■ CACTACEAE		
Samaipaticereus corroanus	cárdenas	SAm
Sansevieria ■ DRACAENACEAE / AGAVACEAE		
Sansevieria abyssinica		Afr
Sansevieria aethiopica	common bowstring hemp	Afr
Sansevieria angustifolia		Afr
Sansevieria arborescens		Afr
Sansevieria aubrytiana		Afr
Sansevieria bagamoyensis		Afr
Sansevieria caespitosa		Afr
Sansevieria canaliculata		Afr
Sansevieria caulescens		Afr
Sansevieria conspicua		Afr
Sansevieria cylindrica		Afr
Sansevieria dawei		Afr
Sansevieria deserti		Afr
Sansevieria ehrenbergii		Afr, As
Sansevieria fasciata		Afr
Sansevieria fischeri		Afr
Sansevieria gracilis		Afr
Sansevieria grandicuspis		Afr
Sansevieria grandis	Somali hemp	Afr
Sansevieria hyacinthoides	African bowstring hemp	Afr
Sansevieria kirkii	star sansevieria	Afr
Sansevieria liberica		Afr
Sansevieria longiflora		Afr
Sansevieria metallica		Afr
Sansevieria nilotica		Afr
Sansevieria parva	Kenya hyacinth	Afr

292

Sansevieria pearsonii	spear plant, rhinoceros grass	Afr
Sansevieria phillipsiae		Afr
Sansevieria pinguicula		Afr
Sansevieria × powellii (= *S. arborescens* × *S. robusta*)		Afr
Sansevieria raffillii		Afr
Sansevieria roxburghiana		Afr
Sansevieria scabrifolia		Afr
Sansevieria schweinfurthii		Afr
Sansevieria senegambica		Afr
Sansevieria stuckyi		Afr
Sansevieria subspicata		Afr
Sansevieria trifasciata	mother-in-law's tongue, snake plant	Afr
Sansevieria volkensii		Afr
Sansevieria zeylanica	Ceylon bowstring hemp	As
Sarcocaulon ■ GERANIACEAE		
Sarcocaulon crassicaule	candle bush	Afr
Sarcocaulon l'heritieri		Afr
Sarcocaulon patersonii		Afr
Sarcocaulon salmoniflorum		Afr
Sarcostemma ■ APOCYNACEAE		
Sarcostemma australe		Aus
Sarcostemma brunonianum		As
Sarcostemma decorsei		Afr
Sarcostemma insigne		Afr
Sarcostemma madagascariense		Afr
Sarcostemma pearsonii		Afr
Sarcostemma resiliens		Afr
Sarcostemma socotranum		As
Sarcostemma stoloniferum		Afr
Sarcostemma subterraneum		Afr
Sarcostemma vanlessenii		As
Sarcostemma viminale	viney milkweed	Afr
Sceletium ■ MESEMBRYANTHEMACEAE		
Sceletium compactum	living skeleton, skeleton plant	Afr
Sceletium emarcidum	*kougoed*, living skeleton, skeleton plant	Afr
Sceletium expansum	living skeleton, skeleton plant	Afr
Sceletium namaquense (=*S. tortuosum*)		Afr
Sceletium tortuosum	*kougoed*, canna, living skeleton, skeleton plant	Afr
Schlumbergera ■ CACTACEAE		
Schlumbergera ×buckleyi	Christmas cactus	SAm
Schlumbergera obtusangula		SAm
Schlumbergera opuntioides		SAm
Schlumbergera orssichiana		SAm
Schlumbergera russelliana	Christmas cactus	SAm

Schlumbergera truncata	Christmas cactus, orchid cactus, lobster's claw, crab cactus	SAm
Schwantesia ■ MESEMBRYANTHEMACEAE		
Schwantesia species		Afr
Sclerocactus ■ CACTACEAE		
Sclerocactus brevihamatus	shorthook fishhook cactus	NAm
Sclerocactus erectocentrus	needle-spined pineapple cactus	CAm, NAm
Sclerocactus glaucus	Uinta Basin hookless cactus	NAm
Sclerocactus intertextus		CAm, NAm
Sclerocactus johnsonii	pygmy barrel cactus	NAm
Sclerocactus mariposensis	Lloyd's mariposa cactus	CAm, NAm
Sclerocactus papyracanthus	paper-spined cactus	NAm
Sclerocactus polyancistrus	red-spined fishhook cactus	NAm
Sclerocactus scheeri		CAm, NAm
Sclerocactus tobuschii		NAm
Sclerocactus uncinatus	Chihuahuan fishhook cactus	CAm, NAm
Sclerocactus unguispinus		CAm
Sclerocactus warnockii		NAm
Sclerocactus whipplei	Whipplei's fishhook cactus	NAm
Sclerocactus wrightiae	Wright's fishhook cactus	NAm
Scopelogena ■ MESEMBRYANTHEMACEAE		
Scopelogena gracilis		Afr
Scopelogena veruculata		Afr
×Sedadia ■ CRASSULACEAE		
×Sedadia amecamecana (Sedum dendroideum × Villadia batesii)		CAm
Sedum ■ CRASSULACEAE		
Sedum acre	common stonecrop, stone crop, wall pepper, goldmoss sedum	Eu, Afr
Sedum adolphii	golden sedum	CAm
Sedum aizoon		Eu, As
Sedum alamosanum		CAm
Sedum album		Eu, As, Afr
Sedum allantoides		CAm
Sedum alpestre		Eu
Sedum alsinefolium		Eu
Sedum anglicum		Eu
Sedum annuum		Eu, As
Sedum anopetalum		Eu, As
Sedum atlanticum		Afr
Sedum atratum		Eu
Sedum batallae		CAm
Sedum bellum		CAm
Sedum borissovae		As
Sedum borschii		NAm
Sedum brevifolium		Eu, Afr
Sedum brissemoretii		Afr
Sedum caducum		CAm

Sedum caeruleum		Eu
Sedum caespitosum		Eu, As
Sedum cepaea		Eu
Sedum chontalense		CAm
Sedum clavatum		CAm
Sedum cockerellii		NAm
Sedum commixtum		NAm
Sedum compactum		NAm
Sedum compressum		NAM
Sedum confertiflorum		Eu, As
Sedum confusum		CAm
Sedum craigii		CAm
Sedum crassularia		Afr
Sedum cupressoides		CAm
Sedum cuspidatum		CAm
Sedum dasyphyllum		Eu, NAm
Sedum debile		NAm
Sedum dendroideum		NAm
Sedum diffusum		CAm
Sedum divergens		NAm
Sedum ebracteatum		NAm
Sedum farinosum		Afr
Sedum floriferum		As
Sedum formosanum		As
Sedum forsterianum		Eu
Sedum frutescens		CAm
Sedum furfuraceum		NAm
Sedum fusiforme		Afr
Sedum glabrum		CAm
Sedum glaucophyllum		NAm
Sedum grandipetalum		CAm
Sedum greggii		CAm
Sedum grisebachii		Eu
Sedum griseum		CAm
Sedum guadalajaranum		CAm
Sedum gypsicolum		Eu
Sedum hemsleyanum		CAm
Sedum hintonii		CAm
Sedum hispanicum		Eu, As
Sedum hultenii		CAm
Sedum humifusum		CAm
Sedum hybridum		Eu, As
Sedum hyperaizoon		As
Sedum japonicum		As
Sedum kamtschaticum		As
Sedum laconicum		Eu
Sedum lampusae		Eu

Sedum lanceolatum		NAm
Sedum lancerotense		Afr
Sedum laxum		NAm
Sedum leibergii		NAm
Sedum liebmannianum		CAm, NAm
Sedum lineare		As
Sedum litorale		As
Sedum littoreum		Eu, As
Sedum longipes		CAm
Sedum lucidum		CAm
Sedum luteoviride		CAm
Sedum lydium		Eu
Sedum magellense		Eu
Sedum makinoi		As
Sedum mellitulum		CAm
Sedum mexicanum		CAm
Sedum middendorffianum		As
Sedum monregalense		Eu
Sedum moranense	red stonecrop	CAm
Sedum moranii		NAm
Sedum morganianum	donkey's tail	Eu, As
Sedum multiceps		Afr
Sedum nevadense		Eu, Afr
Sedum nevii		NAm
Sedum niveum		NAm
Sedum nudum		Afr
Sedum nussbaumerianum		CAm
Sedum nuttallianum		NAm
Sedum oaxacanum		CAm
Sedum obcordatum		CAm
Sedum obtusatum		NAm
Sedum obtusifolium		As
Sedum oreganum		NAm
Sedum oregonense		NAm
Sedum oxypetalum		CAm
Sedum pachyphyllum		CAm
Sedum pallidum		As
Sedum palmeri		CAm
Sedum pilosum		Eu, As
Sedum potosinum		CAm
Sedum praealtum		CAm
Sedum pruinatum		Eu
Sedum pulchellum		NAm
Sedum pulvinatum		CAm
Sedum quevae		CAm
Sedum radiatum		NAm
Sedum reflexum	blue stonecrop	Eu

Sedum retusum		CAm
Sedum rhodocarpum		CAm
Sedum rubens		Eu, Afr
Sedum ×rubrotinctum	jelly bean plant, pork and beans	CAm
Sedum ruwenzoriense		Afr
Sedum sarmentosum		As
Sedum sediforme	pale stonecrop	Eu
Sedum selskianum		As
Sedum sempervivoides		As
Sedum sexangulare	tasteless stonecrop	Eu, As
Sedum sichotense		As
Sedum sieboldii (see *Hylotelephium sieboldii*)		
Sedum smallii		NAm
Sedum spathulifolium		NAm
Sedum spectabile (see *Hylotelephium spectabile*)		
Sedum spurium	dragon's blood sedum, two-row stonecrop	As
Sedum stahlii	coral beads	CAm
Sedum stefco		Eu
Sedum stenopetalum		NAm
Sedum stevenianum		Eu
Sedum stoloniferum		Eu, As
Sedum suaveolens		CAm
Sedum subulatum		Eu, As
Sedum telephium (see *Hylotelephium telephium*)		
Sedum tenellum		As
Sedum tenuifolium		Eu
Sedum ternatum		NAm
Sedum torulosum		CAm
Sedum treleasei		CAm
Sedum trullipetalum		As
Sedum tuberiferum		Eu
Sedum urvillei		Eu
Sedum versadense		CAm
Sedum villosum		Eu
Sedum viride		CAm
Sedum wrightii		CAm, NAm
Selenicereus ■ CACTACEAE		
Selenicereus anthonyanus		CAm
Selenicereus atropilosus		CAm
Selenicereus donkelaarii		CAm
Selenicereus grandiflorus	queen of the night	CAm
Selenicereus hamatus	queen of the night	CAm
Selenicereus inermis		CAm, SAm
Selenicereus innesii		CAm
Selenicereus macdonaldii		CAm

Selenicereus megalanthus	yellow pitaya	SAm
Selenicereus murrillii		CAm
Selenicereus pteranthus		CAm
Selenicereus setaceus		SAm
Selenicereus spinulosus	vine-like moonlight cactus	CAm, NAm
Selenicereus testudo		CAm
Selenicereus urbanianus		CAm
Selenicereus vagans		CAm
Selenicereus wercklei		CAm
Selenicereus wittii		SAm

Semnanthe lacera (see *Erepsia lacera*)

Sempervivum ■ CRASSULACEAE

Sempervivum altum		Eu
Sempervivum arachnoideum	cobweb houseleek, spider web houseleek	Eu
Sempervivum armenum		Eu
Sempervivum atlanticum		Afr
Sempervivum ballsii		Eu
Sempervivum borissovae		Eu
Sempervivum calcareum	chalky houseleek	Eu
Sempervivum cantabricum		Eu
Sempervivum caucasicum		Eu
Sempervivum ciliosum		Eu
Sempervivum davisii		Eu, As
Sempervivum dolomiticum		Eu
Sempervivum erythraeum		Eu
Sempervivum glabrifolium		Eu
Sempervivum grandifolium		Eu
Sempervivum ×giuseppii		Eu
Sempervivum ingwersenii		Eu
Sempervivum kindingeri		Eu
Sempervivum kosaninii		Eu
Sempervivum leucanthum		Eu
Sempervivum macedonicum		Eu
Sempervivum marmoreum		Eu
Sempervivum minus		Eu
Sempervivum montanum		Eu
Sempervivum nevadense		Eu
Sempervivum octopodes		Eu
Sempervivum ossetiense		Eu
Sempervivum pittonii		Eu
Sempervivum ×praegeri		Eu
Sempervivum pumilum		Eu
Sempervivum sosnowskyi		Eu
Sempervivum tectorum	roof houseleek, common houseleek	Eu
Sempervivum thompsonianum		Eu
Sempervivum transcaucasicum		Eu

Sempervivum ×vaccarii		Eu
Sempervivum ×widderi		Eu
Sempervivum wulfenii		Eu
Sempervivum zeleborii		Eu
Senecio ■ ASTERACEAE		
Senecio acaulis		Afr
Senecio articulatus	candle plant, hot-dog cactus, sausage crassula	Afr
Senecio barbertonicus		Afr
Senecio citriformis		Afr
Senecio crassimus		Afr
Senecio ficoides		Afr
Senecio hallianus		Afr
Senecio haworthii	cocoon plant	Afr
Senecio herreianus		Afr
Senecio kleiniiformis	spearhead	Afr
Senecio macroglossus	wax vine, Natal ivy	Afr
Senecio mandraliscae	blue finger	Afr
Senecio radicans	creeping berries, string of pearls	Afr
Senecio rowleyanus	string-of-beads	Afr
Senecio serpens	blue-chalksticks	Afr
Senecio spiculosus		Afr
Senecio tamoides	canary creeper	Afr
Sesamothamnus ■ PEDALIACEAE		
Sesamothamnus benguillensis		Afr
Sesamothamnus busseanus		Afr
Sesamothamnus guerichii		Afr
Sesamothamnus lugardii		Afr
Sesamothamnus rivae		Afr
Sinocrassula ■ CRASSULACEAE		
Sinocrassula indica	Indian stonecrop	As
Sinocrassula yunnanensis	Chinese stonecrop	As
Sphalmanthus ■ MESEMBRYANTHEMACEAE		
Sphalmanthus species		Afr
Stapelia ■ APOCYNACEAE		
Stapelia acuminata		Afr
Stapelia ambigua		Afr
Stapelia arenosa		Afr
Stapelia asterias		Afr
Stapelia clavicorona		Afr
Stapelia concinna		Afr
Stapelia conformis		Afr
Stapelia desmetiana		Afr
Stapelia divaricata		Afr
Stapelia erectiflora		Afr
Stapelia flavirostris		Afr
Stapelia flavopurpurea	carrion plant	Afr
Stapelia fuscopurpurea		Afr
Stapelia gariepensis		Afr

Stapelia gettliffei		Afr
Stapelia gigantea	giant carrion flower, giant stapelia	Afr
Stapelia glabricaulis		Afr
Stapelia glanduliflora		Afr
Stapelia grandiflora	purple carrion flower	Afr
Stapelia hirsuta		Afr
Stapelia juttae		Afr
Stapelia kwebensis		Afr
Stapelia leendertziae	red carrion flower, *aaskelk*	Afr
Stapelia nouhuysii		Afr
Stapelia nudiflora		Afr
Stapelia olivacea		Afr
Stapelia pearsonii		Afr
Stapelia peglerae		Afr
Stapelia pillansii		Afr
Stapelia portae-taurinae		Afr
Stapelia pulvinata		Afr
Stapelia rubiginosa		Afr
Stapelia rufa		Afr
Stapelia schinzii		Afr
Stapelia stultitoides		Afr
Stapelia surrecta		Afr
Stapelia tsomoensis		Afr
Stapelia vetula		Afr
Stapelianthus ■ APOCYNACEAE		
Stapelianthus species		Afr
Stapeliopsis ■ APOCYNACEAE		
Stapeliopsis species		Afr
Stenocactus ■ CACTACEAE		
Stenocactus coptonogonus		CAm
Stenocactus crispatus	book cactus	CAm
Stenocactus multicostatus	brain cactus, wave cactus	CAm
Stenocactus obvallatus		CAm
Stenocactus ochoterenanus		CAm
Stenocactus phyllacanthus		CAm
Stenocactus sulphureus		CAm
Stenocactus vaupelianus		CAm
Stenocereus ■ CACTACEAE		
Stenocereus alamosensis	octopus cactus	CAm
Stenocereus beneckei		CAm
Stenocereus dumortieri	candelabra cactus	CAm
Stenocereus eruca	creeping devil cactus	CAm
Stenocereus griseus		SAm
Stenocereus gummosus		CAm
Stenocereus martinezii		CAm
Stenocereus pruinosus		CAm
Stenocereus queretaroensis		CAm
Stenocereus stellatus		CAm

Stenocereus thurberi	organ pipe cactus	CAm, NAm
Stenocereus treleasi		CAm
Stephanocereus ■ CACTACEAE		
Stephanocereus leucostele		SAm
Stephanocereus luetzelburgii		SAm
Stetsonia ■ CACTACEAE		
Stetsonia coryne	toothpick cactus	SAm
Stomatium ■ MESEMBRYANTHEMACEAE		
Stomatium agninum		Afr
Stomatium ermininum	*tierbekvygie* (tiger mouth mesemb)	Afr
Stomatium loganii		Afr
Stomatium meyeri		Afr
Stomatium murinum		Afr
Stomatium mustellinum	*kussingvygie* (cushion mesemb)	Afr
Stomatium niveum		Afr
Stomatium suaveolens		Afr
Strombocactus ■ CACTACEAE		
Strombocactus disciformis		CAm
Synadenium ■ EUPHORBIACEAE		
Synadenium compactum		Afr
Synadenium cupulare	dead man's tree	Afr
Synadenium glaucescens		Afr
Synadenium grantii	African milk bush	Afr
Tacinga ■ CACTACEAE		
Tacinga funalis		SAm
Tacitus bellus (see *Graptopetalum bellum*)		
Talinum ■ PORTULACACEAE		
Talinum arnottii		Afr
Talinum caffrum		Afr
Talinum calycinum	largeflower flameflower	NAm
Talinum guadalupense		NAm, CAm
Talinum mengesii		NAm
Talinum okanoganense		NAm
Talinum paniculatum	flameflower, jewels-of-opar	NAm, CAm
Talinum parviflorum		NAm
Talinum portulacifolium		CAm
Talinum reflexum		SAm
Talinum rugospermum		NAm
Talinum spinescens	spiny flameflower	NAm
Talinum teretifolium		NAm
Talinum triangulare		NAm
Tanquana ■ MESEMBRYANTHEMACEAE		
Tanquana archeri		Afr
Tanquana hilmarii		Afr
Tanquana prismatica		Afr

Tavaresia ■ Apocynaceae		
Tavaresia angolensis		Afr
Tavaresia barklyi		Afr
Tavaresia meintjesii		Afr
Thelocactus ■ Cactaceae		
Thelocactus bicolor	glory of Texas	CAm, NAm
Thelocactus conothelos		CAm
Thelocactus hastifer		CAm
Thelocactus heterochromus		CAm
Thelocactus hexaedrophorus		CAm
Thelocactus leucacanthus		CAm
Thelocactus macdowellii		CAm
Thelocactus rinconensis		CAm
Thelocactus setispinus		CAm, NAm
Thelocactus tulensis		CAm
Thompsonella ■ Crassulaceae		
Thompsonella minutiflora		CAm
Thorncroftia ■ Lamiaceae		
Thorncroftia succulenta	wild sage	Afr
Titanopsis ■ Mesembryanthemaceae		
Titanopsis 'Primosii'		Cult
Titanopsis calcarea	wart plant, sheep's tongue, little tortoise feet	Afr
Titanopsis fulleri		Afr
Titanopsis hugo-schlechteri		Afr
Titanopsis luederitzii		Afr
Titanopsis schwantesii		Afr
Trichocaulon (see *Hoodia*)		
Trichodiadema ■ Mesembryanthemaceae		
Trichodiadema species		Afr
Tridentea ■ Apocynaceae		
Tridentea species		Afr
Tylecodon ■ Crassulaceae		
Tylecodon cacalioides		Afr
Tylecodon paniculatus	butterbush, butter tree, *botterboom*	Afr
Tylecodon reticulatus		Afr
Tylecodon schaeferianus		Afr
Tylecodon wallichii	common *krimpsiek*	Afr
Uebelmannia ■ Cactaceae		
Uebelmannia buiningii		SAm
Uebelmannia gummifera		SAm
Uebelmannia meninensis		SAm
Uebelmannia pectinifera		SAm
Umbilicus ■ Crassulaceae		
Umbilicus erectus		Eu, As
Umbilicus horizontalis		Eu

Umbilicus rupestris	navelwort, penny wort, pennywort	Eu, As

Vanheerdia ■ Mesembryanthemaceae		
Vanheerdia divergens		Afr

Villadia ■ Crassulaceae		
Villadia batesii		CAm
Villadia cucullata		NAm
Villadia elongata		CAm
Villadia grandyi		SAm
Villadia guatemalensis		CAm
Villadia imbricata		CAm
Villadia jurgensenii		CAm

Weberocereus ■ Cactaceae		
Weberocereus biolleyi		CAm
Weberocereus bradei		CAm
Weberocereus glaber		CAm
Weberocereus imitans		CAm
Weberocereus panamensis		CAm
Weberocereus rosei		SAm
Weberocereus tonduzii	ballerina flower	CAm
Weberocereus trichophorus		CAm
Weberocereus tunilla		CAm

Welwitschia ■ Welwitschiaceae		
Welwitschia mirabilis	welwitschia	Afr

Whitesloanea ■ Apocynaceae		
Whitesloanea crassa		Afr

Xerosicyos ■ Cucurbitaceae		
Xerosicyos danguyi	dollar plant	Afr

Yucca ■ Agavaceae		
Yucca aloifolia	Spanish bayonet, dagger plant	CAm, NAm
Yucca aloifolia 'Variegata'	variegated Spanish bayonet, variegated dagger plant	Cam, NAm
Yucca angustissima		NAm
Yucca arizonica		NAm
Yucca baccata	Spanish bayonet, blue yucca, banana yucca	Cam, NAm
Yucca brevifolia	Joshua tree	NAM
Yucca carnerosana	Spanish dagger, giant Spanish dagger	NAm
Yucca constricta	Buckley's yucca, white rim yucca	CAm, NAm
Yucca desmetiana		CAm
Yucca elata	soap tree, soap tree yucca, soap weed, palmella	CAm, NAm
Yucca elephantipes	palm-lily	CAm
Yucca filamentosa	Adam's needle, Adam's thread, spoonleaf yucca, needle palm, St Peter's palm	NAm
Yucca filifera		NAm

Yucca flexilis		NAm
Yucca gilbertiana		NAm
Yucca glauca		NAm
Yucca gloriosa	Spanish dagger, Roman candle, palm lily	NAm
***Yucca gloriosa* 'Variegata'**		NAm
Yucca guatamalensis (see *Yucca elephantipes*)		
Yucca harrimaniae		NAm
Yucca ×karlsruhensis (=*Y. filamentosa* × *Y. glauca*)		Cult
Yucca louisianensis		NAm
Yucca neomexicana		CAm
Yucca pallida		NAm
Yucca recurvifolia	pendulous yucca, weeping yucca	NAm
Yucca reverchonii	San Angelo yucca	NAm
Yucca rigida	blue yucca	CAm
Yucca rostrata	beaked yucca, big bend yucca	NAm
Yucca rupicola	twisted leaf yucca	NAm
Yucca schidigera		NAm
Yucca schottii		NAm
Yucca smalliana	Adam's needle, bear grass	NAm
Yucca thompsoniana	Thompson's yucca	NAm
Yucca torreyi	Torrey's yucca	CAm, NAm
Yucca treculeana	Spanish dagger, palma pita	CAm, NAm
Yucca ×vomerensis (=*Y. aloifolia* × *Y gloriosa*)		Cult
Yucca whipplei	Our Lord's candle	CAm, NAm
Zygophyllum ■ Zygophyllaceae		
Zygophyllum album		Afr, As
Zygophyllum fabago	Syrian bean caper	As
Zygophyllum foetidum	pungent tortoise bush	Afr
Zygophyllum morgsana	tortoise bush, *skilpadbos*	Afr
Zygophyllum prismatothecum		Aus

Index

Names in **bold italics** = treated species
Page numbers in **bold** = treated or illustrated species

316